Delta Heritage Trail
(Missouri Pacific's Wynne Subdivision):
History Through the Miles

Barton Jennings

Delta Heritage Trail (Missouri Pacific's Wynne Subdivision): History Through the Miles
Copyright © 2021 by Barton Jennings

All rights reserved. This book may not be duplicated or transmitted in any way, or stored in an information retrieval system, without the express written consent of the publisher, except in the form of brief excerpts or quotations for the purpose of review. Making copies of this book, or any portion, for any purpose other than your own, is a violation of United States copyright laws.

Publisher's Cataloging-in-Publication Data
Jennings, Barton

Delta Heritage Trail (Missouri Pacific's Wynne Subdivision): History Through the Miles
364p.; 21cm.
ISBN: 978-1-7327888-5-5

Library of Congress Control Number: 2021932836

Top front cover photo by Barton Jennings.
Bottom front and back cover photos by Sarah Jennings.
All interior photos by Barton Jennings unless otherwise noted.

Please send comments or corrections to sarah@techscribes.com

TechScribes, Inc.
PO Box 2199
Alma, AR 72921
www.techscribes.com

Printed in the United States of America

Contents

Acknowledgments 7
The Delta Heritage Trail 11
   The Delta Heritage Trail Corridor 13
   Building the Delta Heritage Trail 16
   The Delta Heritage Trail Experience 18
Driving the Delta Heritage Trail 25
Creating a Delta Heritage Trail Route Guide 29
   The Language of the Delta Heritage Trail Guide 33
Helena Junction to Rohwer – The History of the Railroad Route of the Delta Heritage Trail 39
   Delayed by the Bridges 41
   Early Railroad Operations 42
   Helena Southwestern Railroad Company 43
   Consolidation and Changes on the Line 45
   The End of the Memphis, Helena & Louisiana Line ... 55
   The Author's Story – The End of the Wynne 56
Helena Junction to Rohwer – The Guide to the Railroad Route of the Delta Heritage Trail 65
Helena Junction Trailhead to Elaine Trailhead – Active Delta Heritage Trail 69
   Lexa (Missouri Pacific Milepost 325.5) 72
   Latour Junction (Missouri Pacific Milepost 326.3) 74
   Helena Junction (Missouri Pacific Milepost 326.5) 75
   Helena, Arkansas 76
   Helena's Delta Cultural Center 80
   The Railroads of Helena 81
   Passenger Trains #343 and #344 83
   Dawkins Spur 86
   The Cotton Gin 88
   The Railroad Pole Line 93

Coolidge Addition 99
The Railroad Layout at Barton Junction 100
Barton, Arkansas 102
The Lakeview Resettlement Project 118
The Howe Lumber Company 129
Shay Locomotives 133
The Missouri Pacific at Wabash 134
Wabash and the 1919 Elaine Massacre 135
The Railroad at Hoop Spur 140
Elaine, Arkansas 145
Gerard B. Lambert Company 149
The 1919 Elaine Massacre 151
Today's Elaine 155

Elaine to Watson – Future Delta Heritage Trail 159
Continental Gin Company 176
The Change to Mechanical Farming 183
The Great Mississippi River Flood of 1927 192
The Drought of 1930-1931 193
White River National Wildlife Refuge 201
Lift Bridge Operations 222
McClellan–Kerr Arkansas River Navigation System 223
The White River 225
County Line 226
Trusten Holder State Wildlife Management Area 230
Building and Rebuilding the Bridge 235
County Line 240
Ernest Hemingway and Yancopin 246
Red Fork 247

Watson Trailhead to Rohwer Trailhead – Active Delta Heritage Trail 253
The Railroad at Watson 254
The Community of Watson Switch 256
Watson and the Timber Industry 260
Perkins Land & Lumber Company 271
The Town of Kelso 272

Rohwer Relocation Camp.. 276
The Railroad at Rohwer 283
The Railroad South to McGehee, Arkansas 287
Rohwer to Arkansas City – The History of the Levee Route of the Delta Heritage Trail..291
Rohwer Trailhead to Arkansas City Trailhead – The Guide to the Levee Route of the Delta Heritage Trail 297
Bar Pits.. 312
Mound Cemetery 317
Freddie Black Choctaw Island Wildlife Management Area 323
Arkansas City.. 326
The Timber Companies of Arkansas City................. 339
The Railroads of Arkansas City 347
About the Author 363

Other books by Barton Jennings

History Through the Miles

Arkansas & Missouri Railroad: History Through the Miles
Alaska Railroad: History Through the Miles
Iowa Interstate Railroad: History Through the Miles
Everett Railroad: History Through the Miles
Tennessee Central Railway: History Through the Miles
Whitewater Valley Railroad: History Through the Miles
Oregon's Joseph Branch: History Through the Miles
Missouri & North Arkansas Railroad:
History Through the Miles
Hennepin Canal Parkway: History Through the Miles
Idaho's Payette River Railroads: History Through the Miles

Textbook

The Basics of Transportation: Policies, Practices and Pricing – An Applied Perspective

Acknowledgments

The Memphis, Helena & Louisiana route was torn apart about thirty years ago, and the levees were built almost eighty years ago, so you can't just go out and see how things were done back then. The author has been fortunate enough to know some of the employees who worked for the railroad over the last few years of its operation, and was even there to help manage its final days. Additionally, he has had the pleasure to get to know a number of the people who have researched the area. The staff of the Delta Heritage Trail State Park have been enthusiastic about the efforts to produce this book, and Molly Elders and Ryan Smith have been extremely helpful in sharing information about the trail and its future plans. They have also been excited about the information that this book has uncovered, and plan to share much of it at the park's visitor center, various trailheads, and during special events. These people all deserve a thanks for their help and support.

A number of documents were also used in writing this book. It is amazing what can be found on the internet these days. Copies of *The Official Guide of the Railways*, the annual reports of various state railroad and corporation commissions, reports of the Interstate Commerce Commission and U.S. Corps of Engineers, Congressional committee reports, and other such documents are great resources.

The Missouri Pacific Railroad itself produced numerous documents that are still available. These include timetables, track charts, lists of stations, and contracts. Related sources such as the *Arkansas Marketing and Industrial Guide*, *The Coal Dealers Blue Book*, local histories published by the Goodspeed Publishing Company, Sanborn Insurance

Maps, and others were a great aid. Newspapers also reported heavily on the construction and operations of the Memphis, Helena & Louisiana Railway. David Hoge is a master of newspaper research, and his collection of more than 3000 pages of railroad-related newspaper articles from Arkansas is a masterful source of information. He deserves thanks for sharing this resource. The *Arkansas Railroad History* website is also a jewel with some of the best researchers around sharing information. Copies of trade magazines about the timber, lumber, farming, and banking industries also provided a great deal of information. Finally, the author has a basement with several rooms full of books, timetables and other documents about this and other railroads – important research items from a time long before today's internet. Thanks go out to everyone who helped.

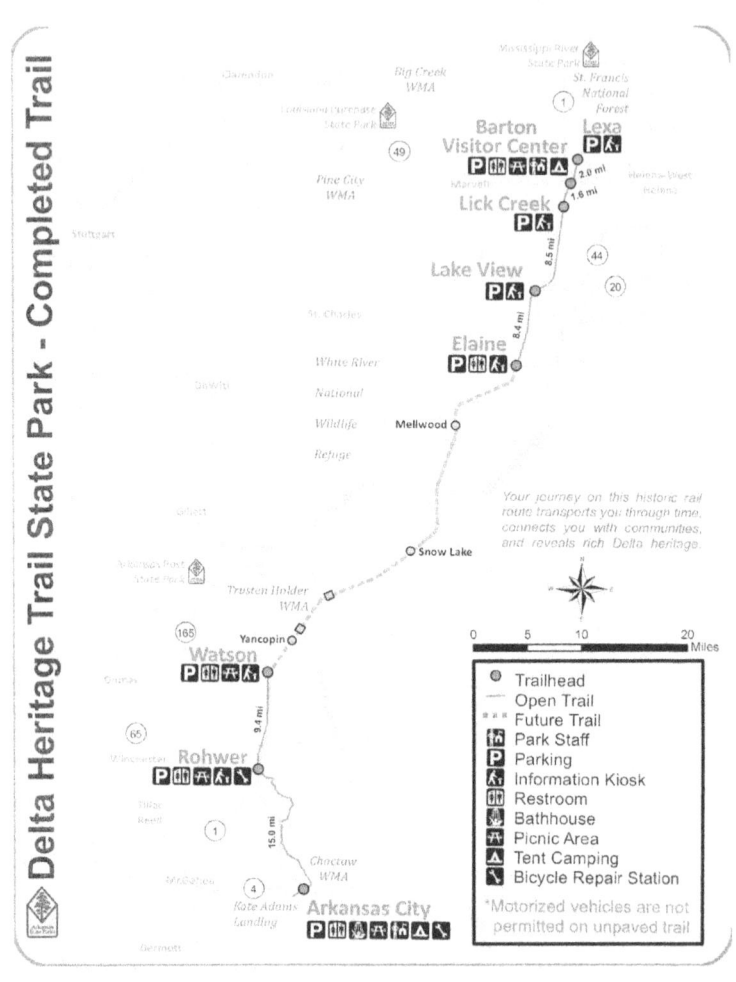

Map courtesy of the Delta Heritage Trail State Park.

The Delta Heritage Trail

The Delta Heritage Trail, a part of the Delta Heritage Trail State Park, is a planned 85-mile trail through Phillips, Arkansas, and Desha counties in southeastern Arkansas. Most of this route was originally through swampy bottomlands, later converted to farmland through logging, the construction of drainage canals and levees, and then the clearing of land. The territory covered by the trail features large farms that grow cotton, rice, soybeans, winter wheat, and many other crops. It also includes the river bottoms along the White and Arkansas rivers, and views of the backwaters of the Mississippi River from the levees along the southern end of the trail. Numerous small towns, many with populations of less than one hundred, show where sawmills and other industries once hummed along, employing thousands. Locations along the trail also mark the struggle of sharecroppers and tenant farmers to obtain equal rights and respect with the landowners.

The route generally dates to the construction of the Memphis, Helena & Louisiana Railway, built during the earliest years of the twentieth century. This railroad went through several owners until Union Pacific Railroad determined that the line was not needed and that it would be abandoned. In 1991, Union Pacific officials informed the Arkansas Department of Parks and Tourism that the right-of-way might become available for other uses. With this, the State of Arkansas began to work with the Interstate Commerce Commission to save the right-of-way for a possible trail and park.

After more than a year and several funding delays, the Arkansas Highway and Transportation Department and the Arkansas Department of Parks and Tourism jointly reached an agreement with Union Pacific to obtain the route through donation. According to the departments, on December 23, 1992, the state was assured that it would receive the 73-mile corridor from near Lexa (Phillips County, Arkansas) to near Cypress Bend (Desha County, Arkansas). Using the railbanking provisions of the National Trails System Act, the state received almost 900 acres of natural lowlands, 58 bridges, and an important route across the White River and Arkansas River.

Railbanking is a practice where a former rail line can be removed, but its route is preserved for other uses, with the possibility of the rail line being installed again in the future if demand requires it. In return, the railroad transfers all rights and liabilities of the corridor to a public agency sponsor to allow public use. Therefore, thanks to Union Pacific Railroad, the State of Arkansas, and several federal laws and agencies, the Delta Heritage Trail State Park and its trail now exist. In addition, thanks to gifts such as those by the Walton Family Foundation, the trail is being expanded and completed for its entire 85-mile route between Helena Junction and Arkansas City.

This sign welcomes visitors to the Delta Heritage Trail State Park facility at Barton Junction.

The Delta Heritage Trail Corridor

The Delta Heritage Trail State Park is located in the Delta Region of Southeast Arkansas. During the first several decades of the twentieth century, the railroad route used by the trail handled local farm and timber products, as well as freight moving from the Gulf Coast to the industries of the North. Today, it is a lightly populated rural area based upon farming and hunting, and the trail route can essentially be broken down into four parts.

[1] The northern part of the park is built on a former railroad grade between Helena Junction and Snow Lake. The route generally passes through farm fields and small communities, and much of the trail is lined with trees. The Helena Junction-Elaine area was the first part of the trail constructed and opened. The route between Elaine and Snow Lake was being engineered as this book was being written.

[2] The second part is the isolated railroad stretch between Snow Lake and Yancopin. Almost all of this route passes through the bottomlands of the White River and Arkansas River, much of which are part of the White River National Wildlife Refuge and the Trusten Holder Wildlife Management Area. This territory is almost all heavily wooded, and the route passes by few buildings and no communities. It is almost all elevated on bridges (almost 20,000 feet) or earthen embankments, providing views down into the surrounding land. This area is heavily populated with wildlife and the trail has not been built through this area.

[3] The third part is the southern end of the rail-to-trail project, located between Yancopin and Rohwer. It also primarily passes through farm fields and small communities on an abandoned railroad grade. Most of this part of the trail opened in 2018.

[4] The southern-most part of the corridor and trail is the most unique of the project. It is the sixteen miles that uses roads on the levees of the Mississippi River. No communities exist on the route except at the two endpoints of Rohwer and Arkansas City. The rest of the route generally separates the farm fields of Desha County and the floodplain of the Mississippi River. This part of the trail also opened in 2018.

All four sections are located in the Mississippi River Embayment, also known as the Mississippi Alluvial Plain, or simply the Delta. It was all historically covered by heavy forests. During the 1500s when Hernando de Soto explored the area, this was part of the largest forested wetland in North America. The 24 million acres of woods lined the Mississippi River from Louisiana through Arkansas and north to Missouri and Illinois. Today, about twenty percent of the Arkansas Delta is still covered by forests, and the Delta Heritage Trail passes through the largest part of these woods. These Arkansas bottomlands were declared to be a "Wetland of International Importance" by the United Nations in 1989, and efforts continue to protect and even expand them.

The Delta Hertitage Trail

The railroad once passed through miles of wetlands and bottomlands, and now the Delta Heritage Trail does the same.

The trail also passes through some of the richest farmland in the world. Soybeans, cotton, corn, rice, and winter wheat are grown all along the route, with most farms relying upon the international market demand for their commodities. Large groves of pecan trees also stand, and are used as healthy and tasty additions to many foods. Tree farms have also been developed along the route, often used as pulp for area paper mills or timber for local sawmills. Basically, the trail passes through rural Southeastern Arkansas and its small farming communities.

Building the Delta Heritage Trail

The Delta Heritage Trail State Park was planned from the start to be built in multiple phases. After the property acquisition on December 23, 1992, numerous plans were studied as to what to do with the right-of-way. Proposals to turn it into a highway, a tourist train route, and a series of trails were all made and evaluated. The first few miles of the trail opened from Helena Junction to near Barton during 2002, and the park was officially dedicated on October 25, 2002. Barton is the official headquarters of the state park and features a visitor center with park information, a gift shop, restrooms, a campground, and picnic tables. The visitor center can also help with area tours, including bike and kayak rentals.

The visitor center at Barton Junction, located in a former cotton gin, ties together much of the trail's history. It features trail information, route history, and basic supplies for those traveling the Delta Heritage Trail.

By 2020, about twenty miles of compacted gravel trail were completed on the north end from Helena Junction to Elaine, with more work underway. On the south end of the trail, a creative proposal was made to get the trail south of Cypress Bend. A plan was developed that would take the trail east from Rohwer, and using the roads on the Mississippi River levees, get the trail to a terminus at Arkansas City. Almost fifteen miles of shared-use road heads north from Arkansas City to Rohwer, where another ten miles of compacted gravel trail use the railroad grade to reach Watson.

On October 18, 2018, a dedication was held for the Arkansas City Trailhead, a facility that features parking, picnic areas, a water fountain, a bicycle repair station, a playground, a large group charcoal grill, an open pavilion, and bathhouse facilities. The bathhouse building, constructed in the style of a former railroad station, also houses administrative offices.

In early 2020, the park received a $20 million gift from the Walton Family Foundation, which had previously funded a series of hiking and biking trails in Northwest Arkansas. Matching funds from Arkansas Parks and Tourism will be used to complete the trail between Elaine and Watson, a distance of about forty miles. Work is already underway to extend the trail southward from Elaine and to add additional trailhead locations. A big part of the effort is the various studies being conducted to determine the best way to cross the two large rivers along the route, certainly some of the highlights of the entire project. Keep your eyes on the website of the Delta Heritage Trail State Park for updates.

The Delta Heritage Trail Experience

The Delta Heritage Trail is a well-maintained trail that links many of the small communities of Southeastern Arkansas. Where trains once operated, the trail surface is packed crushed stone, generally high and dry except during the hardest rains. More than 20,000 feet of bridges span waterways along this part of the trail – some new and some historic railroad bridges rebuilt for pedestrian use. Because the railroad elevated their grade, even during times of local flooding the trail is generally above the water levels. Between Rohwer and Arkansas City, the trail uses the raised Mississippi River levees and the trail is paved. From end-to-end, the trail is almost level, with the only climbs located where you get on and off the levee.

On most of the trail, travel is limited to walking and bicycling, with provisions made for those with disability needs. Powered vehicles, with a few exceptions, are prohibited on this part of the trail, as are equestrian riders. Between Rohwer and Arkansas City, motorized vehicles are allowed since the Delta Heritage Trail shares the right-of-way with paved levee and farm roads.

Courtesy is probably the primary rule when using the Delta Heritage Trail. This yield to pedestrians sign is a reminder about this basic policy.

The Delta Hertitage Trail

The Delta Heritage Trail uses packed crushed stone on the former railroad grade, and motorized vehicles are not allowed. As shown at Elaine, the trail is gated at most grade crossings to limit users to bicycles and their feet.

The rail-trail that has opened between Helena Junction and Rohwer has trailhead facilities scattered along the route. Additionally, benches are available at a number of places along the trail. This part of the Delta Heritage Trail passes through some areas of heavy woods and shade, and then other areas of open farmland.

The Rohwer to Arkansas City trail is on top of large levees and shade is almost non-existent. There are also no benches along the route between the two trailheads, but there is plenty of sloping grass that you can sit on. On this part of the route, cyclists should keep their eyes open for the cattle guards that are used to separate farms and herds. Also be sure to look out for the cows that happily wander back and forth across the road.

Watch for cows on the levees of the Rohwer to Arkansas City portion of the trail. Cyclists should also beware of cattle guards in the pavement.

The weather can be hot and humid in the summer, and cool and rainy in the winter. However, the long spring and fall seasons are often described as terrific by visitors and locals alike. The area experiences a four-month summer (mid-May to mid-September), with the highest temperatures in late July and early August. Temperatures during the peak of summer average 92 degrees as a high and 74 as a low. Winter is generally Thanksgiving to Valentine's Day, with an average of 53 degrees as a high and 36 degrees as a low. Late fall and early spring have the rainiest days of the year. Note the weather forecast and come prepared.

The Delta Hertitage Trail

The Delta Heritage Trail is a great place to just sit and enjoy nature, due to the number of benches scattered along the route. This bench is located at the Helena Junction Trailhead and sits where Helena Junction once allowed trains to head north towards Memphis, or east towards Helena.

Come prepared with sunscreen, a hat, and sunglasses. Wear appropriate clothes and shoes. Also, carry plenty of water and snacks as this is rural country, and only a few convenience and grocery stores are open near the trail. These stores are noted in the trail guides, but there is no guarantee that they will be open the day or time that you pass them.

Please do not spoil the trail for others – pick up your trash and make sure all fires are out before leaving a grill or other location. If you have any questions about the rules of the park and trail, check with the staff or the park's website.

Currently, the Delta Heritage Trail is a daytime activity, with camping available at Barton and Arkansas City. This may change as the trail is completed through the Arkansas and White River bottomlands.

Wildlife

And what about wildlife? It is everywhere. Bird watchers will love the trail. The many ponds and waterways attract almost any waterbird that passes through the region. Many other bird species make their homes here all year long. Animals also inhabit the area, especially the wooded terrain. Everything from squirrel, rabbit and deer, to foxes and bear, can be seen by a lucky visitor. Don't be afraid of them as they are probably more afraid of you. However, don't bother or approach them. Just stand and watch as they scamper or wander around. The trail also provides an opportunity to view some of the oldest and largest trees around, patches of prairie grasslands that survived on the railroad right-of-way, the many native flowers that mark the various seasons, and areas of second growth timber that are returning to the conditions found hundreds of years ago. Also note the daylilies and daffodils, old fruit trees, and other plants that often mark the locations of now-gone homes and communities.

Alligators

One common question is whether there are alligators along the Delta Heritage Trail. The answer is yes! The American Alligator has lived in Arkansas for thousands of years, and their current population is again growing, with 45 of Arkansas' 75 counties having documented alligators. Much of east, central, and south Arkansas were the home of alligators when the state was first settled, but the draining of wetlands and unregulated hunting for hides for use in making purses, belts, shoes, and other products almost eliminated the population.

However, beginning about 1960, efforts were made to restore the population. This was done through both state and federal protection, plus restocking efforts by multiple agencies and organizations. Between 1972 and 1984, the Louisiana Department of Wildlife and Fisheries provided 2841 alligators to the Arkansas Game and Fish Commission for release across the state. Since then, the population has been stable enough to allow alligator hunting, generally over two weekends in mid-September. Of the about forty permits issued for public lands, more than half are for the Lower Arkansas River Wetland Complex. One interesting bit of information about the hunt is that it takes place at night, from ½ hour after sunset through ½ hour before sunrise.

So where can a user of the Delta Heritage Trail see an alligator? Basically, any waterway along the trail is a potential alligator habitat. A study by the Arkansas Game and Fish Commission has found that the area harbors a high alligator density. In particular, alligators are found in the "large areas of shallow water marsh and swamp habitat." This means that the areas near the White and Arkansas Rivers, as well as along the Mississippi River levee, are some of the best places to see an alligator.

Warning – although an alligator may seem to be a slow creature, do not approach it. For short distances, they can run faster than a human. They are also often hard to see, resembling a dried log on land, or floating just below the surface of a pond. In winter, they seldom eat as their body temperature is not warm enough to digest food. Instead, on sunny days, they bask in the sun trying to warm up. However, in warmer weather, they are aggressively trying to eat up for winter.

Driving the Delta Heritage Trail

For those without the time or ability, or who just want to experience the Delta Heritage Trail from the comfort of their own vehicle or tour bus, pretty much the entire trail from Helena Junction to Arkansas City can be closely followed from adjacent paved highways, except for the 14.5 miles between Snow Lake and Yancopin.

If you are north of the Arkansas and White Rivers, any visit should include the visitor center at the Barton Trailhead. From the park's visitor center, turn west on U.S. Highway 49 and then south on Arkansas Highway 85 at Walnut Corner. Highway 85 closely follows the trail from the Barton Trailhead to near Lake View, where you take Arkansas Highway 44 on to Snow Lake. While there are a few short stretches where the trail and highway are not immediately side-by-side, they are always close enough that this route guide will tell the story of what you are seeing. You can also stop along the way at the various trailheads to walk a bit of the trail and to read the information panels.

South of the Arkansas and White Rivers, the roads follow the trail even more closely. Here, Arkansas City is a good start with its larger trailhead facility and the Kate Adams Lake complex. For more than fourteen miles, you can literally drive the Delta Heritage Trail as it uses the paved roads on top of the Mississippi River levees between Arkansas City and Rohwer. At Rohwer, you can drive north on Arkansas Highway 1 all the way to Watson, making stops along the way as desired. A visit to the Rohwer Relocation Center is certainly worth the little effort required. At Watson, take Desha County Road 41 (Yancopin Road) on to Yancopin. Just like north of the rivers, you can stop along the way at the various trailheads to walk a bit of the trail and to read the information panels.

Please remember to yield the right-of-way to cyclists and hikers. Check your gas gauge as services are limited in this rural part of Southeastern Arkansas, as can be cell service. Descriptions are provided in the route guide about driving to the Arkansas and White River bridges. Note that these roads, while generally in good condition, are not paved. In rainy weather, or when the river levels are high, you should not attempt to drive to these locations. There are no services and no cell coverage along these country roads.

Got it? Okay, now sit back and enjoy the Delta Heritage Trail!

Modern parking lots that include handicapped parking are available at every trailhead, as shown by this sign at the Helena Junction Trailhead.

Arkansas Highway 1 closely follows the Delta Heritage Trail between Rohwer and Watson. It can also be used between Watson and Barton via Backgate, Arkansas, to connect the north and south parts of the trail together.

Creating a Delta Heritage Trail Route Guide

The purpose of this book is to provide a description of the route used by the Delta Heritage Trail and to tell its history. This description includes things that you can see now and what you would have experienced decades and even a century or more ago. It includes details about the railroad, the communities along its route, many of the people who lived here, and information about the various roads that the trail crosses. While the park includes approximately 900 acres over about 85 miles, the history that is visible includes much more. Nearby cities and towns, area farms, major national companies, and international demand for farm and timber products all play a role in what you see today.

The Delta Heritage Trail crosses a number of local and county roads, and signs generally alert trail users of these locations.

Delta Heritage Trail: History Through the Miles

Because most of the Delta Heritage Trail has been built on the former right-of-way of the Memphis, Helena & Louisiana Railway, then St. Louis, Iron Mountain & Southern, later the Missouri Pacific Railroad, and eventually Union Pacific Railroad, the history of the railroad often takes center stage for the trail between Helena Junction and Rohwer. The tracks, stations and customers at each location help to tell the story of what happened, but many railroad stations cannot be found today. This alone tells part of the story of the Delta Region of southeast Arkansas.

Times change, and much of the physical history along the Delta Heritage Trail can no longer be seen, such as this former railroad depot at Arkansas City. Today, the area is the home of the Arkansas City Trailhead.

Following the trail southward, this guide identifies communities, railroad stations and their mileposts as used by the Delta Heritage Trail. These mileposts and distances start at the Helena Junction Trailhead at what was once called Latour Junction. This trail guide uses the mileposts as they existed when the book was printed. However, as the middle of the trail is completed, it is possible that the mileposts could be slightly moved. Any changes will be reflected in future editions of this book.

It should be noted that the mileposts used by the railroad were very different, and were actually changed over the years. The final railroad mileposts started at Valley Junction, near Dupo, in the East St. Louis, Illinois, area. Because many historic records use the old railroad mileposts, they are often noted in the route description. This allows those who research the route on their own to use these railroad records to locate items along the route. Additionally, the bridges along the railroad were once known by their Memphis, Helena & Louisiana Railway (MH&L) number. Used for reporting purposes, these MH&L bridge numbers are also often cited.

Once a location is identified, the history is then told in a number of eras, including during the railroad's construction, the line's peak during the 1910s and 1920s, the retreat of the 1940s and 1950s, and then the last days of the railroad during the 1980s. Changes since then are also noted. Fortunately, the book's author was here during the last days of the railroad's operations, and information from those days is included. Additionally, trips over the trail's route during the past few years have added to the "what can you see now" part of the route description.

There is always the question about how much detail to provide. One reader told the author that in a previous book, if someone once tied a mule to a she-shed along the line, it was reported. While that is not quite the goal, there is an effort to explain the history of each community along the line, what businesses and shippers were located there, and what facilities the railroad had. Obviously, all of these changed over the nearly one hundred years of the railroad's history, so the challenge is how much information to report. In writing this book, the author attempted to include information about the original settling of the area, the first few years of the railroad's existence and the efforts to log and farm the land, the peak of each community's activity, and what still exists today. Not everything is told, but enough history is provided to give the reader an idea of what happened at each location.

Please note that these details continue to change as businesses open and close, brush is cut back or grows, new trailheads are added, and other changes take place. Every effort has been made to have this book as current as possible when it was written. New information will be included as time permits.

A help in following the Delta Heritage Trail and knowing what was at many of the locations, are the many maps available on the internet. County road maps, topographic (topo) maps, and many other maps from the era can be found. Comparing these older maps with newer maps can often make finding the history of the area easier. The U.S. Geological Survey has been very active making their Historical Topographic Map Collection available through TopoView. Some of these maps date from the 1930s and show the region just after its peak of activity. It is amazing how much things can change in so little time.

Another thing that should be recognized is that what will be seen along the trail can vary greatly by the season of the year. Winter allows views without the leaves, but it is also a wetter time of the year. Summer is drier, but it is also much hotter. If you want to discuss extremes – its 107F in summer and 10F in winter. Rainfall averages 52 inches a year, but more than half occurs in winter. Snow is rare and usually melts the same day. The growing season lasts from mid-March to mid-November.

It cannot be overstated that this is a rural area, something many people are not used to. Bring plenty of food and water because it can be many miles between open stores where you can get more. The two ends of the trail system are often directly next to roads, but the center between Snow Lake and Watson is isolated, so understand where you are heading and how long it will take to get there. This guide attempts to provide this type of information where appropriate.

The history of the route of the Delta Heritage Trail varies greatly between the two major parts. The route from Helena Junction to Rohwer is being built on a former railroad grade with a strong history. From Rohwer to Arkansas City, the route uses local paved roads on the Mississippi River levee system. Because of these differences, the description of the trail will be broken into these two parts: the Railroad Route and the Levee Route.

The Language of the Delta Heritage Trail Guide

Railroading, farming, logging, river boating, and the Mississippi River Delta all have some unique words and phrases that may seem strange. Therefore, an attempt will be made to explain what they mean. Explanations about cotton gins, the change from hand to mechanical farming, and other items are included in this book. A number of other terms are explained here.

Bottomland, swamp, bayou, wetland, and floodplain are all used along the route. A bottomland is defined as low-lying land along a watercourse. The term floodplain is often used for the same area as during high water, the area can easily flood. Swamp, bayou and wetland are terms used for areas that are partially or intermittently covered with water.

The term **plantation** was commonly used for the large farms in the area. Typically, a plantation was a farm which was worked by resident labor, often tenant farmers or sharecroppers during the late 1800s and early 1900s. Sharecropper, tenant farmer, and wage worker are often mentioned, especially as they relate to the Elaine Massacre. These are old farming terms that actually were used across the country. A **sharecropper** is a farmer who works the land owned by someone else. The farmer receives a percentage of the crop or of the crop's value – thus a share of the crop. However, the sharecropper was also generally charged for the seed, tools, living quarters, and food, meaning that they seldom produced any significant profit for their work.

A **tenant farmer** is similar to a sharecropper. The term dates back to at least 1745 and represents a farmer who works the property of others, paying a rent or a share of their harvest. Generally, tenant farmers are more independent than sharecroppers, and some work the property of multiple farms. The practice is very common today as a great amount of farmland is owned by companies or estates, and the land is rented out to farmers or ranchers to work. In 2016, the United States Department of Agriculture's Economic Research Service reported that "approximately 39 percent of the 911 million acres of farmland in the contiguous 48 States was rented. More than half of cropland is rented, compared with just over 25 percent of pastureland. In general, rental activity is concentrated in grain production areas; cash grains such as rice, corn, soybeans, and wheat, and also cotton, are commonly grown in areas where over 50 percent of farmland is rented."

Just as with almost all businesses, there are also workers who are simply hired to do certain tasks. A **wage worker** or **farm laborer** is a person that simply gets paid on an hourly or daily basis for their work. Many of these individuals work only seasonally on the farm, generally during the spring planting and fall harvest. They often hold other jobs which allow them the flexibility to also work some in agriculture.

The facilities and equipment of farming can also be a bit confusing. A **grain elevator** is a building used to store grain until needed. The term elevator came about because the buildings were often tall, and the grain was elevated to the top to be placed in the proper bin. A **gin** is a machine used to separate a product from seeds and waste material. A cotton gin is a machine that separates the cotton fiber from the seed and dirt. A **harvester** is the device that is used to pick the crop. A cotton picker, also known as a stripper, is a specialized harvesting machine. Most plantations also featured a **commissary**, or what was essentially a company store for those who worked on the farm.

The timber industry was closely related to many of the farms, as they cleared the land and then operated farms or sold the land off. A **sawmill** is simply a mill that cuts the large trees into boards. The next step was a **planing mill** that cut the boards to size and smoothed their surfaces. Because the timber was generally cut live and from wetlands, the wood often needed to be dried. This could be done by setting the wood outdoors, or through the use of a **dry kiln** that heated up the wood like a kitchen oven heats up food. The timber towns also commonly featured a commissary.

The railroad also had its workers who lived in the region. Many of the communities along the Delta Heritage Trail once had housing for **section gangs**. Railroad tracks require a great deal of maintenance, and laborers were stationed along the tracks to inspect them and make repairs – thus gangs that covered a section of the track. Because railroad workers often moved about to where the work was taking place, or where their seniority would allow them to hold a good job, basic lodging was often provided by the railroad. In some cases, this was done using permanent houses, and in other cases simple railroad bunkcars were provided.

The larger communities, or where there were large volumes of freight and passenger movements, had a railroad **agent**. These agents could sell passenger train tickets, issue waybills (a document prepared by the carrier that contains details of the shipment, route, and charges for freight movements), send and receive telegraph messages, handle express freight and mail, and issue train orders to passing trains. The railroad also provided housing for these workers in most communities, often by having an apartment on the second floor of the depot.

Directing all of the movements over the tracks was a **dispatcher**. This dispatcher gave authority to trains, track crews, and others to be on the tracks and to move in a certain direction between specific locations. The dispatcher also issued train orders which provided additional information to employees. These instructions could include things like a change in a train's schedule, where to pick up or drop off freight cars, and any changes in the speed limits along the line. Many of these train orders were issued to the station agents who would pass them on to the trains as they passed. Signals were often placed on a depot so that the agent could tell a train crew to get new orders. These signals became known as train order signals. Telephones located along the line were also used to exchange information. Eventually, the use of radios allowed the dispatcher to talk directly to the train crews even while on their trains.

Most stations – railroads call any named location a station, even if there is not a depot building – had a number of **tracks**. A siding is a long track that a train can enter to allow another train to pass. These tracks are generally located at regular intervals along a line. House or team tracks are shorter tracks that can be used by local shippers to load or unload freight. Some shippers were large enough to have their own tracks, generally called a spur track. In some places, such as at Barton Junction, a track once headed off several miles to serve multiple customers. These tracks are often known as industrial leads or branch lines.

Walking the trail, you will see a number of types of **bridges**. A timber trestle is simply a timber bridge that uses vertical piles to hold up the short spans. These were easy to build, and could extend to almost any length. The beam-span bridges use the same basic design, but use steel I-beams instead of timber stringers between the groups of piles. Often, these piles were built with steel I-beams or poured concrete.

Plate girder bridges are very popular with railroads and can be longer that timber and I-beam spans. A plate girder is a large manufactured I-beam, and two are attached to form a bridge span. A deck plate girder has the track on the top of the bridge span, while a through plate girder has the track passing between the plate girders, with the connecting components below the track. Through truss spans are used to cross the Arkansas and White Rivers because of the great lengths required. A truss structure is like the roofing trusses found on many buildings, a top and a bottom connected by many triangular units. Typically, railroads pass between the trusses with the structure both above and below the track.

On top of all of these terms are the local accents that can create even bigger challenges. These accents led to the term bar pit for borrow pit, a source of fill dirt. Visitors will also find that many area names have a distinct sound to them, not always exactly how they look on paper. One example is Rohwer (pronounced Ro-ar).

Delta Heritage Trail: History Through the Miles

Helena Junction to Rohwer –
The History of the Railroad Route of the Delta Heritage Trail

Most of the Delta Heritage Trail has been built on the grade of the former **Memphis, Helena & Louisiana Railway** (Missouri Pacific Railroad) between Helena Junction and Rohwer, both in Arkansas. Built during the early 1900s, this rail line was actually a late addition to the nation's systems of railroads. While proposals were made for decades to build a railroad south from the Memphis area on the west side of the Mississippi River, the White and Arkansas river channels kept construction from happening.

It wasn't until the late 1890s that a true effort began to build the railroad, thanks to the financing provided by George Gould. The Gould family had been involved with the Missouri Pacific Railway and the St. Louis, Iron Mountain & Southern Railway for several decades. The Missouri Pacific company actually started as the Pacific Railroad, with the first track built from St. Louis in 1851. The railroad was reorganized as the **Missouri Pacific Railway** in 1872. Jay Gould, a major railroad owner and financial speculator who was one of the so-called "robber barons," gained control of the railway in 1879.

Meanwhile, the **St. Louis, Iron Mountain & Southern Railway** was built during the 1870s to haul iron ore from Iron Mountain, Missouri, to St. Louis. Jay Gould acquired control in 1883. His son George Gould took control of both railroads in 1892 when his father died of tuberculosis. George Gould continued to expand the railroad empire and wanted to build rail lines into parts of the country without rail service, thus blocking the expansion of competing companies. For eastern Arkansas, this meant that railroad along the west bank of the Mississippi River.

While many rumors about construction of the line had been reported for decades, one of the first serious reports was in the *Helena Weekly World* (June 5, 1901). It reported that engineers Elliott (chief engineer of the Yazoo & Mississippi Valley) and Gordon were making a railroad survey south from Helena, after having made one from Memphis to Helena three years earlier. Reports at the time stated that the survey was for Reed Northrup, president of the American Refrigerator Transit Company (ART). However, Northrup was a cousin of George Gould, leading to reports that this was a Missouri Pacific Railway project. Interestingly, the Missouri Pacific acquired ART in 1903, and the firm is still a subsidiary of the Union Pacific Corporation.

A concern for Helena was whether the community would be on the mainline, or simply on a branch line. This fear was realized when *The Railway Age* (March 21, 1902) reported on the incorporation of the Memphis, Helena & Louisiana. The article stated that the railroad would be built from a point opposite of Memphis, and then south to the Louisiana state line, for a total of 187.5 miles. The construction would include two branches to Helena: from the Saint Francis River southeast to Helena (9 miles) and from Helena southwest to the new main line (11 miles). Later, Henry Rohwer, chief engineer of the Missouri Pacific, reported that the Memphis, Helena & Louisiana Railway would be built from a point near West Memphis, to Prippe Junction on the St. Louis, Iron Mountain & Southern. Some existing track would be used in that area, and then new track would be built from Halley, Arkansas, to Tallulah, Louisiana. Rohwer also stated that there were plans to build on to Clayton, Louisiana, to connect with the New Orleans & Northwestern Railway. This would create a new

Memphis to New Orleans route that would be controlled by George Gould.

The Memphis, Helena & Louisiana was actually just a paper railroad, and it never operated a train. Instead, the company was created to build the railroad for the St. Louis, Iron Mountain & Southern. Two companies were actually created. The Memphis, Helena & Louisiana Railway was chartered in Arkansas, while the Memphis, Helena & Louisiana Railroad was chartered in Louisiana. The officers of the two companies were the same as those of the Missouri Pacific Railway and the St. Louis, Iron Mountain & Southern Railway. This relationship led newspapers to state that the railroad was being built in the interest of the Missouri Pacific, and thus it was a "Gould Road." This relationship became even more clear when the Memphis, Helena & Louisiana was sold to the St. Louis, Iron Mountain & Southern on April 30, 1903. However, the Memphis, Helena & Louisiana name was still used for several years in the construction reports, and for more than several decades in other government reports.

Construction continued, but the bottoms around the Arkansas and White rivers were still a challenge. In July 1904, only forty miles of track remained to be completed, primarily around the two large bridges. An interesting bit of news came from Russell Harding, General Manager of Missouri Pacific, who stated that the line would also be used by the St. Louis & San Francisco (Frisco), although this would never occur.

Delayed by the Bridges

These last forty miles of track took another eighteen months to complete, no matter the optimism of the company officials. The key delay was the construction of the two large bridges needed to cross the Arkansas River and the White River. Both bridges were authorized by Congress on February 24, 1902, and the Secretary of War on August 14, 1902.

The annual flooding in the river bottoms limited much of the actual foundation work. The White River bridge had its piers installed by December 1904, and steel work began soon after. However, the Arkansas River bridge was more of a challenge. The river had a wide channel and its main course changed frequently. Therefore, there was a major engineering project to reroute the river under the proposed location of the drawspan. Both bridges were erected in 1905, but the Arkansas River attacked the railroad again when it completely changed its channel and went back to an older route. As reported in the December 23, 1905, *Arkansas Gazette*, the new Arkansas River bridge was left "standing high and dry a mile from the stream." Before the railroad could open, the river had to be rerouted back under the bridge.

Early Railroad Operations

The Memphis, Helena & Louisiana route was put into service on December 26, 1905. Service at first was basic as the line was still being improved and finished. Passenger service didn't begin until March 1, 1906, and this service was not very impressive as it was simply a passenger car on the local freight train. As reported by the *Arkansas Gazette* on that date: "It is announced that local mixed service will be started on the Memphis, Helena and Louisiana railroad between Helena and McGehee, beginning today. Under the schedule the train will leave McGehee at 7 a.m. and arrive at Helena at 4:25 p.m., and returning will leave Helena at 8:10 a.m. and arrive at McGehee at 5:15 p.m. Trains will be run daily except Sunday."

More service began by the end of the month with the announcement about new St. Louis to Ferriday (Louisiana) service, where trains would connect with the Texas & Pacific's line to New Orleans. St. Louis to Helena "fast mail service" was also starting on two trains each way. Much of the early freight service handled timber and lumber, as the railroad opened up about 100 miles of eastern Arkansas. Almost every new station featured a logging railroad and sawmill until the late 1920s. As the timber was cut, agricultural products such as cotton, rice, corn, wheat and fertilizer started to dominate. Additionally, a number of trains simply carried freight between the Gulf of Mexico and cities like Memphis, St. Louis, and Chicago. So much freight was moving right after World War II that five scheduled freight trains operated over the line in each direction, plus a number of daily extra trains.

Helena Southwestern Railroad Company

Early statements had been made that the St. Louis & San Francisco would also use this line, but that never happened. However, the Helena Southwestern Railroad Company did operate their trains over the line, generally handling timber shipments to West Helena.

The Helena Southwestern Railroad started as a private line built to support the Chicago Mill & Lumber Company's operations at Helena. The 2.321-mile line, with 3.249 miles of yard tracks and sidings, was built by the lumber company in 1913 and then sold to the Helena Southwestern Railroad Company, which was incorporated on November 7, 1913. The sale took place in two steps on December 30, 1913, and May 1, 1914. This gave the railroad a mainline from West Helena to Helena Southwestern Junction and a connection with Missouri Pacific. There were a number of plans for expansion, and the *Railway Review*, dated February 28, 1914, stated that the railroad planned to build southwest from West Helena to Pillows Hills, Arkansas, a total of 20 miles.

The proposed line was never built, but instead other Chicago Mill properties were assigned to the railroad. During 1916, the Helena Southwestern acquired Arkansas railroad property in Prairie and Woodruff Counties from the Chicago Mill & Lumber Company. The lumber company also had properties in northern Louisiana. To connect to these properties, the railroad had trackage rights on other area railroads. One of these was 57.8 miles of trackage rights over the Missouri & North Arkansas between West Helena and McClelland, Arkansas, a route known as the McClelland Division.

The railroad company also operated over the Memphis, Helena & Louisiana route, using almost 220 miles of Missouri Pacific track from Southwestern Junction near West Helena, through Barton to near Tallulah, Louisiana (the Main Line Division), and Chimile, Louisiana (the White River Division). These routes connected with several other Chicago Mill properties and allowed the movement of logs and lumber. Most of these trackage rights and secondary operations were retired by the 1930s.

The railroad operated quietly for many decades, but according to the Railroad Retirement Board, the Helena Southwestern "ceased to be an employer effective with the close of business December 31, 1986." The property was sold to P. E. Barnes & Sons, Ltd., as a private carrier in April 1987. The mill and the railroad were eventually closed and abandoned. While the Chicago Mill & Lumber Company and its Helena Southwestern is gone, there is a unique survivor of the company. The two-truck, 53-ton Heisler #10 railroad locomotive still exists, displayed at the Railroad Museum of Pennsylvania. The Heisler was built in 1918 with serial number 1375, for the W. T. Smith Lumber

Company in Chapman, Alabama. It was sold to Angelina Hardwood of Ferriday, Louisiana, and then the Chicago Mill & Lumber Company in Tallulah, Louisiana.

Consolidation and Changes on the Line

The Memphis, Helena & Louisiana (MH&L) was sold to the St. Louis, Iron Mountain & Southern Railway Company on April 30, 1903. This company had been created in 1874, and over the next several decades grew closer and closer to the Missouri Pacific Railway, although not always in a willing way. The control of the company by Jay Gould in 1883 made it a part of a 10,000-mile system of lines. This system greatly expanded as Gould acquired and built more lines, including the Helena to McGehee line.

On August 19, 1915, both the Iron Mountain and the Missouri Pacific Railway Company entered receivership. On February 21, 1917, the two railroads were sold at foreclosure to the creditors of the lines. Most of the two systems were then merged into the new Missouri Pacific Railroad Company on May 12, 1917. While this helped the company financially, it also provided alternative routes for the movement of passengers and freight. These alternative routes sometimes came in handy. Although the MH&L line was generally built using high fills, flooding still impacted the railroad. For example, during February 1907, late winter and early spring of 1916, and in March and April of 1917, the line was flooded between Snow Lake and Watson and all rail service was stopped.

Passenger service was never heavy on the Helena to McGehee line. In 1909, a single passenger train (#341 southbound, #342 northbound) operated each way daily between Helena and McGehee, each taking about nine hours. By 1926, two trains operated daily in each direction between Memphis, Helena and McGehee. Trains #343 and

#344 were the daytime locals, making all stops and taking less than four hours to make the run between Helena and McGehee. At the same time, trains #330 and #331 provided overnight service, carrying a Memphis-Ferriday, Louisiana sleeping car. This train only made stops at larger stations. This sleeper service did not last the Great Depression.

	341	Ms	October 31, 1909. LEAVE / ARRIVE	342	
	A M			P M	
	†8 10	0	Helena	4 00	
	9 53	12	Barton Junction	2 00	
	10 35	18	Oneida	1 10	
	11 05	23	Lake View	12 43	
	11 59	30	Elaine	11 59	
	12 45	39	Mellwood	11 00	
	1 10	45	Ferguson	10 30	
	1 40	52	Snow Lake	10 00	
	3 10	70	Watson	8 30	
	3 41	76	Kelso	7 55	
	3 53	79	Rohwer	7 40	
	4 20	85	McArthur	7 20	
	5 00	91	McGehee	†7 00	
	P M		ARRIVE / LEAVE	A M	

Dated October 31, 1909, this time table shows one of the first schedules for the Memphis, Helena & Louisiana route. From *The Official Guide to the Railways and Steam Navigation Lines of the United States,* January 1910, page 921.

Helena Junction to Rohwer – History of the Railroad Route

Table 55—MEMPHIS, HELENA, McGEHEE AND NATCHEZ.

397	331	343	Mls.	January 24, 1926.	330	344	398	854
	P M	A M		LEAVE] [ARRIVE	A M	P M		
.....	*8 00	*9 00	0	+... **Memphis** ...ⓢ	6 50	5 40	.....	.....
.....	— —	9 28	8.8	......Hulbert......	— —	5 10	.....	.....
.....	8 50	9 48	17.9	......Neuhardt ...ⓢ	5 42	4 47	.....	.....
.....	9 04	10 01	23.4	......Chatfield......	5 25	4 34	.....	.....
.....	9 17	10 13	28.9	......Hughes....ⓢ	5 07	4 20	.....	.....
.....	9 28	10 23	33.4	......Bledsoe......	4 54	4 08	.....	.....
.....	9 40	10 37	38.1	......Brickeys....ⓢ	4 38	3 56	.....	.....
.....	9 51	10 50	42.9	......Soudan......	4 24	3 45	.....	.....
.....	10 14	11 12	50.8	+... **Mariana** ....ⓢ	4 00	3 24	.....	.....
.....	11 17	12 14	76.3	arr..+**Helena**ⓢ .lve.	3 00	2 25	.....	.....
.....	11 27	1 45	76.3	lve....**Helena**...arr.	2 50	2 10	.....	.....
.....	12 15	2 32	94.1	......Oneida......	2 00	1 22	.....	.....
.....	12 25	2 43	98.6	.....Lake View.....	1 48	1 11	.....	.....
.....	12 40	2 58	105.9	......Elaine ....ⓢ	1 28	12 57	.....	.....
.....	— —	3 06	110.3	......Mary......	— —	12 47	.....	.....
.....	1 02	3 17	115.4	......Mellwood....ⓢ	1 02	12 36	.....	.....
.....	1 13	3 28	122.5	.....Ferguson.....	12 50	12 25	.....	.....
.....	1 27	3 45	128.7	......Snow Lake...ⓢ	12 37	12 10	.....	.....
.....	— —	4 03	134.8	......Mozart.....ⓢ	— —	11 55	.....	.....
.....	2 08	4 40	146.9	......Watson....ⓢ	11 58	11 25	.....	.....
.....	2 30	5 02	156.2	......Rohwer......	11 37	11 04	.....	.....
Mix.	2 45	5 19	162.3	......McArthur.....	11 23	10 48	Mix.	.....
†A M	3 00	5 35	167.9	arr.+**McGehee**ⓢlve.	11 10	*10 35	P M	.....
‡7 45	3 30	P-M	167.9	lve...**McGehee**...arr.	10 25	A M	‡1 25	.....
.....	— —		171.2	......Masonville.....	— —			.....
.....	3 55		175.4	+....**Dermott**....ⓢ	10 05			.....
8 00	.....		172.6	..**Trippe Junction.**..	.....		1 10	.....
8 15	4 15		177.0	......**Halley**.....ⓢ	9 40		12 55	.....
8 40	4 30		184.4	.....Macon Lake.....	9 26		12 30	.....
9 20	4 52		191.5	.....**Lake Village**..ⓢ	9 03		12 01	.....
9 40	5 05		196.9	......Jennie......	8 53		11 15	.....
10 00	5 14		200.3	......Chicot......	8 44		11 00	.....
10 30	5 30		207.0	+.....**Eudora**.....ⓢ	8 30		10 30	.....
11 00	5 40		210.9	.....Readland.....	8 12		9 40	.....
11 15	5 48	855	213.9	.....Arkla, Ark.....	8 04		9 20	.....
11 50	5 58	Mix.	218.1	....Millikin, La...ⓢ	7 56		9 00	Mix.
12 45	6 12	A M	223.5	......Shelburn.....	7 44		8 30	P M
1 30	6 30	†7 00	230.5	+.Lake Providence.ⓢ	7 30		†8 00	2 30
P M	6 50	7 25	239.0	....Transylvania...ⓢ	7 09		A M	1 55
.....	7 05	7 40	243.1	......Alsatia......	6 57			1 35
.....	7 15	7 50	246.0	.....Roosevelt.....	6 50			1 15
.....	7 23	8 00	247.9	.....Sondheimer.....	6 45			1 05
.....	7 30	8 10	249.2	......Enoka......	6 40			12 50
.....	7 45	8 30	253.8	......Mansford.....	6 31			12 25
.....	8 05	9 10	258.9	......**Tallulah**...ⓢ	6 20			11 50
.....	8 15	9 25	262.7	......Laclede......	6 02			11 25
.....	8 28	10 00	268.2	...Alligator Bayou...	5 51			11 00
.....	8 38	10 40	272.0	......Quimby.....ⓢ	5 43			10 40
.....	8 52	11 00	276.5	......Somerset......	5 32			10 20
.....	f —	f —	278.3	.....Durrossett.....	f —			
.....	9 15	11 40	283.8	.....Newellton....ⓢ	5 15			9 55
.....	9 30	12 01	289.2	....Lake Bruin.....	5 03			9 30
.....	9 42	12 45	294.2	....St. Joseph....ⓢ	4 51			8 55
.....	10 00	1 10	301.1	....Locust Ridge....	4 33			8 05
.....	10 10	1 25	304.8	.....Goldman......	4 24			7 50
.....	10 15	1 35	306.6	+...Waterproof....ⓢ	4 20			7 40
.....	10 45	2 20	317.7	.**Clayton Junction**.	3 53			7 00
.....	11 00	2 45	323.2	arr...**Ferriday** ⓢ lve.	*3 40			†6 45
.....	1 00	P M	336.5	arr...**Natchez**.ⓢlve.	*2 30			†5 00
.....	P M	.....		(Natchez & South.)	P M			A M

For Through Sleeping Car Service, see pages 722-724.
For Index of Stations, see pages 718-720.

This January 24, 1926, schedule shows the Memphis, Helena & Louisiana route at about its peak of passenger service. From *The Official Guide to the Railways and Steam Navigation Lines of the United States*, February 1926, page 735.

Delta Heritage Trail: History Through the Miles

Table 54.
MEMPHIS, HELENA, McGEHEE AND NATCHEZ.

Bus.	Bus.	331	341	335	Mls.	April 15, 1934.		346	334	330	Bus.	Bus.
P M	A M	P M	P M	A M		LEAVE]	[ARRIVE	A M	P M	A M	A M	P M
*7 00	*1000	*7 00	*1045	*9 00	0	+...Memphis...ð		7 10	6 35	10 35	10 10	5 20
....	....	f7 25	⊙	f9 31	8.8	......Hulbert......		▲	f6 05	f1005	....	....
f7 57	f1057	f7 40	....	f9 50	17.9	.....Neuhardt....ð		....	f5 60	f9 50	f9 09	f4 21
8 14	11 14	f7 50	....	f9 59	23.4	.....Chatfield.....		....	f5 40	f9 40	8 56	4 06
8 28	11 28	8 00	....	f1008	28.9	......Hughes.....ð		....	5 31	9 31	8 44	3 52
8 39	f1139	f8 09	....	f1016	33.4	......Bledsoe......		....	f5 21	f9 21	f8 36	f3 41
f8 51	f1151	8 18	....	10 24	38.1	......Brickeys....ð		....	5 13	9 13	f8 26	f3 29
f9 02	f1202	f8 28	Via Little Rock.	f1029	42.9	......Soudan......	Via Little Rock.	....	f5 03	f9 03	f8 17	f3 18
9 20	12 20	8 45		10 40	50.8	+...Marianna....ð		....	4 48	8 48	8 00	3 00
10 20	1 20	9 35		11 40	76.3	arr.+Helena ð.lve.		....	4 00	*8 00	*7 00	*2 00
P M	P M	P M		1 30	76.3	lve...Helena...arr.		....	3 30	A M	A M	P M
....	....	....		2 17	94.1	......Oneida.....		....	f2 38	....	....	....
....	....	....		f2 29	98.6	...Lake View...ð		....	f2 29	....	....	....
....	....	....	Motor.	2 43	105.9	......Elaine....ð		....	2 17	Motor.	....	....
....	....	....		2 59	115.4	....Mellwood....ð		....	2 01		....	....
....	....	....		f3 10	122.5	.....Ferguson....△		....	f1 50		....	....
....	....	....		3 25	128.7	...Snow Lake...ð		....	1 35		....	....
....	....	....		f3 37	134.8	......Mozart....ð		....	f1 25		....	....
....	....	....		4 11	146.9	......Watson....ð		....	12 47		....	....
....	....	3 97		4 32	156.2	......Rohwer.....		....	12 27	....	....	3 96
Bus.	....	Mix.		f4 46	162.3	......McArthur....		....	f12 15	Bus.	....	Mix.
P M		†A M	5 35	5 00	167.9	arr.+McGehee ð lve.		11 55	*1205	P M	>....	P M
*1260	....	⁊7 00	6 30	P M	167.9	lve..McGehee..arr.		11 05	P M	3 25	....	⁊8 30
1 01	....	- -	- -	....	172.6	..Trippe Junction..		- -	....	3 14	....	....
1 16	....	- -	6 48	....	177.0	......Halley....ð		10 40	....	3 04	....	- -
1 35	....	- -	f7 02	....	184.4	...Macon Lake...		f10 24	....	2 52	....	- -
1 55	....	- -	7 17	....	191.5	+..Lake Village..ð		10 10	....	2 37	....	- -
2 07	....	- -	f7 26	....	196.9	......Jennie......		9 56	....	2 27	....	- -
2 17	....	- -	f7 34	....	200.3	......Chicot.....		8 48	....	2 20	....	- -
2 35	....	- -	7 55	....	207.0	+.....Eudora.....ð		9 35	....	2 07	....	- -
2 50	....	- -	8 03	....	210.9	......Readland...		9 17	....	1 55	....	- -
....	....	f1032	- -	Bus.	213.9	......Arkla, Ark....		- -	....	....	....	f3 40
3 14	....	f1042	f8 16	Bus.	218.1	....Millikin, La....ð		f9 00	Bus.	1 40	....	3 25
....	....	f1056	f8 25	A M	223.5	.....Shelburn.....		f8 49	P M	....	....	f5 10
3 50	....	11 20	8 40	*6 35	230.5	+.Lake Providence.ð		8 35	7 05	1 14	....	2 45
4 12	....	f1140	8 54	6 51	239.0	...Transylvania...ð		8 15	6 36	12 57	....	f2 20
4 22	....	f12 10	f9 03	6 59	243.1	......Alsatia.....		8 04	6 28	12 48	....	f2 00
4 31	....	f12 15	f9 09	7 04	246.0	.....Roosevelt....		f7 57	6 23	12 43	....	f1 40
4 36	....	12 20	9 14	7 08	247.9	....Sondheimer...ð		7 52	6 19	12 40	....	1 30
4 39	....	12 25	f9 17	7 10	249.2	......Enoka......		f7 48	6 17	12 37	....	f1 20
4 50	....	f1235	f9 26	7 18	253.8	.....Mansford....		f7 39	6 09	12 29	....	f1 05
5 00	....	12 50	9 40	7 30	258.9	......Tallulah....ð		7 30	6 00	12 20	....	12 50
5 12	....	f1 25	f9 48	7 42	262.7	......Laclede....		f7 15	5 48	10 53	....	f1120
5 25	....	f1 40	f9 56	7 55	268.2	...Alligator Bayou..		f7 07	5 32	10 40	....	f1110
....	....	f2 00	10 05	....	272.0	......Quimby....ð		f7 00	....	....	....	f1100
5 44	....	f2 15	f1015	8 16	276.5	.....Somerset....		f6 50	5 08	10 20	....	f1045
6 01	....	2 40	10 28	8 34	283.8	.....Newellton...ð		6 38	4 48	1004	....	10 28
6 13	....	f3 00	f1037	8 54	289.2	.....Lake Bruin...		f6 28	4 31	9 45	....	f1010
6 31	....	3 30	1048	9 00	294.2	.....St. Joseph...ð		6 18	4 26	9 31	....	9 55
6 48	....	f3 50	f1102	9 30	301.1	...Locust Ridge....		f6 02	4 05	9 13	....	f9 35
7 02	....	f4 00	f1110	9 46	304.8	.....Goldman.....		f5 53	3 50	8 57	....	f9 20
7 09	....	4 47	11 14	9 54	306.6	+...Waterproof...ð		5 50	3 44	8 50	....	9 15
....	....	....	11 35	....	317.7	.Clayton Junction.		5 28	....	....	....	8 45
7 50	....	....	11 45	10 40	323.2	arr.+Ferriday ð lve.		5 15	3 05	8 10	....	†8 30
8 20	....	....	P M	12 40	11 15	332.6	arr...Vidalia ð..lve.		4 35	2 45	....	A M
8 45	....	....	....	1 30	11 40	336.5	arr...Natchez ð lve.		*4 00	*2 25	*7 20	....	....
P M				P M	A M		(Natchez & South.)	P M	P M	A M		

This April 15, 1934, schedule shows that Missouri Pacific cut the level of passenger service during the Great Depression, and most of it never returned. From *The Official Guide to the Railways and Steam Navigation Lines of the United States*, May 1934, page 701.

On May 11, 1941, Missouri Pacific inaugurated the railroad's first diesel-powered streamlined train in Arkansas – the *Delta Eagle*. This train was an attempt to increase services but cut costs on rural routes, and it featured a diesel locomotive with a baggage section at the rear, and only two coaches. Nothing about the train was normal. The diesel locomotive was custom built by the Electro Motive Corporation as a model AA-6 with only one 1000-horsepower diesel engine instead of two. The unused space housed a baggage compartment with additional space used for a steam generator that provided steam heat to the train.

The two coaches were built by the St. Louis Car Company in early 1941. Car #760 had a 15-foot Railway Post Office section that was used to sort mail that was picked up or dropped off along the route. The car also included sixty coach seats that were assigned to black passengers due to state segregation laws. The second coach was #732, a 51-seat grill-chair car that provided basic meals. There was a small counter and a pair of tables that sat eight. This car was assigned to white passengers. As the train needed maintenance or repair, the cars and locomotive would be replaced for a few days, generally with older equipment that was being held in reserve.

The *Delta Eagle* passenger train initially operated between Memphis, Tennessee, and Tallulah, Louisiana, and it was financially very successful through World War II. As roads were built, traffic declined and the route was cut back to Memphis-McGehee on January 1, 1952, and Helena-McGehee on October 27, 1954. The last use of the name *Delta Eagle* was in the Missouri Pacific timetable dated October 19, 1954.

Delta Heritage Trail: History Through the Miles

Delta Eagle
STREAMLINED - DIESEL POWERED

TABLE R

335-336-335 Daily Example	Miles			334-337-334 Daily Example
4.15 Su	.0	Lv	MEMPHIS...Ar	11.45 Su
4.31	7.8		......Wimef........	11.20
4.58	28.9		.....Hughes......	10.52
f5.08	38.1		.....Brickeys......	f10.38
5.26	50.8		....MARIANNA....	10.21
5.42	63.2		.......Lexa........	10.04
6.04 Su	76.3	Ar	...HELENA... Lv	9.43 Su
6.10 Su	76.3	Lv	Ar	9.41 Su
6.47	94.1		......Oneida......	9.08
f	98.7		....Lake View......	f
7.05	105.9		......Elaine......	8.50
7.18	115.4		.....Mellwood......	8.35
7.38	128.7		.....Snow Lake.....	8.14
f7.47	134.8		......Mozart......	f8.04
f	137.8		......Benzal.......	f
f7.58	140.8		......Medina......	f7.54
8.11	146.9		......Watson......	7.44
8.26	156.2		......Rohwer......	7.29
f8.35	162.3		.....McArthur.....	f7.22
8.45 Su	167.9	Ar	Lv	7.15 Su
			...McGEHEE...	
9.10 Su	167.9	Lv	Ar	7.05 Su
9.45 Su	191.5	Ar.	LAKE VILLAGE. Lv	6.31 Su
Ⓐ10.29 Su	191.5	Lv.	.Lake Village...Ar	Ⓐ5.44 Su
Ⓐ11.20 Su	.....	Ar	Lv	Ⓐ5.00 Su
			.GREENVILLE.	
Ⓐ8.30 Su	.....	Lv	Ar	Ⓐ8.05 Su
Ⓐ9.21 Su	191.5	Ar.	..Lake Village...Lv	Ⓐ7.14 Su
9.45 Su	191.5	Lv.	LAKE VILLAGE. Ar	6.31 Su
f9.57	200.3		.......Chicot.......	f6.18
10.06	207.0		.....EUDORA......	6.10
10.37	230.5		...Lake Providence...	5.39
Ⓖ10.48	239.0		.....Transylvania.....	Ⓖ5.28
11.00	247.9		.....Sondheimer.....	5.16
11.20 Su	258.9	Ar.	..TALLULAH...Lv	5.00 Su

CONNECTION TO NEW ORLEANS

103				116
9.10 Su	.....	Lv....McGehee....Ar		7.00 Su
12.10 Mo	.....	Ar.....Monroe.....Lv		4.25 Su
2.55 Mo	.....	Ar....Alexandria....Lv		1.55 Su
8.20 Mo	.....	Ar..New Orleans...Lv		8.30 Sa

Ⓐ Missouri Pacific Transportation Co. Bus.
f Flag stop.
Ⓖ Stops for revenue passengers to or from McGehee or beyond.

CONSISTS
DIVIDED COACH — Memphis-Tallulah
GRILL COACH — Memphis-Tallulah

As shown by this schedule, in 1946 the Delta Eagle operated between Memphis and Tallulah. From Missouri Pacific passenger timetable, Issued February 10, 1946. From the collection of Barton Jennings.

Helena Junction to Rohwer – History of the Railroad Route

Missouri River Eagle
Between: St. Louis - Kansas City - St. Joseph - Lincoln - Omaha.

Colorado Eagle
Between: St. Louis - Kansas City - Pueblo - Colorado Springs - Denver.

Delta Eagle
Between: Memphis - Helena and Tallulah, La.

Schedules and Equipment Shown on Pages 5, 6 and 9.

STREAMLINED DIESEL-POWERED

The Delta Eagle debuted in 1941. Missouri Pacific heavily promoted the service after World War II. From Missouri Pacific passenger timetable, Issued February 10, 1946. From the collection of Barton Jennings.

Within a year, the traditional train was replaced by the *Eaglette* #670, a 75-foot-long self-propelled motor car, built by American Car and Foundry in 1942. This car featured a passenger and baggage section, putting an entire train in one car. However, it did not include a post office section, indicating the loss of the railway post office service on the route as the Memphis & McGehee Railway Post Office route had been discontinued on October 28, 1954. Reports state that closed pouch mail service did continue almost until the end of the McGehee-Helena motorcar service. For those who want to learn more about railway post offices, check out the Railway Mail Service Library.

Despite the cost savings, the lack of riders led to larger and larger losses. Missouri Pacific stated that the company had lost $217,244 running the *Delta Eagle* between 1956 and 1959. In late 1959, Missouri Pacific announced plans to end the passenger service provided by trains #334 and #335. A series of petitions and a number of public statements fought the abandonment. One of the common themes was the isolation of the communities along the line. For example, the twenty rail miles between Snow Lake and Watson required more than 100 miles by road. Other examples of the importance of the passenger service was the use of the passenger trains by children going to and from school, and law enforcement using the trains to reach remote parts of the counties. However, passenger service ended on February 27, 1960.

Helena Junction to Rohwer – History of the Railroad Route

TABLE 10-11-59 **25**   **HELENA — McGEHEE**

Miles		335 Daily	Miles		334 Daily
0	Lv HELENA..........	5.40	0	Lv McGEHEE	9.30
13	Lv Lexa.............	6.01	6	Lv McArthur........	f 9.37
23	Lv Oneida...........	6.23	21	Lv Watson..........	9.58
35	Lv Elaine...........	6.42	27	Lv Medina..........	f10.07
44	Lv Mellwood.........	6.56	39	Lv Snow Lake.......	10.26
58	Lv Snow Lake........	7.14	53	Lv Mellwood........	10.44
70	Lv Medina...........	f 7.32	62	Lv Elaine..........	10.56
76	Lv Watson	7.46	74	Lv Oneida..........	11.11
91	Lv McArthur.........	f 8.07	84	Lv Lexa............	11.33
97	Ar McGehee..........	8.20	97	Ar HELENA..........	11.59

f—Stops on signal.
★—Stops to receive or discharge revenue passengers.
T—Stops for revenue passengers to or from Opelousas and points beyond.

This is the last public timetable released by Missouri Pacific (December 6, 1959) that showed the Helena to McGehee passenger service. From Missouri Pacific passenger timetable, dated December 6, 1959. From the collection of Barton Jennings.

Just as the passenger train was ending on the line, the railroad also changed from operating steam locomotives to using diesel locomotives. This allowed the many water towers along the line to be closed, as well as the steam shops at McGehee and elsewhere. The use of radios and the loss of local freight eliminated the need for agents at many of the stations along the line, meaning that depots could be torn down. During the 1950s, the rail line continued to be used by trains heading to and from the Gulf Coast, with about a half-dozen freight trains heading in each direction every day. Many of these handled the chemical business that was so important to the railroad. However, the construction of the new single-crest (hump) classification yard in North Little Rock in 1961 started moving service to the lines that passed through that terminal. During May 1962, Missouri Pacific announced that two freight trains would move off the Memphis, Helena & Louisiana line and start operating through North Little Rock. Both of these trains originated in Dupo, Illinois, and the plans were to reclassify the cars at the new yard so they could be blocked for points south such as Alexandria, New Orleans and Houston. About a dozen trainmen living in Paragould, Arkansas, were impacted by the change.

A study of the 188.1-mile line between Paragould and McGehee was conducted by the railroad in 1970. It stated that less than one million tons of freight moved over the line in each direction, with the principal commodities being "cotton, cotton seed, paper products, wood chips, limestone, feed, soybeans, soybean mill and oil, caustic soda, chemicals, rubber products, wood products, and Chicago Mill products." At the time, the line was served by a series of local trains, with a tri-weekly local freight operating between McGehee and Helena. It left McGehee Monday, Wednesday and Friday, and then returned the next day, with Sunday as the off day. The study also commented that the "line between Snow Lake and McGehee has some unstable fills that get irregular during rainy seasons or extended dry weather periods, but we generally keep them up in fair condition without extra forces, due to the light traffic over this segment of the line."

As the traffic increased across the railroad during the 1970s, Missouri Pacific began operating blocked trains that did not need switching along the route. This led the company to again move freight over the Memphis, Helena & Louisiana line. In April 1980, Missouri Pacific began rebuilding the line between McGehee and Paragould with plans to operate chemical trains over the route. The railroad installed 127 miles of welded rail, 125,000 new ties, and centralized traffic control (CTC) trackside signals along the line. The railroad also extended the sidings at Snow Lake and Watson, replaced about ninety turnouts, and improved 197 grade crossings. The company also made bridge repairs and had plans to fill or replace many of the older timber trestles. By Spring 1981, a series of chemical trains were again using the line daily. With this, the tonnage over the line grew substantially, with 3.7 million tons moving southbound and 10.8 million tons moving northbound over the McGehee-Helena Junction route in 1985.

The End of the Memphis, Helena & Louisiana Line

At the same time, a series of railroad mergers across the country were taking place. One of these included Missouri Pacific, Union Pacific, and Western Pacific. On January 8, 1980, the Union Pacific Corporation had announced an agreement to buy the Missouri Pacific Railroad. Approval was finally received on September 13, 1982, after a series of hearings and lawsuits. It finally took a Supreme Court ruling to allow the merger on December 22, 1982. A unique detail not known by many was that the Missouri Pacific had a number of outstanding bonds that prevented a full merger of the two companies. The bonds were finally closed during the mid-1990s, and the merger became final on January 1, 1997.

With the merger, traffic routing changed as duplicate routes were added by the merger and subtracted by sale and abandonment. By the mid-1980s, new operating plans began moving the freight traffic off of the Memphis, Helena & Louisiana line. During the Thanksgiving holiday of 1986, the last of the traffic was moved again to lines that operated though the North Little Rock terminal. The MH&L line was used for some special moves after that, but it was soon embargoed and left to sit unused for several years. During this time, many of the newly installed train signals were relocated to the Sedalia Subdivision in Missouri.

The May 20, 1991, *Federal Register* covered the final details of the line's abandonment. The report stated that Missouri Pacific Railroad was abandoning "a 73.53-mile portion of its Wynne Branch line of railroad, milepost 326.27 near Helena Junction, and milepost 399.8, near Cypress Bend." The abandonment application stated that [1] no local traffic had moved over the line for at least 2 years; [2] any overhead traffic on the line could be rerouted over other lines; and [3] no formal complaint had been filed by a user of rail service on the line. The Interstate Commerce Commission approved the abandonment on May 13, 1991. In 1992, Union Pacific donated the 73-mile abandoned right-of-way to the State of Arkansas, allowing the creation of the Delta Heritage Trail.

The Author's Story – The End of the Wynne

The following was first written for the Arkansas Railroad Club and printed in their August 2006 newsletter. The article marked the twentieth anniversary of the closing of the line between Cypress Bend and Helena Junction. It has been edited and updated for inclusion in this book.

The year 1986 marked the effective end of the Helena to McGehee line of the Memphis, Helena & Louisiana. The line had become part of the Missouri Pacific's (later Union Pacific's) Wynne Subdivision, which once ran from McGehee, northward to Paragould, through east Arkansas. This line was once part of the route of the famous Missouri Pacific *Delta Eagle*, a unique little two-car train that operated between Memphis, Tennessee, and Tallulah, Louisiana. This train operated from 1941 to 1952, making it one of the shortest-lived *Eagle*-named trains on the Missouri Pacific.

The history of the line's construction is a bit complicated. Starting near Jonesboro, Arkansas, the line branched off from the Texas & St. Louis Railroad (later Missouri Pacific's St. Louis to Texas mainline). Construction started in 1882 by the St. Louis, Iron Mountain & Southern Railway and extended just over sixty miles to a connection with the Rock Island line at Forrest City, Arkansas. From the south, the Iron Mountain & Helena Railroad (IM&H) had built into Forrest City in 1881 from Marianna, Arkansas. South of there, the railroad had been built in 1880 from Helena as a 3' 6" gauge line by the IM&H, but it was standard gauged in 1881 when the line was extended. This part of the Wynne Subdivision still exists, some of it now operated in the Helena area by the Arkansas Midland, the rest as a lightly used branch of Union Pacific.

South of Helena Junction, the line is now a combination of hiking and biking trails and abandoned right-of-way between railroad mileposts 327 and 399. This part of the Wynne Subdivision was built by the Memphis, Helena & Louisiana Railway, starting in McGehee, Arkansas, in 1904, and finishing at Helena Junction in 1906. Little of the physical line remains with the only rail service being between McGehee and the former Potlatch paper mill lead at Cypress Bend. The Helena to Cypress Bend part of the line was always the hardest to justify operating, with almost no on-line business and the high cost of two major bridges (Arkansas River – 6020' of timber, steel and turnspan, White River – 4260' of bridge, including a lift span).

While today not much more than a wide spot on U.S. Highway 65/165 in southeast Arkansas, McGehee was once one of the most important points on the Missouri Pacific Railroad. At one time it featured a roundhouse, fueling facilities, a busy freight car repair track, a 24-hour office, and a very busy yard. In fact, the hump yard in North Little Rock, Arkansas, was originally proposed for McGehee.

In 1986, the author of this book was working for Union Pacific as the Manager of Track Maintenance (MTM) out of McGehee. This was just a few years after the merger between the Missouri Pacific, Western Pacific, and Union Pacific railroads. Arriving in McGehee, my territory covered the former Missouri Pacific trackage to Little Rock through Pine Bluff, as well as the southern end of the Wynne Subdivision. At the time, Union Pacific track, bridge and signal forces were finishing up a large project to rebuild the line to handle additional chemical traffic that was planned to be moved off of various routes through Little Rock. Ties had been installed north of Cypress Bend, a large surfacing gang was working south from Helena Junction, and bridge forces were working to fill in one of the large timber trestles in the Arkansas/White River bottoms.

McGehee was also changing. While it featured local trains operating in five directions (toward Little Rock, Monroe, Cypress Bend, Warren, and Tallulah), some mainline trains were beginning to operate through McGehee without stopping for train orders or to change crews. However, the two yards (old and new) were kept busy enough to require several switch crews. The station had lost its 24-hour status and the author took the train order signals down off the station. Additionally, it wasn't long before the diesel fueling facilities were removed and the diesel tanks torn down.

My first trip across the line was by hi-rail (a vehicle that can operate both on road and rail tracks) on July 7, 1986, to just get a feel for what was where, but a trip on July 16th involved much of the divisional management to get a status report on the various projects that were underway. My notes indicate that most of the work left was clean-up, including installing new guard rails on bridges and removing scrap materials. A week later, the railroad operated a special chemical train across the line during the early morning of July 24th which required manually locking switches in front of it and inspecting the track afterwards. This was a train that had obtained the nickname "The Bhopal Special." It was a unit train of methyl isocyanate, the chemical which just a year earlier had escaped a plant in India and killed many people in and around Bhopal. This was a good example of why the line was being rebuilt – getting hazardous chemicals from the Gulf Coast to industrial users in the north while risking exposure to as few people as possible.

A sign that the railroad still had major plans for the Wynne Subdivision again shows up in my notes on July 30th. On that day, I hi-railed the line to inspect the rail to make recommendations for future rail replacement and grinding programs. I was back on the line two days later on August 1st to inspect the track in front of a Houston-Chicago (HOCH) chemical train. By the way, my track-and-time to be on the track started at 1:27am. The train's reverse move, the CHHO, derailed at the south end of Snow Lake siding on August 5th, but it rerailed itself without the crew ever knowing. On August 18th, the Potlatch local, with Missouri Pacific locomotives 2223 and 2310, hit a rice truck just two miles north of McGehee. Just some of the excitement taking place along the line at the time.

On August 20th, it was back to the hi-rail for a trip between Watson and McGehee to plan for unloading thirty cars of ballast to begin track tamping in this area. August 27th saw me back on the line between McGehee and Snow Lake escorting a Federal Railroad Administration (FRA) employee on an inspection trip. Oh, and there are notes about four separate derailments in August at the Potlatch paper mill and on its lead – just some of the joys of being in maintenance-of-way!

The first week of September saw ballast still being unloaded on the Wynne Subdivision just north of McGehee. Also, a full inspection of the White River bridge was made with notes about the need to replace some ties around the fire breaks on the structure. Meanwhile at least two freights a day in each direction continued to operate over the line between McGehee and Jonesboro/Paragould. A note on September 10th indicates that 21 cars of ballast had been unloaded and 15 more were needed to complete the surfacing on the Wynne line. The rest of September saw quite a bit of ballast unloading and tamping, as well as more fill for that timber trestle project out in the bottoms. Additionally, the derailments on the Potlatch lead continued through the month.

October started with Union Pacific's track geometry car EC-3 heading north out of McGehee on the 8th. I rode as far as Lexa and then caught a ride with Union Pacific #2529 (INHO - INdianapolis-HOuston) back south to McGehee. My notes show only a few geometry problems left on the line. There were also some comments about management wanting copies of track inspection reports for the Potlatch Lead at Cypress Bend as I campaigned for some work there.

A comment should be made here about my trips over the Wynne Subdivision. Many more hi-rail trips over the line were made than is indicated here. I was on duty every other weekend and the territory on those days included all the way up to Helena and beyond. These trips often included a stop for lunch with my folks in Caldwell, north of Forrest City. Additionally, routine trips were often made to check on the progress of various projects and to observe the different gangs at work.

Things got real interesting on October 16th when a work train derailed an axle at Vestal, a seldom used spur track between the Arkansas and White River bridges. Vestal had once been an important point on the line as the Corps of Engineers had located a rotary car unloader here to dump rock from railcars into barges for navigation work on the two rivers. However, by 1986, it was used only by maintenance forces and access was only by rail. Notes indicate that the bridge forces using the train to unload fill at that timber trestle got the locomotive rerailed, but a number of managers, including myself, visited the site the next day. For those interested, the locomotive involved was Missouri Pacific #2095, a GP38-2 built by EMD of General Motors. The track gauge wasn't too good and 54 of the 83 ties in the area did not meet the FRA's definition of a good tie.

November got started in an interesting fashion when a semi-truck missed the turn at Watson and bounced across the ditch and onto the mainline before 6am. The next day, time was again spent on the line checking the progress of the surfacing gang and checking for any final cleanup work needed. On October 13th, the center of activity was at Medina as the work train had again derailed. This time it was an empty rock hopper (Missouri Pacific 582121) and it was a tough one to rerail. From my notes, it had climbed the rail at a joint so at least ties and gauge weren't to blame this time.

On Thursday, November 20th, DAPCO (a rail inspection company like Sperry) was on the property inspecting rail and worked between McGehee and Watson. The next day, a survey team was checking on bridges on the Wynne Subdivision while an inventory of available rail for relay on the line was conducted by the author. On the 24th, DAPCO was back and tested north of Watson. On the 25th, the rail inspection was followed up with another inspection of surfacing needs, bouncing on and off the track between the trains HOCH (HOuston-CHicago) and CHHO, the regular freights along with the INHO (INdianapolis-HOuston) and HOIN.

The next trip over the Wynne Subdivision was on November 28th, the day after Thanksgiving. There were no comments about trains in my notes. This would be something realized a day or two later. On Saturday the 29th, I was again at Cypress Bend inspecting a derailed car for the paper mill. Returning to McGehee, we were able to get all of the time we wanted on the Wynne Subdivision, but didn't think much of it as there was a planned train shutdown for the holiday.

Over the next week or two, it became obvious that the freights had not returned to the line, but that we were still spending great amounts of money maintaining track and upgrading bridges. More ballast for tamping was ordered, filling in bridges continued, and on December 12th we did some minor work to the White River lift bridge when it got stuck down in front of several barges. On Sunday, December 14th, I rode train LAI773 (the Potlatch Local) to inspect the line and had a talk with the crew about if the through trains would come back. The dispatcher also told me we could have all the time we wanted as all of the through trains were being diverted to other routes. Within a few days, there were some notes about the surfacing gang tamping on the Potlatch Lead. Obviously it was felt that the line to the paper mill was seeing more action then the mainline. The end of the Wynne was at hand!

Suddenly, all of my notes about the Wynne Subdivision focus on the paper mill lead at Cypress Bend. On December 22th, there are lots of notes about using the mainline surfacing gang to rebuild about 80 feet of track on the lead, including digging down to grade and building an entirely new fill. Additionally, the highway department was rebuilding Arkansas Highway 1 and a new crossing was going in. With all of this work, it wasn't long afterwards that we got caught and the gang was sent elsewhere and the last hi-rail project inspection trip over the Wynne Subdivision was made on Saturday, December 27, 1986.

While this was the end of regular freight service over the Wynne Subdivision, this wasn't quite the final death of the line. A bit of track and bridge work continued for some time and track inspections continued to be made just in case the line was needed. On January 8, 1987, I took the Division's Superintendent over the line to see its current status. A trip on January 16th noted that there were still 14 hoppers of rock at Medina for unloading. On March 19th, the White River bridge again locked down, blocking barge traffic and causing a rush of work.

Apparently top Union Pacific management still didn't know what they wanted to do with the Wynne Subdivision as the EC-3 geometry car made an inspection from McGehee to Jonesboro on April 2nd and 3rd, 1987. On April 13th, a weed spray train operated across the line using Union Pacific #1630. On the 23rd, UP management was again on the line, this time doing the yearly switch inspection.

The unusual happened on June 22nd when a note indicates that a storm had blown several cars over at Watson and that they would be rerailed, and the LAI73 (Potlatch Local) would run over the line to pick up any cars left on the line and take them to McGehee. I do remember a lot of chainsaw work and flagging of crossings. Another train ran over the line on July 20, 1987, when train RLMGMG (RaiL-McGehee-McGehee) operated south over the line and turned north toward Little Rock at McGehee to unload new welded rail. And guess what, the EC-3 car was back on September 1, 1987. However, after this time, travel on the line was down to a once-a-month hirail trip to just make sure that the railroad was still there.

Things picked up on March 30, 1988, when the MMGME (Maintenance-of-Way McGehee to Memphis) operated over the line. This train was nothing more than a contract weed spray train, but as it turned out, this was the last train that I ever saw cover the entire line. A note said that the crew was called at 6am at Lexa and was brought down to McGehee by taxi for the trip back. A sign that the line wasn't coming back for a while happened on April 5th when the EC-3 car only operated as far as Cypress Bend from McGehee (and didn't even cover the Potlatch Lead). By this time the track north of Cypress Bend was out of service (as noted in the May 31, 1988, track profile) and wasn't even being hi-railed to see if it was still there.

Even though the tracks were out of service, that didn't stop us from using them. On July 8, 1988, LAI73 took 60 covered hoppers to Watson for storage as McGehee yard was getting pretty full. This move involved another hi-rail trip to cut brush and a lot of flagging of crossings. For some reason, I hi-railed from Watson to McGehee on March 14, 1989, but no explanation was made in my notes. On June 20, 1989, I took the EC-3 geometry car from McGehee to the White River bridge, where it was handed off to the MTM from Memphis. There are notes that the bridge wouldn't come down but that it was working by the time the car got there.

This was my last trip to the bridge by rail. After that, issues on other parts of the railroad took priority. With the tracks now gone, the most recent visits have all been by driving various local roads.

Helena Junction to Rohwer –
The Guide to the Railroad Route of the Delta Heritage Trail

The almost seventy miles of trail from Helena Junction to Rohwer are on the abandoned grade of the Memphis, Helena & Louisiana Railway, later Missouri Pacific, and then Union Pacific Railroad. This route was considered as running north to south by the railroad, so that description will be used for the trail. In most cases, the trail actually does run north to south, but in a few places it can swing far to the east or west. However, the north-south direction will still be used. In referring to items along the trail, east and west will generally be used to describe their location. In the various towns along the route, street names will be used when possible.

One challenge is the names of the many streams along the route. Some have had their name changed over time, while others have been moved as part of the development of various drainage systems. This information will be provided when known to clarify any issues.

Along the entire Delta Heritage Trail are mileposts to help you keep track of where you are. These mileposts are new and are based upon the route used by the Delta Heritage Trail. The railroad had their own mileposts that started at Valley Junction, near Dupo, in the East St. Louis area. Both mileposts will be noted.

As of 2021, the Helena Junction to Rohwer rail-trail is open in two sections – Helena Junction to Elaine, and Watson to Rohwer. The middle forty miles is not yet open, but planning is underway to complete this section over the next few years. Information about all three of these sections is included here so that as the trail is expanded, information about the route is available.

Helena Junction to Rohwer – Guide to the Railroad Route

Delta Heritage Trail: History Through the Miles

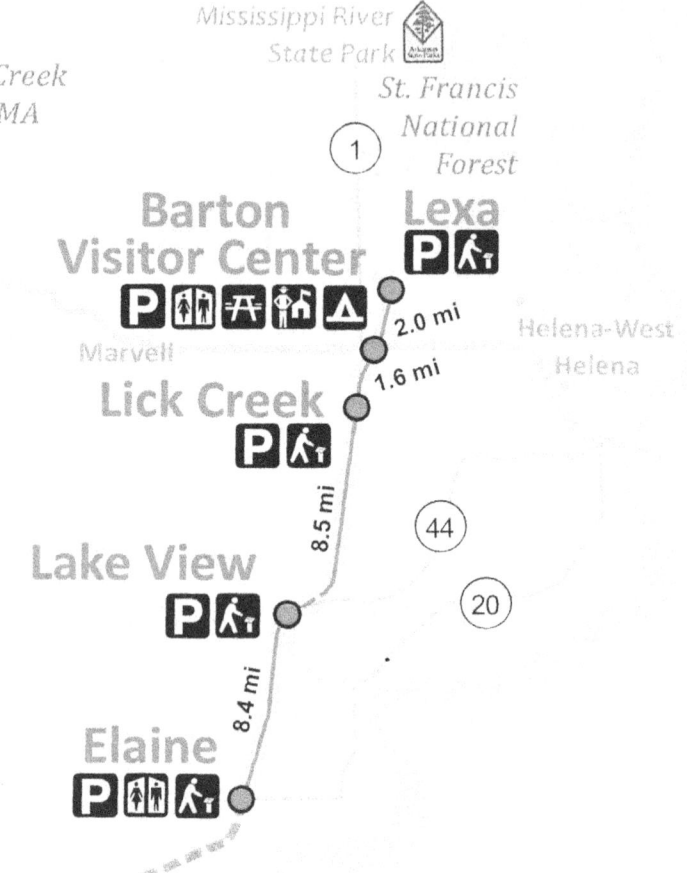

Trail map from Helena Trailhead to Elaine Trailhead. Map courtesy of the Delta Heritage Trail State Park.

Helena Junction Trailhead to Elaine Trailhead –
Active Delta Heritage Trail

0.0 **HELENA JUNCTION TRAILHEAD** – Located on Phillips County Road 251 not far south of Lexa is the Helena Junction Trailhead of the Delta Heritage Trail. For the railroad, this was DD Junction, later Helena Junction, a large wye track junction that connected tracks going in three directions. To allow train crews to communicate with the railroad's dispatcher, there was a telephone booth here for decades. To the north is a rail line through Lexa and on to St. Louis, Missouri. To the east is a line to Helena, Arkansas. To the south was a line to McGehee, Arkansas, today's Delta Heritage Trail. Information about the communities to the north and east are included below to help explain the importance of this location.

The Helena Junction Trailhead is clearly marked. All trailheads along the Delta Heritage Trail are marked with similar signs.

Delta Heritage Trail: History Through the Miles

Looking north from the Helena Junction Trailhead, the abandoned railroad grade can clearly be seen passing through the woods. The grade of the wye track to the east can also be spotted.

Where the south leg of the Helena Junction wye once connected with the McGehee mainline at Missouri Pacific Milepost 326.7, there is now a parking lot at the north end of the Delta Heritage Trail. This is the the Helena Junction Trailhead, located at an elevation of 212 feet, the highest point on the trail. The trailhead features several information signs and a few benches to simply enjoy the surrounding woods. If you look carefully, the old grade for the wye can be found as it curves off to the northeast.

The Delta Heritage Trail is marked with milepost signs, with the distance measured from Helena Junction.

This sign at the Helena Junction Trailhead shows that the Lick Creek Trailhead is 3.6 miles to the south. This is one of the most popular parts of the trail due to the distance between trailheads.

Lexa (Missouri Pacific Milepost 325.5)

Located a mile north of here in Phillips County is Lexa, Arkansas. Highway 242, running east-west, serves as First Street and is the only grade crossing across the Union Pacific Helena Subdivision rail line in Lexa. Today, Lexa is a town of approximately 300 residents at an elevation of 204 feet. Unfortunately, the town has few businesses and primarily serves as a residential community for the Helena area. The Arkansas Midland Railroad, a part of the Genesee & Wyoming family of railroads, now operates the Helena Branch between Lexa and Helena, and bases many of its operations in the small metal railroad office and yard in downtown Lexa.

The original plans for Lexa were much greater than today's results. Lexa was created when the Iron Mountain & Helena Railroad Company built through the area. The railroad used the land of Nathaniel Lexington Graves, and a small town developed on his plantation land. A post office opened in 1880 on property owned by Graves, reportedly using his middle name – Lexington. However, other sources credit his son, Alexander "Lex"" Graves as the source of the name. Because the name was somewhat common, it was shortened to Lexa in 1885. The town grew when the St. Louis, Iron Mountain & Southern (former Iron Mountain & Helena) built a small shop complex for repairing locomotives, cars, and equipment at Lexa in 1908.

According to the *Encyclopedia of Arkansas History & Culture*, "by 1911, Lexa had five general stores, three hotels, a restaurant, a drugstore, several boarding houses, and more than 100 private residences. Three schools were built – two for African-American students and one for white students. A Methodist church was established, followed shortly by a Baptist church." However, as the railroad was merged into the Missouri Pacific Railroad in 1917, the shops were closed and moved to other locations. Many businesses also moved away, starting a steady decrease in population. As an attempt to end the losses, Lexa was incorporated on April 15, 1925, but few things improved.

The 1921 *Arkansas Marketing and Industrial Guide* listed three significant industries at Lexa. The first two were the Lexa Gin Company and the Hicks & Solomon cotton gin, a common industry found in many towns in eastern Arkansas. In 1904, gins in Phillips County had produced 35,053 bales of cotton, more than any other county in Arkansas. The third major industrial activity was the Missouri Pacific Railroad feeding yard, used to rest and feed cattle in transit. During the early 1960s, these pens were shown to measure 37' x 107'. None of these can be found at Lexa today.

While industry and businesses moved away, farming continued in the area, and is still active today. A number of plantations existed in the area by the 1850s, and the fields were regularly flooded by high water on the Mississippi River. This natural fertilizer made the area some of the richest farmland in the state.

Phillips County is still a leader in agricultural production for Arkansas, with more than 80% of the county being farmland. Soybeans (245,000 acres), corn (35,000 acres), cotton (25,500 acres), wheat (10,500 acres), and pecans (500 acres) all ranked in the top five for county production in the state in 2016. Other crops like rice (5000 acres), peanuts

(600 acres) and sorghum (200 acres) are also grown. Most or all of these will be seen along the Delta Heritage Trail.

Latour Junction (Missouri Pacific Milepost 326.3)

The community of Latour was once to the southeast of here, located on what is now known as the Helena Lead, or the Arkansas Midland Railway. It was located where Phillips County Road 251 comes beside the railroad and curves to the southeast. A few houses remain in this area.

The community of Latour was never large, with a population of about 50 listed in 1915. However, it was large enough to gain a post office in 1881 which lasted until 1920. The only major industry listed for the community was farming. It is likely that the community was named for Géraud Calixte Jean Baptiste Arsène Lacarrière Latour (1778–1837), or more simply Major L. Latour. Latour, who was trained as an architect, surveyor and engineer, traveled quite a bit with Jean Lafitte and mapped large parts of the south and southwest. He developed one of the early plans for the City of Baton Rouge, and later served as a military engineer for Andrew Jackson at the Battle of New Orleans. It is known that Latour and Lafitte visited this part of Arkansas during their travels.

For many years, Latour Junction was the railroad switch for the line to Latour, and on to Helena. This junction location was known as New Latour in the description of the Missouri Pacific Railroad Company's 1917 incorporation. Records show that the 81.64 miles of track to McGehee was built by the Memphis, Helena & Louisiana Railway (MH&L), while the northward 106.93 miles of track to Paragould, and the 20.93 miles on to Knobel, both in Arkansas, were built by the Iron Mountain & Helena Railroad and the St. Louis, Iron Mountain & Southern Railway.

The initial arrangement at Latour had the mainline from the north curve east to Helena. Southbound trains would head to Helena, handle any local business, and turn. For several decades, a locomotive roundhouse stood at Helena, allowing steam locomotives to be swapped. Train crews also changed on some trains. When ready to head south, the train could come out to Latour Junction and turn south on the wye, or head to Barton Junction and turn south there. Eventually, it was decided that not all trains needed to head to Helena. The west side of the wye became a mainline and many trains simply headed north-south through the area without stopping at Helena.

The junction was later known as the switch to the Helena Lead. Today the tracks are still in service to Helena, but have been abandoned to the south on what was the mainline. The May 20, 1991, issue of the *Federal Register* reported on this abandonment. The Union Pacific Railroad track abandoned was "a 73.53-mile portion of its Wynne Branch line of railroad milepost 326.27 near Helena Junction, and milepost 399.8, near Cypress Bend." Milepost 326.26 was the cited location of Latour Junction in various railroad records.

Helena Junction (Missouri Pacific Milepost 326.5)

Located at an elevation of 207 feet, in 1969 Missouri Pacific Railroad showed this to be H. L. Junction, or Helena Lead Junction. The location is actually about the middle of the large wye that was once located here. A wye is a three-sided set of tracks that can be used to turn trains, and to allow trains to head in multiple directions. In this case, trains from the north could turn to the southeast to reach Helena using a line built by the Iron Mountain & Helena Railroad, or continue south to McGehee, Arkansas, on the line built by the Memphis, Helena & Louisiana Railway. The third leg allowed trains from McGehee to also turn east to reach Helena. For many years, the railroad had a telephone booth located here that allowed train crewmen and track workers to communicate with the railroad's dispatcher.

Helena, Arkansas

Helena is located at the south end of Crowley's Ridge on the west bank of the Mississippi River. Local digs have unearthed pottery, various types of stone points, and large burial mounds. Many of these relics indicate that this was a trading center located on ground above the annual floods. Helena is also believed by some to be the location of the first non-native religious service west of the Mississippi River (other evidence suggests the location to be at Parkin Archeological State Park in Arkansas), conducted when Spanish explorer Hernando Desoto crossed the river near here in 1541. Other reports indicate that Father Jacques Marquette and fur trader Louis Joliet visited Indian settlements in the area in 1673 during their four-month exploration of the Mississippi River. The first white settlement reportedly was in 1800 when William Patterson built a dock and river terminal. His son, John Patterson, is claimed to be the first white child of American parents born in Arkansas. In 1820, Phillips County was created, being named for Sylvanus Phillips. The same year, Helena was surveyed and mapped by New Yorker Nicholas Rightor. The name of the town, Helena, came from the daughter of Sylvanus Phillips.

Helena was made the county seat in 1830, the same year that Sylvanus Phillips died. A post office opened in 1831 and trade on the Mississippi River led to the Town of Helena being incorporated in 1833. It is now recognized as the second-oldest incorporated city in Arkansas, incorporated as a city in 1856. Because of its position on the river, it attracted a number of merchants, bankers, and steamboat owners. This led Helena to resemble the many river towns up and down the river with expensive houses on the ridges, large warehouses and docks along the river, and the typical taverns, brothels, and housing for the working class.

During the Civil War, Helena was a key blockade point on the Mississippi River and Union forces occupied the town in 1862. From here, campaigns against Vicksburg and Little Rock were planned and supported. Because of this, the capture of Helena and then the defeat of Confederate forces attempting to retake the town on July 4, 1863, have been listed as one of the three critical Union victories, along with Gettysburg and Vicksburg, that are considered the turning point of the Civil War. One point of pride for locals during the war was that seven Confederate generals were from the Helena area. Among these was Patrick Cleburne, a famous local businessman. Cleburne, two other generals, and many veterans are buried in the Confederate section of Maple Hill Cemetery in Helena.

Because of the presence of Union forces, Helena was an early target for runaway slaves. So many slaves showed up and were given their freedom that two black regiments were formed at Helena. In 2011, Helena's Freedom Park was designated by the National Parks Service as a site on the National Underground Railroad Network to Freedom, the first site in the state of Arkansas to receive that designation. A number of other era remains also still exist. The remains of four Union batteries are still visible, with Battery C being restored. A replica of Fort Curtis has also been built to explain the city's Civil War history.

After the war, Helena recovered quickly due to its location on the Mississippi River. It regained its reputation as a major cotton town, and a place where almost every vice could be obtained with ease. Mark Twain visited and wrote about Helena, stating that "Helena occupies one of the prettiest situations on the Mississippi" in his book *Life on the Mississippi*. He also wrote that Helena was "exceptionally productive" and "the commercial center of a broad and prosperous region."

The late 1800s and early 1900s saw railroads arrive and a move away from the river to other modes of transportation. Industry, especially those related to timber, located on the edge of town, creating communities such as West Helena. However, the Eighteenth Amendment and its prohibition of alcoholic beverages closed many of the businesses related to barrel making. During January 1927, Helena opened a new $400,000 river terminal, hoping to expand shipping. Within months, Helena was struck by the Mississippi River Flood of 1927. The Depression hit before the town recovered, a second flood in 1937 did more damage, and railroads that served the town were lost over the next decade or two. With the timber gone, Helena reverted back to a large farm town, moving cotton, fertilizer, and other farm crops.

Helena was the location of the first broadcast of *King Biscuit Time*, a show dedicated to Southern blues music. First aired on November 21, 1941, the show is still on the air on the original KFFA. It is the longest-running daily American radio broadcast in history, and has won numerous broadcasting awards. The show is broadcast live from the studio at the Delta Cultural Center and visits are encouraged. World War II provided some economic boost for the community, especially with car parts and box manufacturing companies. Immediately after the war in 1946, the school systems of Helena and West Helena were merged.

Like many southern cities, the 1950-1970s were hard as industry and the economy changed, civil rights and school desegregation were pushed, and many workers moved away for better jobs. The century of segregated communities and the history of conflict between Helena and West Helena led to years of efforts to try to consolidate the cities. Finally, on January 1, 2006, the two merged creating the city of Helena-West Helena, Arkansas. In 2010, the combined population was 12,282.

The Helena-West Helena area has been the hometown of a number of famous people. For example, John Hanks Alexander, the first African-American officer to hold a regular command position, and the second African-American graduate of the U.S. Military Academy, is from here. Country Music Hall of Famer Conway Twitty once lived here, as his father was the captain of one of the automobile ferries used on the Mississippi River before the Helena Bridge was built in 1961. Baseball stars Alex Johnson and Ellis Valentine claim the area as home. Finally, the first African-American president of the Board of Commissioners of Cook County, Illinois, John Stroger Jr., came from Helena.

Helena's Delta Cultural Center

In 1915, the old Arkansas Midland Railroad station was replaced with a new red brick building with limestone accents. Today listed on the National Register of Historic Places, the two-story building is described as having been built with "detailing from the Craftsman period as well as subtle Classical Revival influences." The station was built with a two-story northern section, with upstairs offices designed as the regional headquarters for the St. Louis, Iron Mountain & Southern. The southern end served as a one-story freight house. Originally, the freight and baggage sections were separated by a breezeway which was enclosed early in the building's existence. It later became the station of Missouri Pacific Railroad.

Located in the Missouri Pacific depot and a series of nearby storefronts on Cherry Street is the Delta Cultural Center. This is another must stop for any exploration of the area. The center provides an opportunity to wander this former passenger depot and freight house. The displays in the Missouri Pacific depot include items about area railroads, industry, farming, the Civil War, and the 1927 Flood. A noted feature is the bell from Illinois Central Railroad's *Pelican* ferryboat.

Attached to the station is Missouri Pacific caboose 13461, which can be toured. This caboose was built at the Sedalia (Missouri) shops of Missouri Pacific in 1950. Originally numbered 1196, it was one of 180 welded cabooses built by the railroad. The caboose was modernized in the late 1960s. When Missouri Pacific became a part of Union Pacific, the caboose became a member of class CA-21. The caboose was finally retired on April 1, 1987, and donated to Helena during May 1989.

The Railroads of Helena

At one time, five different railroads served Helena. The local railroad was **The Citizens Street Railway Company**, chartered on March 8, 1887. The system originally operated up Cherry Street through the business district, and then connected with the neighborhoods to the north. It became the Helena Street Railway Company by 1890, and still used horse-pulled cars. By 1912, the line was extended to West Helena as an electric interurban system, known as the Helena Street & Interurban Railroad Company. The streetcar system shut down on August 5, 1933, and was replaced by the buses of the Twin City Transit Company.

Besides the electric interurban railroad, there were four different steam railroads that once served Helena. From the west, the first two were the **Arkansas Central Railway**, later the Arkansas Midland Railroad, and the Iron Mountain & Helena. Then there was the Missouri & North Arkansas, also from the west. The final railroad was the Yazoo & Mississippi Valley from the east, crossing the Mississippi River to reach Helena.

The **Iron Mountain & Helena** was the first steam railroad at Helena. It and the Arkansas Midland both later became a part of Missouri Pacific in 1917. The Arkansas Midland route out of Helena through Barton was abandoned during the 1930s. During the 1940s, Missouri Pacific ran five passenger trains in and out of Helena each day, and they also ran a "doodlebug" (a self-propelled railcar) from Helena to Memphis every day. One of these trains was the regionally famous *Delta Eagle*. The *Delta Eagle* was Missouri Pacific's first diesel-powered streamlined train serving Arkansas. The train featured a unique consist using a diesel locomotive which was built with a baggage section at the rear, plus two coaches. The train initially operated between Memphis and Tallulah, Louisiana, but was cut back to running between Helena and McGehee on October 27, 1954. The passenger train last operated on February 27, 1960.

The Missouri Pacific Railroad became part of Union Pacific in 1982. In 1992, the line from Lexa to Helena was turned over to the Arkansas Midland Railroad, owned by the Pinsley Railroad Corporation. In late 2014, Pinsley sold their Arkansas railroads to Genesee & Wyoming.

The third steam railroad was the **Louisiana, New Orleans & Texas Railroad**, which used a transfer boat (ferry) to bring cars across the Mississippi River starting in 1889. The trackage in Arkansas was technically the Louisville, New Orleans & Texas Railway Company of Arkansas. The Interstate Commerce Commission stated that the railroad consisted of a terminal yard in Helena, a total of 0.895 miles of track. The railroad was later the Yazoo & Mississippi Valley (Y&MV), and then the Illinois Central

Railroad in 1946. The end of ferry service became official with a March 23, 1973, ruling of the Interstate Commerce Commission, and its tracks at Helena were sold to Missouri Pacific.

The final railroad to arrive at Helena was the **Missouri & North Arkansas Railroad Company**, which reached here in 1906 and operated until 1946. This line was never prosperous and went through several reorganizations until most of it was abandoned. The Helena & Northwestern Railway operated the south end of the line from 1949 until 1951. After that, the line was abandoned and tracks removed, except for a few isolated industrial tracks that were kept to protect rail shippers.

Passenger Trains #343 and #344

For many years, Missouri Pacific Railroad operated passenger trains #343 and #344 between Memphis, Tennessee, and Arkansas City, Arkansas. Since the route of the Delta Heritage Trail generally follows this route, these trains will be followed across the route, giving users of the trail a bit of the feel for what it was like a century ago. The times provided are based upon a schedule published on January 24, 1926, about the time of peak passenger service over the line.

In 1926, passenger trains #330 and #331 also operated over the line, running between Memphis and Ferriday, Louisiana, with connecting ferry service on to Natchez, Mississippi. These two trains operated overnight and featured a 12-section drawing room, buffet broiler dining car, chair car, and divided coach between Memphis and Ferriday.

Train #343 would depart Memphis daily at 9:00am and arrive at Helena at 12:14pm. It would leave at 1:45pm, providing plenty of time for passengers to find lunch. Train #343 would then arrive at McGehee at 5:35pm, passengers would then have a chance for dinner, and then the passenger train would depart at 6:35pm for a 7:15pm arrival at Arkansas City. Northbound #344 would depart Arkansas City at 9:35am and arrive at McGehee at 10:15am. #344 would then depart at 10:35am and arrive at Helena at 2:10pm and depart at 2:25pm. It was scheduled to reach Memphis at 5:40pm.

0.4 **COUNTY ROAD 251** – Not far south of the Helena Junction Trailhead, the trail has an at-grade crossing with Phillips County Road 251, which heads east to Latour and then on south to U.S. Highway 49. Throughout this area, the trail is shaded by a narrow line of trees.

Note the gates across the trail. The Delta Heritage Trail is designed for hiking and biking, and these gates are designed to discourage vehicular traffic from using the route.

1.6 **BRIDGE** – The trail and former railroad grade crosses a small stream that has been channeled as part of the local drainage system. This practice is common in the area. The stream essentially flows to the southeast and into Lick Creek. The railroad had a 60-foot TPTOD (timber pile trestle with an open deck) bridge. Located at Missouri Pacific Milepost 328.3, this five-panel bridge was known as Bridge No. 2 of the Memphis, Helena & Louisiana Railway.

All of the stream crossings on the Delta Heritage Trail between Helena Junction and Elaine use the original railroad bridges, rebuilt with new decks to allow use by hikers and bikers. Many of these bridges had open decks, meaning that they had ties as the deck of the bridge, with space between them. Some bridges were built with ballast decks. These had a full solid bridge deck that was covered with ballast, with the track on top of and in the rock.

2.0 U.S. HIGHWAY 49 OVERHEAD BRIDGE – Missouri Pacific Railroad records show that an overhead highway bridge was installed here in 1922, with a replacement built in 1949. Later, the railroad showed this to be a pair of overhead viaducts. U.S. Highway 49 is one of the original federal highways, connecting Gulfport and Clarksdale, Mississippi. In 1963, it was extended across the new Mississippi River bridge at Helena, all the way to Brinkley, Arkansas. It was extended several more times and the north end of the highway is now a junction with U.S. Highway 62 at Piggott, Arkansas. This makes U.S. Highway 49 about 520 miles long.

Piggott was once the home of the Pfeiffer family, the in-laws of novelist Ernest Hemingway. Hemingway actually visited this area a number of times, especially the river bottoms south of Snow Lake, where hunting, fishing and drinking were popular pastimes.

The Milepost 2.0 sign marks where the Delta Heritage Trail passes under U.S. Highway 49.

Dawkins Spur

Dawkins Spur was once located just north of where the overpass now exists at Missouri Pacific Milepost 328.7. This location was listed in the 1922 *Bullinger's Postal and Shippers Guide for the United States and Canada*. The guide stated that the station was served by the Memphis Division of the Missouri Pacific Railroad. The line used was the Latour District which at the time covered Latour Junction to McGehee. The Dawkins Spur track once headed to the southwest from the mainline, but it was removed in 1923.

2.1 DELTA HERITAGE TRAIL STATE PARK'S VISITOR CENTER

– The visitor center is located at what is known as the **Barton Trailhead**. Located on U.S. Highway 49, the visitor center uses a retired cotton gin, and includes historic displays, a gift shop and park offices. Outside are 24-hour access restrooms, five primitive campsites with tent pads, picnic tables, standing grills, and a community water spigot. There is also plenty of vehicle parking. The trail in this area is heavily wooded, as is much of the Barton Trailhead property.

Not far to the west on U.S. Highway 49 is Walnut Corner, the intersection between U.S. Highway 49 and Arkansas Highway 1. The intersection can be very busy, and it includes a gas station and convenience store, a bank, restaurant, and several other businesses. The Barton-Lexa High School is also located here. This is probably the busiest place along the entire Delta Heritage Trail, and the location with the most services.

This sign marks the Barton Trailhead, located near the visitor center of the Delta Heritage Trail State Park.

There are five primitive campsites at the Barton Trailhead, and the sites are marked by this sign.

The Cotton Gin

The cotton gin used by the visitor center was purchased by others after it closed, with the buildings cleared of all of their machinery. Its new owners started to convert the structure into a house, and the seed house was rebuilt into a small apartment. When the Delta Heritage Trail State Park opened, the cotton gin building was acquired and a new visitor center built into the structure.

The former cotton gin and about 3.5 acres was purchased by the Arkansas Department of Parks and Tourism from Wanda and Chip Franklin during February 2001. The metal gin building was built about 1950 and includes 4254 square feet of space. To the south is an 864-square-foot seed house.

The Delta Heritage Trail State Park visitor center at Barton Junction is housed within a former cotton gin, very appropriate for the region that the trail passes through.

Cotton gins were and still are an important part of the southern agricultural scene. At first, the cotton lint was separated from the seed by hand. It was a slow and hard process that produced only about one pound of cotton lint a day. The cotton gin dates back to about a thousand years ago with the creation of the Churka gin. This type of roller gin was hand operated and consisted of two hard rollers that ran together at the same surface speed, pinching fiber from the seed. Reportedly, a good Churka gin could produce about five pounds of cotton lint a day. As cotton production grew in the United States, improvements had to be made, especially since the cotton grown in the South had fiber that was strongly attached to the seed.

This improvement came about on March 14, 1794, when Eli Whitney received a patent on a machine to gin cotton. According to the *Cotton Ginners Handbook*, published in December 1994 by the United States Department of Agriculture, this machine used "saws or metal spikes driven into a wooden cylinder in concentric rows. The spikes or saws passed through narrow slots to remove cotton fiber from the seed one batch at a time. To operate the gin, the ginner placed a few handfuls of seed cotton in the machine and then turned the cylinder by hand; the gin then removed the fibers from the seed and brushed them into a pile behind the machine. The gin was then stopped, the seeds were removed, and the process was repeated."

Improvements were quickly made by additional inventors, blacksmiths, and many others. One of the most important was by Henry Ogden Holmes, a plantation blacksmith from South Carolina. Holmes received a patent on May 12, 1796, for his gin which featured slots that allowed cleaned seeds to fall out of the bottom of the gin. This allowed gins to be used continuously, and about four million bales of cotton were ginned annually by 1860, more than half of the world's supply.

Improvements continued, and better machinery became available, leading to the construction of more and larger cotton gins. By 1920, there were 18,440 cotton gins in the United States, producing 13,271,000 bales, or 720 bales per gin. In 1940, there were 11,650 cotton gins that produced 12,298,000 bales, or 1056 on average. Since then, the number of cotton gins has continued to decrease even while the production of cotton has increased. This came about due to larger and more efficient gins, with 5395 gins producing 14,265,000 bales in 1960 (2644 per gin) and 1533 gins producing 15,065,000 bales (an average of 9826) in 1990. Many gins also added drying and cleaning equipment, and by 1960, "most gins used two stages of seed cotton drying, three or four seed cotton cleaners, and two lint cleaners to clean and dry cotton," according to the United States Department of Agriculture. Therefore, old retired cotton gins can be found throughout the south, with the remaining active cotton gins now standing larger and busier than ever.

While we describe production in bales of cotton, what is a bale? The National Cotton Council of America states that a bale of cotton weighs 500 pounds, and is 54-55 inches long, 20-21 inches wide, and about 33 inches thick. However, the National Cotton Council also states that these "are approximate values and some normal variations are to be expected."

The equipment in the field also pushed the need for larger and more efficient cotton gins. The use of mechanical harvesting equipment reduced the time required to pick the cotton; thus, more cotton reached the cotton gins in shorter periods of time. The harvester, or cotton stripper, also increased efficiency in the field, picking up to 99 percent of the cotton from the plant. Moving the cotton from the field to the gin also changed, led by the Arkansas Cotton Caddy. The Caddy "was the first device to make a compacted, free-standing stack of harvested cotton used for both storage and transport." Thanks to the Caddy, and the similar box press, more than half of the U.S. cotton crop was stored in modules before ginning by 1992.

For the past few years, even newer machinery is assisting the farmer in harvesting their cotton crop. For example, John Deere builds a round module cotton picker that cleans the cotton and creates its own round bales of cotton, all while picking the field.

This speeds up the harvesting process and reduces the number of machines required to pick, clean and transport the cotton. Thanks to these machines, cotton is now moved more efficiently and in larger single volumes from the fields, leading to many cotton gins now owning their own trucks to haul modules and bales for their customers, allowing better scheduling of the cotton ginning process.

This cotton box press stood ready, not far from the Delta Heritage Trail, for the 2020 harvest. This device is an example of the modernization that reduced the need for farm labor across the region.

While cotton gins were an essential part of the cotton farming business, few farmers could afford to buy and install the expensive ginning outfits. Therefore, cotton gins were owned either by large plantations, corporations, or cooperative associations. Many of the cotton gins offered other services such as selling cotton seed, tools, farming equipment, and other farm supplies.

From late August through late December, cotton was picked and brought to the gin, requiring it to operate eighteen to twenty-four hours a day. The route to a cotton gin was easy to find as it was often lined by lost cotton and hundreds of wagons hauling that day's production. To pay for the ginning, farmers often sold their cotton seed to the ginners. Sharecroppers and tenant farmers often simply obtained a credit for their cotton that could be used in the nearby company store. Cotton buyers often had a representative at the cotton gin who would make offers directly to farmers based upon the grade, color and quantity of cotton available. Therefore, the gin location was busy each fall for many years, with the rest of the year being spent conducting routine maintenance.

For those that want to know more about cotton gins, their history and their design, check out the *Cotton Ginners Handbook*, known as Agricultural Handbook Number 503. It was released by the United States Department of Agriculture in December 1994.

The Railroad Pole Line

There are several former railroad telegraph poles on the west side of the Delta Heritage Trail near Barton Junction. Most railroads were once followed by a pole line that served different purposes. The primary purpose of the poles was to carry electrical circuits. These included telegraph, telephone, signaling, and power lines. Today, these have generally been replaced by things like fiber optics, microwave, radio, and local power lines, and most pole lines have been removed.

The railroad pole line had different names on different railroads. These included code line poles, telephone poles, telegraph poles, utility poles, signal poles, and simply line poles. On different routes, the wires were used for different purposes. For example, the first poles along the Memphis, Helena & Louisiana carried telegraph wires. On many railroads, the telegraph lines were actually installed by a company like Western Union. In many cases, Western Union would install extra lines for the railroad as payment for the use of the right-of-way. Then, the railroad would handle local messages for Western Union at the depot, and the railroad's own messages on their lines. On rural routes, a single set of telegraph lines might be used due to the low volume of messages.

Railroads used the telegraph for many years, but telephone service was adopted during the early to mid-1900s. Lines for this service were added to the pole line, sometimes using the same basic method of sharing with local telephone companies. By World War II, a number of telephones were located along the MH&L route, allowing train crews and track employees to talk to the railroad's dispatcher. A surprisingly large number of telephone lines were often used as there could be circuits dedicated to dispatchers, station to station messages, and system communications.

Because electrical power was not always available along the railroad, some railroads had their own power lines on the poles. These were generally clearly marked to save lives. As rural electrification took place, the electrical lines were often shortened and only existed between a public connection and where the power was needed.

Reminders about the railroad heritage of much of the Delta Heritage Trail can be found all along the trail. For example, this former telegraph/signal line pole still stands at the Barton Trailhead.

Pole lines also carried signal line wires. Little of the MH&L was signaled until the 1980s except for some short sections around junctions and between McArthur and McGehee, south of Rohwer. Initially, these signal lines required a number of wires, but improvements reduced them to only two to four wires. Today, most signals are handled through signal pulses using the steel rails of the track, microwave, radio, or satellite communications.

A final use of the pole line was as information for the train crews and track gangs. Poles were marked with their railroad location and carried the mileposts of the railroad. Railroads often referenced these poles as part of a station's location. For example, the telephone booth at Barton Junction was shown to be at Milepost 329 Pole 8.

Today, the once-common pole line is rare. Between the new technologies replacing the wires, and the value of the copper and steel wires and the poles they rest on, few lines remain. The few poles that can still be found along the Delta Heritage Trail are reminders of these historic technologies.

Heading south toward Barton Junction, the trail crosses this small bridge near Milepost 2.3. Note the pile of old bridge timbers nearby. Reminders of the railroad can be found all along the Delta Heritage Trail.

Helena Junction to Elaine

Look for the 2.5 milepost to find the Barton Junction area. This location was once very busy with two railroads and a number of connecting tracks. Today, it is a quiet spot in the woods along the Delta Heritage Trail.

2.5 **BARTON JUNCTION** – This location, at Missouri Pacific Milepost 329.2, was once the crossing with the Arkansas Midland Railroad Company, known as Barton Junction or Barton Crossing, and later the switch for the Holly Grove Industrial Lead. The Arkansas Midland rail line actually had a fairly complex history. It started as the Arkansas Midland Railroad, created on November 7, 1853, and chartered on January 20, 1855. The route was planned as a 115-mile line from Helena to Little Rock, and some discussion had it as a narrow gauge line. While some grading was done, the company never built any track due to a lack of funding and the Civil War. On August 31, 1870, the Arkansas Central Railway Company was organized and acquired the work of the Arkansas Midland. The firm completed track with a gauge of 3'-6" from Helena to Duncan and on to Clarendon, a total of approximately fifty miles. Train service began in 1872.

That year, a railroad map was published by G. W. & C. B. Colton & Company that showed the Arkansas Central as a part of a much larger network of railroads. The map was labeled as showing "the Arkansas Central, the Helena & Corinth, and the Pine Bluff & Southwestern Railways, together forming the Texas & Northeastern Railway." The map showed an existing route from Corinth (Mississippi) to Helena to Pine Bluff (Arkansas), and on to Shreveport (Louisiana), with projected lines and connections to places like Nashville (Tennessee), Chicago (Illinois), Houston and San Antonio (Texas), and even Los Angeles (California).

However, the railroad almost immediately failed financially and was sold to the new Arkansas Midland Railroad Company (chartered May 15, 1878) on January 3. 1880. On the same date, the Arkansas Midland acquired the Little Rock & Helena Railroad Company. The new owner of the combined railroad system was Sidney Hornor, a member of the Hornor family that would later develop West Helena and the interurban railroad between Helena and West Helena.

When the Cotton Belt built through Arkansas in 1883, the Arkansas Midland converted its track to 3-foot gauge so freight cars could be interchanged between the two railroads. The line then converted to standard gauge in 1887 when most railroads in the region did the same thing. The Arkansas Midland expanded further on August 1, 1891, when it bought the Helena & Indian Bay Railroad which ran from Pine City to Brinkley, and then changed its track to standard gauge from its original 3-foot gauge. In 1901, Jay Gould bought the railroad and then it was merged into the St. Louis, Iron Mountain & Southern on September 1, 1909. For a number of years, trains from Helena heading south toward McGehee used the Arkansas Midland line to Barton Junction, where they turned south on the Memphis, Helena & Louisiana. However, because Missouri Pacific had two routes west from Helena, the Arkansas Midland route was abandoned east of Barton Junction in 1932.

The line west of here was eventually shortened until it became the 25.3-mile-long Holly Grove Industrial Lead, and the mainline switch received the name H G Junction (Holly Grove Junction). This line was still clearly listed in the 1969 employee timetable of Missouri Pacific. In 1975, the lead was abandoned between Marvell and Holly Grove, leaving a ten-mile rail line known as the Marvell Industrial Lead. This was abandoned in 1979, leaving the Barton spur track, which lasted until the end of the railroad.

Coolidge Addition

In 1905, a Coolidge Addition to Barton was platted around Barton Junction. A map of the plan showed a depot on the west side of the MH&L mainline, just south of the junction. A connecting track between the two lines was located on the southeast corner of the junction.

Coolidge Addition was large, with six east-west streets north of the junction and four to the south. There were five north-south streets west of the junction and two to the east. In total, there were 82 blocks planned for the community, with most having eighteen lots, except for the planned business district to the west of the depot which had 32 lots. Little of the Addition ever developed and nothing of the project exists today.

The Railroad Layout at Barton Junction

The layout of Barton Junction changed over the years, and a few minutes spent wandering through the woods will result in visitors finding a number of old grades and foundations. The Arkansas Central Railway grade can be easily found as it crosses the Delta Heritage Trail. Just to the north, the grade of the interchange track built after the track east of here to Helena was abandoned can be found on the west side of the trail.

South of the former diamond (railroad crossing) location and to the west were at least three tracks. Just south of the diamond was a short connecting track, removed in December 1948. Further south was a second connecting track that was retired in 1938. An industry track was even further to the south, and it was removed in 1946. To the southeast of the location of the railroad diamond was also a connecting track, used until the Arkansas Midland track was abandoned between Helena and here in 1932. On the east side of the MH&L mainline, and south of Barton Junction, was once an 89-car siding that went as far south as Missouri Pacific Milepost 330. This track was removed during Spring 1943.

Helena Junction to Elaine

Besides the tracks, Barton Junction also featured a number of buildings and other structures. A water tank, water column, pump house, and fuel oil tank had been improved in 1925, but were retired in late 1943. A telephone cabin was retired in 1956 and replaced by a telephone booth that was moved from Vanndale, a station north of Wynne, Arkansas. Train order signals also once stood here, removed as the junction became less important and the agency closed. Almost until the end of the Arkansas Central Railway line west towards Clarendon, Barton Junction was a train register station where conductors recorded their use of the line.

At one time, the railroad had a number of facilities at Barton Junction – a station, water tower, pump house, and others. A few of their foundations can still be found.

Despite all of this, Barton was not a major station along the MH&L line. During 1920, a new shelter shed with a 135-foot platform was installed to handle the local passenger and freight business. A few changes in its design took place over the years, but what was described as a freight and passenger shelter was removed in 1953.

Barton, Arkansas

Barton was an early community in Phillips County, located at an elevation of 191 feet. The community was reportedly named for Barton W. Green, Sr., a Swiss immigrant who homesteaded the area before the Civil War. Green invited other Swiss settlers to move to the area, with the last major immigration happening in 1903.

A post office opened at Barton in 1873, and it is still open. Efforts were made during the late 1800s and early 1900s to bring industry to the Arkansas Delta, and the Premier Cotton Mill was built in Barton in 1904 as a yarn mill, but it was moved to Helena in 1913. While manufacturing left Barton, the W. H. Gibson cotton gin still processed local cotton for many decades.

Barton is the home of the Barton Bears, long a powerhouse in high school football. Between 1978 and 2011, the school won eight state championships and finished second three times. Between 1985 and 1990, Barton won 63 consecutive football games, a state record. Football isn't the school's only activity, as the Lady Bears were state track champions in 1995 and state slowpitch softball champions in 1996. The boys track team won the state championship in 1994 and 2001. Barton High School is part of the

Barton School District which serves Barton, Lakeview, Lexa, and Oneida.

Barton High School is located not far west of the Delta Heritage Trail visitor center. The school proudly boasts of the football success of the Barton Bears.

Today, Barton is an unincorporated community in Phillips County. The remains of the cotton gin still stand next to the abandoned Arkansas Midland Railroad grade. A few houses also remain in the community, which lines Arkansas Highway 85 to the west.

3.1   COUNTY ROAD 300 – The trail crosses this county road at grade, so watch the traffic. The most common name for this road is the Old Little Rock Road. This route was an early military road used to connect Little Rock with the Mississippi River, and it was later used as a post road. Today, it is only used for local traffic as more modern highways have replaced this narrow and winding road. Just to the west is Arkansas Highway 85, which follows the Delta Heritage Trail until near Lake View.

3.5 LICK CREEK BRIDGE – Look for the long bridge, known as MH&L Bridge No. 5, just north of the Lick Creek Trailhead. Located at Missouri Pacific Milepost 330.2, this bridge was a 135-foot beam open deck structure when used by the railroad. It had been rebuilt from an earlier ten-panel timber pile trestle in 1935. When the bridge was rebuilt, it consisted of five spans built from large steel I-beams, each 27 feet long. Concrete piles were also installed, essentially replacing the timber with concrete and steel.

The Lick Creek Bridge consists of a beam open deck structure resting on concrete piles. It is an example of the type of bridges that were built as heavier trains began to use the line.

Lick Creek is a major stream that drains the lands west of Helena. Lick Creek forms a few miles south of Marianna and flows south on the west side of Crowley's Ridge. It flows just east of Lexa and then turns to the southwest and its waters enter Big Creek about five miles from here. Twenty miles of the waterway is now officially the Lick Creek Canal.

During the Civil War, Lick Creek marked the western limits of Federal control of the Helena area. The Union Army was worried about Confederate forces building up in the area and often sent patrols out to challenge them. One of these small battles, known as the Skirmish at Lick Creek, occurred on January 12, 1863, and involved Powell Clayton (Governor of Arkansas 1868-1871, Senator from Arkansas 1871-1877, and Ambassador to Mexico 1899-1905) and his Fifth Kansas Cavalry. A historical marker at the Lick Creek Trailhead explains the action.

> *After the January 11, 1863, battle at Arkansas Post, General Willis Gorman led troops from Helena on a raid up the White River. Colonel Powell Clayton and 1,200 cavalrymen went to Big Creek west of Helena when a patrol of 25 men of the 2nd Wisconsin Cavalry was sent back with messages. On arriving at Lick Creek, they found the bridge burned. As they forded the creek, around 200 Confederate horsemen attacked the patrol. The Wisconsin men, armed only with pistols, shot five or six attackers, but were quickly overrun. Only 5 of the 25 men made it to Helena.*

Later in March, another large Union force spent five days along Lick Creek fighting a number of small Confederate units. The result was a number of officers from both armies killed or taken prisoner, but no significant strategic advantages were gained. Until later in the year, Federal forces were basically confined to the territory east of Lick Creek.

3.6   LICK CREEK TRAILHEAD – Located on the south bank of Lick Creek is the Lick Creek Trailhead, which features parking, information signs, and easy trail access. The trailhead is located alongside Arkansas Highway 85 about two miles south of the intersection at Walnut Corner. This trailhead features several information signs and a beautiful setting, but offers few other facilities being so close to the park's visitor center.

This sign welcomes visitors to the Lick Creek Trailhead.

Helena Junction to Elaine

4.4 HARBIS SPUR – Harbis was an early community in Phillips County, listed in railroad timetables during the 1910s. However, it wasn't even on maps by the 1940s. Railroad records show that there was once a spur track to the southeast at Missouri Pacific Milepost 331.1, but that it was removed in 1935. Nothing remains here today but a farm road on the west side of the highway.

4.8 DOG BAYOU BRIDGE – The railroad had a 133-foot-long timber pile trestle here, now converted into the trail bridge. For years, this was known as Bridge No. 7, located at Missouri Pacific Milepost 331.5. Dog Bayou forms in the farmland to the east and flows west, eventually entering Big Creek. Much of its route has been channelized and it is used for drainage in the wet season, and irrigation in the dry season.

The Delta Heritage Trail bridges between Helena Junction and Elaine still use the original railroad bridges. An example is this 133-foot-long timber pile trestle that crosses Dog Bayou.

Heading south, the trail continues to be lined by thin rows of trees as it passes through miles of farmland. A number of small streams and drainage/irrigation ditches are also crossed using small timber pile trestles.

For those not accustomed to current farming practices, some of what you see might be a bit surprising. For example, the days of hundreds of laborers hand picking cotton have been gone for more than half a century. After that, large cotton-picking machines would work every row, filling a small bin on the machine. When full, this cotton was dumped into a trailer which was hauled to a cotton gin or storage facility. However, even this process changed starting in the 1970s.

This untitled photo from the Library of Congress shows the traditional method of delivering cotton to the cotton gin – lots of wagons, labor and mules. While untitled, it is believed that the photo was taken in Mississippi in 1939. Photo by Marion Post Wolcott. Library of Congress, Prints & Photographs Division, Farm Security Administration, Office of War Information, Black-and-White Negatives. https://www.loc.gov/item/2017754867/.

If you look at the cotton fields during the picking season, you will often see large blocks of cotton sitting on the ground. This process is often credited to Lambert Wilkes of the Texas A&M Agricultural Extension Service, who was working on a project with Cotton Incorporated in 1971. The process developed uses a box press that is rolled into the field. Cotton pickers unload their cotton directly into these presses that then create trailer-sized bales, equal to as many as a dozen traditional bales. When full, the press is moved, leaving the module of cotton on the ground, covered with a tarpaulin. A large truck can then later move the entire load of cotton in a more efficient manner.

A number of efforts are also underway that include a press directly on the picker that would eliminate the step of transferring the cotton from the picker to the press. One result is the production of round bales wrapped with a protective covering. Each round bale holds 3.8 bales of cotton lint, and the new pickers can actually carry these round bales as they continue picking. This allows more cotton to be picked while allowing less handling of the cotton bales. As advertised, these new pickers eliminate four pieces of machinery and their operators – boll buggy, module builder and two tractors – and also saves money on fuel.

5.7 **COUNTY ROAD 336** – This dirt road heads east from Arkansas Highway 85, and then turns southeast to a junction with Arkansas Highway 44. A number of field and farm roads, as well as driveways to houses, also cross the Delta Heritage Trail.

The Delta Heritage Trail crosses a number of farm and county roads. Signs like this can often be seen near the trail, helping trail users to keep track of where they are.

6.5 MACAULEY SPUR – While Union Pacific documents from 1986 show that this location was Macauley Spur, the 1922 *Bullinger's Postal and Shippers Guide for the United States and Canada* had it listed as Macaulay Spur. Located at Missouri Pacific Milepost 333.2, there was a spur track to the southwest that was retired in 1924. To the west of Arkansas Highway 85 is a farm complex, essentially where Macauley once existed.

6.7 COUNTY ROAD 340 – This dirt road loops through farmland to the east.

8.3 ARKANSAS HIGHWAY 318 – There are actually two highways in Arkansas that carry the Highway 318 number. This is the older road and heads 4.4 miles to the east where it ends at Arkansas Highway 44. This highway was created by the Arkansas State Highway Commission on November 23, 1966.

This sign on Arkansas Highway 85 points the way east for Highway 318.

The second stretch of Arkansas Highway 318 was created in 1973 in response to a new Arkansas law that had the state take over as many as twelve miles of county roads in each county. This Highway 318 is almost ten miles to the west and connects Arkansas Highways 1 and 20.

8.6 ONEIDA – Oneida was founded soon after the railroad was built, and the post office opened in 1907. The town consisted of about six blocks, once located between the tracks and Arkansas Highway 85 at an elevation of 174 feet. The town is now an unincorporated community in Phillips County, the post office is still open, and there is a small grocery store on the highway for those needing some supplies.

In 1921, the cotton gin of the Oneida Planting Company and the Oneida Shingle Mill both operated here. In 1926, Oneida was a regular stop for trains #343 and #344, using a 20' x 50' wooden depot. Train #343 was scheduled to be here at 2:32pm while #344 had a scheduled time of 1:22pm, meaning that the two trains passed each other daily about Helena Junction. The freight and passenger business wasn't much as in 1930 the railroad applied to the Arkansas Railroad Commission to discontinue the company's agent at Oneida. On December 18th, the Commission denied the request, but it did allow the railroad to discontinue Western Union telegraph service at the station.

In December 1931, the Oneida station lost its train order signals and trains no longer relied upon the agent for updated orders and information. With trains no longer stopping, a mail crane was installed in 1933 to allow mail to be picked up and dropped off. Oneida was also the headquarters of a section gang, with two bunk houses and a tool house (all retired in June 1935), a section house (removed January 1942), a 9' x 28' bunk house near the station, and several employee toilets. There was also a 10,000 gallon water tank, a phone booth, and a coal box. The mail crane was removed in 1955 after railroad mail service ended.

The original depot at Oneida, located at Missouri Pacific Milepost 335.3, was retired and a 10' x 28' shelter was built in 1947, located on the east side of the mainline just south of the grade crossing. A 236-foot-long platform stood with the depot, and then the shelter, on the east side of the mainline. A 1212-foot siding ran around the east side of the shelter through the 1960s. At the end of the railroad's operations, there was a short spur track on the east side of the mainline. It was generally used to hold maintenance-of-way equipment during the last few years of the line's operations. This area has been cleared of brush by the State Park as there were once plans to locate a trailhead here.

9.2 **BEAVER BAYOU DITCH BRIDGE** – Located at Missouri Pacific Milepost 335.9, this bridge is easy to find as it is located just south of Oneida and it is one of the longest in the area. Known as Bridge No. 13, the railroad had rebuilt each end by removing the timber piles and installing concrete piles and concrete ballast deck spans. The north end measured 121 feet long, while the south end measured 155 feet. Across the main channel of the stream was a 45-foot deck plate girder steel span. This bridge has had its deck modified for use by the Delta Heritage Trail.

Although the railroad and others called this Beaver Bayou, in early 1979 the United States Board on Geographic Names officially declared that it was Beaver Bayou Ditch. The ditch begins on the southwest side of West Helena and flows to the southwest. From here, the ditch curves to the northwest and enters Big Creek a few miles west of Oneida. The ditch was created and is maintained by the Beaver Bayou Drainage District. The Drainage District was created in 1907, and it has channelized parts of Beaver Bayou, Johnson Bayou, Lick Creek, and Hillside Ditch.

For many years, the south end of the Beaver Bayou Ditch Bridge was the section line between Section Gang #21 to the north and Section Gang #22 to the south.

The railroad used many different bridge designs over the years, especially as the rail line was upgraded for heavier trains. The Beaver Bayou Ditch Bridge is an example as it includes both an older deck plate girder steel span and concrete ballast deck spans that replaced older timber pile spans.

9.5 GORSUCH SPUR – Located not far south of Beaver Bayou Ditch at Missouri Pacific Milepost 336.2 was Gorsuch Spur. A long spur track was located to the west of the mainline, and it ran just inside the property line. Records indicate that the track was leased until 1906, and it was removed in 1919. A community remained for a few more years, and *Bullinger's Postal and Shippers Guide for the United States and Canada* had Gorsuch listed in 1922.

Helena Junction to Elaine

In the Gorsuch Spur area, the Delta Heritage Trail passes through a mix of heavy woods and open fields. The trail has been packed down by users, and almost looks like a country road.

9.7 ARKANSAS HIGHWAY 85 – Heading south, the Delta Heritage Trail crosses Arkansas Highway 85, moving from the east side of the highway to the west. Watch for speeding traffic as you cross the highway.

Arkansas Highway 85 is only 9.73 miles long and connects Arkansas Highway 44 at Lake View, with U.S. Highway 49 at Walnut Corner. This is one of the original state highways created in 1926, and it has not changed its route since its establishment. The entire highway is located in Phillips County.

Just south of this crossing, Phillips County Road 352 heads west to serve several large farms.

10.1 JOHNSONS BAYOU BRIDGE – Johnsons, or Johnson Bayou, is another stream that has been channelized by the Beaver Bayou Drainage District. It is part of the Big Watershed of Phillips County. The bayou ditch starts several miles east of here and flows west less than ten miles before its waters enter Big Creek. The stream is well channelized here and the railroad used a simple 70-foot timber pile trestle, once known as MH&L Bridge No. 14, to cross it at Missouri Pacific Milepost 336.8.

Heading south, the Delta Heritage Trail slowly separates from Arkansas Highway 85 as it approaches Lake View. The property that became part of the Lakeview Resettlement Project actually started just south of Johnson Bayou Ditch, and even included property to the east on both sides of the drainage canal.

10.1 IMHOFF SPUR – Imhoff Spur was located on the south bank of Johnson Bayou. The railroad had a spur track to the southeast that was retired in September 1935. The *Bullinger's Postal and Shippers Guide for the United States and Canada* had Imhoff Spur listed in 1922.

10.8 MAPLE STREET – Maple Street, although a dirt road, is the northernmost street at Lake View, Arkansas. It was also the northern entrance into the Lakeview Resettlement Project and connected to the main street in the community. Heading south, the Delta Heritage Trail begins to curve to the southwest to pass around Old Town Lake.

11.9 ARMISTEAD SPUR – Once located at Missouri Pacific Milepost 338.6 and just north of today's

Market Street was a long spur track to the northeast. This track was leased by a shipper, but was retired in 1922. *Bullinger's Postal and Shippers Guide for the United States and Canada* had Armistead Spur listed in 1922.

12.1 LAKE VIEW TRAILHEAD – Located on the south side of the former Market Street grade crossing is the new Lake View Trailhead for the Delta Heritage Trail. The trailhead features parking, a collection of shaded benches with a number of historical panels, and a bicycle repair station. The remains of a cotton gin stand nearby.

Like most of the trailheads, the Lake View Trailhead features a small shelter with a number of panels illustrating the history of the community, plus a few benches.

Market Street at the Lakeview Resettlement Project was the center of the business district of the new community. The cotton gin was part of this business district, with a syrup mill, machine shop, gas station, store, farm supply store, feed mill, and other businesses located along the street.

To the south on Market Street is the boat ramp and parking for Old Town Lake, an oxbow lake that was once part of the Mississippi River. Fishing for crappie, bream and catfish is common, and finding a parking spot can be difficult on many weekends. The lake averages about 6 feet deep and it is generally lined with cypress trees.

Not far from the Delta Heritage Trail at Lake View is Old Town Lake. The shallow lake is a former channel of the Mississippi River, and is a popular and scenic fishing location.

The Lakeview Resettlement Project

Today's Lake View traces its existence to the Lakeview Resettlement Project, a "New Deal Community." The New Deal was a series of programs enacted by President Franklin Roosevelt between 1933 and 1939, all designed to end the Great Depression and restore prosperity to Americans. This New Deal project replaced the earlier Lakeview, which had existed here for decades.

Besides timber, the Lakeview area also featured a number of small plantations. Never as developed or rich as the plantations further north around Helena, the ones at Lakeview barely survived the Civil War. Some continued with former slaves working as tenant farmers, while others sold timber or leased their properties to larger operations. All of them had to deal with the Flood of 1927, low cotton prices in the late 1920s, the Drought of 1930-1931, and then the Great Depression. Most failed financially during the early 1930s and were unable to pay their taxes.

Many of the plantations and farms were sold to the federal government under foreclosure. This was the beginning of the second iteration of the town. Much of the property was assigned to the Resettlement Administration, which became part of the Farm Security Administration (FSA) in 1937. In that year Lakeview was created as a resettlement community for African-American sharecropper families, one of three created in Arkansas. The community officially opened on January 1, 1938, and included 5600 acres, consisting of ninety-five farms of forty-four acres, each with a farmhouse and barn. The rest of the property was used by the Lake View Cooperative, which owned a general store, a cotton gin, a feed mill, repair shops, and a herd of livestock. There was also a nursery, an elementary school, high school, and a vocational shop. Residents were required to work and pay rent before they could acquire their farm, and a three-to-five-year lease was part of the agreement. One major complaint was that existing black and white tenant farmers who were already living on the property were not allowed to remain, reportedly on the grounds that they were bad credit risks since they had worked on farms that had failed.

Eventually some of the earlier black residents were allowed to settle at Lakeview.

The remains of the former Lake View Cooperative cotton gin still stand along Market Street, near the Delta Heritage Trail. A number of cotton gin buildings remain along the trail, and their standard shape makes them easy to identify.

While the purpose of the Lakeview Resettlement Project was to give the families an opportunity to make a living, most reports indicate that the residents generally remained impoverished for decades, but still better off than before arriving at the community. After many families were able to afford to buy their farms, the area became one of the largest concentrations of black-owned farms in the country.

Helena Junction to Elaine

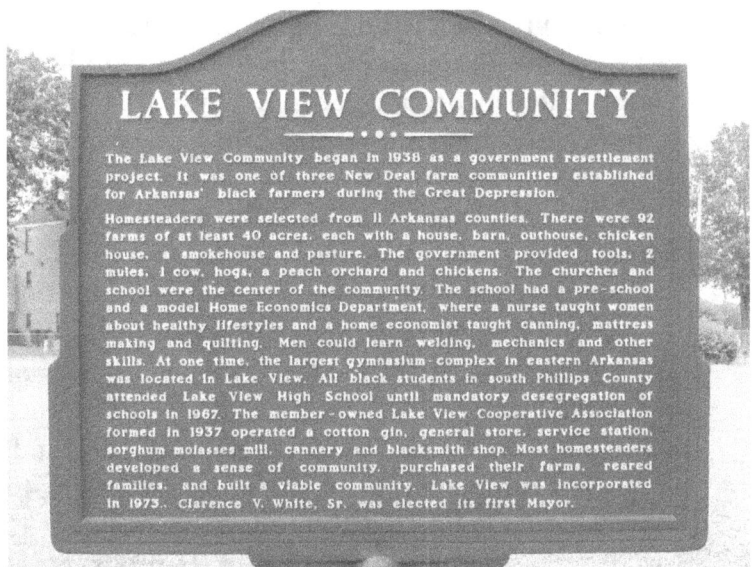

This marker, located alongside Arkansas Highway 44, tells the basic story of the Lake View community.

To make improvements, the town was incorporated as Lake View on December 2, 1980. The name Lake View became official as by this time, there was another Lakeview already incorporated in Arkansas. In 1992, the Lake View School District sued the State of Arkansas, saying that relying upon local property taxes for funding education was unconstitutional because it was both inequitable and inadequate. The suit led to the consolidation of many school districts, causing the Lake View School District to merge with the Barton-Lexa School District, and the local school eventually being closed.

There have been several needed improvements at Lake View, but little of the New Deal-era resettlement still remains. These improvements include a public library, a medical clinic, low-income housing, and an office for Mid-Delta Community Services. Mail is handled through nearby Wabash. Because of the history of the community, Lake View is one of three incorporated communities in Arkansas where African-Americans make up more than ninety percent of the population. In the 2010 census, the population of Lake View was 443 residents. This was down from the 609 that lived here in 1980 when the community was incorporated.

Today, the Lakeview Resettlement Project Historic District is listed on the National Register of Historic Places, added on January 28, 2019. More than a dozen of the original structures still stand, scattered throughout the community. According to the National Register, each of the 95 farms (only 91 were ever settled) included a five or six-room wood-framed house, a barn, a poultry house, a well with an indoor kitchen pump, a wood-frame smokehouse, and an outhouse. For those who are interested, a review of the 58-page registration form for the National Register provides many of the details about the creation of the new community.

Helena Junction to Elaine

House at Lakeview Project, Arkansas. Russell Lee, 1903-1986, photographer. One of the major goals of the Lakeview Resettlement Project was to provide quality housing and an opportunity to make a living for African-American farm families. This is one of almost 100 identical houses built as part of the effort. The photo was taken by Russell Lee in December 1938 as a part of documentation by the Farm Security Administration. Library of Congress, Prints & Photographs Division, Farm Security Administration/Office of War Information Black-and-White Negatives. https://www.loc.gov/item/2017781884/.

Barn with farmer and livestock. Lakeview Project, Arkansas. Russell Lee, 1903-1986, photographer. Each of the 95 farms at the Lakeview Resettlement Project included a new barn like this one. A few of these still stood until the late twentieth century. Library of Congress, Prints & Photographs Division, Farm Security Administration, Office of War Information, Black-and-White Negatives. https://www.loc.gov/item/2017781873/.

Store of the Lakeview Cooperative Association. Russell Lee, 1903-1986, photographer. Most of the businesses operating at Lakeview during the 1930s and 1940s were managed by the Lakeview Cooperative Association, including this store with the typical rural gasoline pump. Library of Congress, Prints & Photographs Division, Farm Security Administration, Office of War Information, Black-and-White Negatives. https://www.loc.gov/item/2017781875/.

13.2 LAKEVIEW – The historical railroad location of Lakeview, often spelled Lake View, has been Missouri Pacific Milepost 339.9. Today, this is at Woodland Street, also known as Phillips County Road 361, a dirt road that marks the south end of Lake View. The City of Lake View, located at an elevation 178, is on the northwest side of Old Town Lake, an oxbow lake created by the Mississippi River. The elevation here is fortunate, as during the flooding of late winter of 1907, the railroad was under water all the way to Lakeview, with the station at Snow Lake completely cut off both north and south.

Over the years, the Lake View area has actually been several towns. Some sources state that the area was originally known as Turkey Scratch, but today's Turkey Scratch is northwest of Lexa. However, the name seemed to have moved around the region. A community known as Red Store was here by 1878 when a post office opened at the site. A report in the October 23, 1903, *Arkansas Gazette* stated that the town changed its name to Powell, but the post office was Red Store until 1906. In that year, it was renamed Lakeview, probably after the nearby Lakeview Plantation. This post office lasted until 1925.

Starting about 1906, there were reports that the Howe Lumber Company had an operation here, although it is likely that the shops were actually at nearby Hugo (today's Wabash). The complex was large enough that the company sent their Shay steam locomotive here about 1926 to have a new firebox installed. The lumber company also reportedly had a standard-gauge logging railroad out of Lakeview for a number of years. Also at Lakeview was once Rhodes & Alderman, a logging firm based at Helena. The firm had a short logging railroad at Lakeview by 1910. With the timber being cut, more land became available for growing crops like cotton, and the Solomon-Chandler Planting Company and its cotton gin operated here for several decades.

Soon after the railroad was built, there were a number of facilities at Lakeview, some for passengers, some for freight, and some for the trains themselves. There was a 24' x 60' wooden depot that was built in 1906, with railroad records showing it being retired in 1935. It was located just south of the road crossing and east of the mainline. An 1196-foot double-ended house track looped around the east side of the station. Lakeview, shown as Lake View in the 1926 timetable, was a regular passenger train stop, and the station also featured a telegraph station. Southbound #343 was to be here at 2:43pm, while #344 had a scheduled time of 1:11pm.

There was also a water tank, pump house and coal bin, all retired in September 1927. At the same time, a 16' x 40' cotton platform was constructed. Right after World War II, the siding here was shown to be LA Siding, and there was a telephone booth. Toward the end of railroad operations, there was a 6953-foot siding at what the railroad called Lakeview. The siding was on the west side of the mainline, with the north switch at Milepost 338.8 (Trail Milepost 12.1 near the Lake View Trailhead), and the south switch at Milepost 340.2 (Trail Milepost 13.5).

In September 1986, Missouri Pacific locomotive #3141 pulls a train northward through Lakeview, just a few months before all freight service ended on the rail line.

13.7 MCGEHEE BAYOU DRAINAGE DITCH BRIDGE – This drainage ditch connects Old Town Lake with Cypress Ditch to the west. The railroad bridge features a 34-foot deck plate girder span with 28 feet of timber pile trestle off each end. Located at

Missouri Pacific Milepost 340.4, this was designated as Bridge No. 20A when it was built in 1941.

The railroad bridge over the McGehee Bayou Drainage Ditch has been rebuilt with a solid deck and handrails, providing a smooth and safe crossing over the waterway.

13.8   PHILLIPS COUNTY ROAD 438 – To the west, the road runs along the top of the local levee which protects the community of Wabash from the McGehee Bayou.

13.9   MCGEHEE BAYOU BRIDGE – This small waterway is the original McGehee Bayou channel. As with many streams in the area, it was channeled and moved to provide drainage to make land available for farming. The railroad used a 79-foot-long timber pile trestle to cross the waterway. Missouri Pacific Railroad knew this as MH&L Bridge No. 21, located at their Milepost 340.6.

Heading towards Elaine, the trail has turned back to the south. Through this area, there is little shade as there are few trees along the right-of-way. After the railroad was abandoned, many farmers continued to mow the right-of-way to help control the spread of insects and weeds into their adjacent crops.

14.4　WABASH – Look for the former grade crossing with Phillips County Road 433 as this is Wabash, an unincorporated community located at an elevation of 176 feet. To the west is the large David Griffin Farms complex, once the site of the Howe Lumber Company. Until the line's abandonment, the railroad had a long spur track that curved through the facility, serving several of the farm's warehouses and cotton gin buildings. A part of David Griffin Farms is Griffin Grain, a dealer in grain which has elevator locations at Wabash, Elaine, Mellwood and Helena. At Helena, the company has acquired the former Planters Service of Helena and set it up as the Griffin River Terminal, a facility with 330,000-bushel storage capacity and the ability to load grain directly into barges operating on the Mississippi River.

Many of the buildings on the Griffin Farms center date back to the Howe Lumber Company, which still had some operations here until the late 1960s. The Howe Lumber Company Store can still be found west of the tracks. To the east of the tracks are about a dozen homes and the Wabash post office. There is also a small grocery and bait shop about a half-mile to the east on the shore of Old Town Lake.

Wabash was one of a number of regional communities where the King Biscuit Entertainers played their music. Performing weekly on the *King Biscuit Time* radio show out of Helena, the group also traveled about and played at stores that sold King Biscuit Flour.

Heading south from Wabash, the old railroad right-of-way is immediately to the west of Arkansas Highway 44 and passes through miles of open farmland. Be sure to have plenty of water as shade is a scarce commodity until near Ferguson.

To the west of the tracks at Wabash is this old grain elevator, now part of the David Griffin Farms complex.

The Howe Lumber Company

Wabash is another town along the Memphis, Helena & Louisiana Railway that grew because of the timber industry. The early name for the community was Hugo, also known as Hugo Station and Hugo Spur after the railroad was built. In December 1906, the Howe Lumber Company was incorporated by Wilmont S. Fernald, Samuel E. Howe, Otis D. Howe, and Wilson H. Howe. The firm built a sawmill here that they named Wabash, after the river at the former home of the Howe family in Logansport, Indiana.

The Howe family had moved to the area a few years earlier and were involved with the incorporation of the Greenfield & Southeastern Railroad Company in May 1905, a firm related to the Greenfield Lumber Company at Harrisburg, Arkansas. The mill at Hugo Spur was successful enough that a post office opened in 1908 using the name of Wabash.

The post office used the name Wabash starting in 1908, several years before the community changed its name from Hugo to Wabash.

To log the surrounding timber, the Howe Lumber Company built a series of logging tracks as far west as Big Creek. To pull the trains, Howe Lumber bought a new Shay steam locomotive. The standard gauge, two-truck, 24-ton locomotive was built in October 1907 as Shop Number 1978 by the Lima Locomotive Works. The Shay became Howe Lumber

Company #1 and was operated by the firm until the late 1920s. It was later scrapped.

On March 13, 1912, W. H. Howe, O. D. Howe, J. C. Howe, W. L. Fernald and W.R. Satterfield chartered the White River Valley Railway Company to build a 10-mile line from Hugo to Webb, both in Phillips County. The charter was announced in numerous magazines such as the *American Lumberman* (March 23, 1912) and *Engineering & Contracting* (March 27, 1912). Even at this time, the railroad station on the Iron Mountain was still known as Hugo, despite the Wabash name used by the post office. The community of Webb doesn't show on maps today and was likely a development planned by the lumber company.

The purpose of this railroad incorporation is not clear, but it is likely that it was done to give the company's railroad the right to participate in published freight rates and tariffs through interchange and rate division agreements with the Iron Mountain. About this time, many industrial railroads were incorporated as common carrier railroads, but in many cases they only served their owners. Many of these were logging railroads which hauled timber to the sawmill, and then maybe moved the finished lumber a short distance to the connecting railroad. The larger railroads like the St. Louis, Iron Mountain & Southern generally provided a rebate or share of the freight rate of about two to three cents per hundredweight (one-hundred pounds) as an encouragement to locate and ship on their line. This sharing of the freight rate often happened even if the larger railroad did the actual switching of the sawmill or manufacturing plant. A series of hearings by the Interstate Commerce Commission, and the U.S. Supreme

Court, eventually established standards for these practices. The White River Valley Railway was not included in these hearings, so it is likely that while the railroad was officially chartered, it was never organized as a common carrier railroad.

The Howe Lumber Company is a good example of what happened during the early 1900s in the state. Lumber production in Arkansas peaked about 1910 and started a slow decline for the next decade, and then the decline accelerated through the Great Depression. In 1917, the sawmills of Arkansas produced almost two billion board feet of lumber, the fifth-most behind Washington, Louisiana, Oregon and Mississippi. However, sawmills were already closing as the supply of standing timber shrank substantially.

Like many such firms, the Howe Lumber Company began farming after the timber was cut. Reports from 1919 stated that the Howe Lumber Company had a successful rice farm with a 20,000-bushel warehouse that was often used for area dances. This was another tenant farming operation that was considered a cause of the 1919 Elaine Massacre, also known as the Phillips County War.

The Howe Lumber Company was still active at Wabash in 1921 with W. H. Howe listed as president. While some sources state that the logging railroad was shut down during the late 1920s, maps produced by the Mississippi River Commission and printed in 1939 still showed a network of rail lines west of Wabash marked "Howe Lumber Company Tramway." The firm still operated at Wabash through the 1960s, and a few of its old buildings can still be found around the tracks.

Helena Junction to Elaine

Shay Locomotives

Some readers may question the reports about Shay and other logging locomotives. However, the Shay locomotive was the most used logging design, with 2767 Shays constructed over 67 years (1878-1945). Having a Shay locomotive generally showed that a logger was serious about operating their logging railroad. Because of their rugged construction, they often lasted decades and were sold from timber company to timber company.

The Shay was known for its low speed (10-20mph), high pulling power, and the ability to climb steep grades and operate on bad track. A Shay had two or three cylinders located on the engineer's side of the locomotive which drove a drive shaft that connected to every axle. To balance the weight, the boiler was moved slightly to the fireman's side of the frame. While almost 120 Shay locomotives still exist, few of them ever operated in Arkansas.

A typical Shay locomotive.

It is interesting to note that while the logging companies were using steam locomotives and other heavy equipment to cut the timber, the farms that followed generally used manual labor for decades.

The Missouri Pacific at Wabash

Railroad maps show that there was a complex network of tracks on the west side of the mainline at Wabash, designated as Missouri Pacific Milepost 341.1. The first tracks apparently looped around the south side of the Howe Lumber Company office. These tracks were removed in 1939 when a new track was built to the north of the office building. Heading south, this track curved off to the west, passing between several seed houses and south of the cotton gin. Several tracks served these buildings, as well as a coal bin and seed platform. The track then connected to about 1500 feet of private tracks that ended west of today's elevator complex, and some of the rails and crossties can still be found in the dirt and road crossings.

The station facilities at Wabash were never fancy. There was a 168-foot-long chat platform on the west side of the mainline, along with a simple station sign. There was also a mail crane for many years. A mail crane allowed a community to have railroad mail service without the train stopping. The mail crane was used to suspend mail pouches or bags for pickup by a passing train. As the train passed, a catcher arm on the Railway Post Office (RPO) car would extend and grab the bag. Meanwhile, the RPO clerk would kick the outgoing pouch out of the car onto the station platform. It was an exiting event that happened daily all across the country. This one lasted until the mail crane was removed in August 1955.

The north end of Wabash also served as the boundary between Track Section Gang 22 to the north, and Section Gang 23 to the south.

Wabash and the 1919 Elaine Massacre

While Elaine is generally considered as the center of the 1919 Elaine Massacre, Wabash must also be considered as having played a role in what was also called the Elaine Race Massacres or the Phillips County War of 1919. The 1919 Elaine Massacre was a major power struggle between the owners and operators of the large farms and logging companies, plus many of the political elite, and the black sharecroppers and tenant farmers who were unable to work their way out of debt.

The event was reported across the country, and the reporting varied from being a legal battle to race riots to lynchings to attempts to overthrow the country. Some reports stated that little happened at Wabash, while some family stories insist that hundreds of black sharecroppers were lynched at Wabash. There is even a legend that a mound at Wabash is the burial site of these victims of the violence. Other stories state that it is an old Indian burial mound or an old forgotten cemetery of the first settlers. The total truth will probably never be known.

15.0 TUGWELL SPUR – Tugwell Spur was a spur track to the southeast on the railroad until the early 1970s, located at Missouri Pacific Milepost 341.7. Construction of the track was authorized in November 1919, and it connected with a private track built by a local customer. In 1951, the railroad reported that it had an eight-car house track, plus the Gin Spur. The grade of the track can still be seen as it drops down to the level of Arkansas Highway 44 and heads east to the unused cotton gin.

Not far south of Wabash, the remains of a cotton gin can be seen to the east. This location was known as Tugwell Spur, and the old grade for the track can still be found.

15.3 WATERWAY BRIDGE – Known as Bridge No. 24 and located at Milepost 342.0 of the railroad, this small three-span, 37-foot-long timber pile trestle bridge has been converted into a trail bridge. The bridge crosses a small drainage and irrigation canal that ties together the fields both east and west of Arkansas Highway 44, which is located just east of the Delta Heritage Trail. Views of the surrounding fields are easy here as there is very little tall vegetation in the area and the former railroad grade stands above almost all of the surrounding terrain.

15.9 EWA SPUR – Today, Ewal (or Ewa) is shown to be simply an unincorporated community. It can be found at the intersection of Arkansas Highway 44 and Phillips County Road 452. Several houses and plenty of grain storage can be seen here. Not far to the south is a low area that was once Ward Bayou. As drainage canals were built throughout the area, a number of the original streams were moved or eliminated.

Ewal Spur, spelled Ewa in many Missouri Pacific and Union Pacific documents, was once another logging company connection to the St. Louis, Iron Mountain & Southern at Milepost 342.7. Maps show that the Howe Lumber Company had a line to here from their series of logging tramways to the west. Ewal Spur was important enough to have a telephone booth installed by the railroad during 1933. This telephone allowed the logging company to contact the dispatcher to get permission to operate over the Missouri Pacific trackage.

The Helena Southwestern Railroad of the Chicago Mill & Lumber Company had trackage rights over Missouri Pacific to serve a number of the logging companies, including here at Ewa. The company called this Ewa Junction, and ran their last train to here in March 1939. The spur track that once headed to the southwest was retired in May of that year.

17.1 GUM BAYOU BRIDGE – This small waterway once drained the fields to the northeast, and took the water westward to Govan Slough. What used to be wandering streams have been turned into a network of organized drainage ditches.

Located at Missouri Pacific Milepost 344.0, this was MH&L Bridge No. 28. The railroad used a

56-foot-long timber pile trestle to cross Gum Bayou, converted for use by the Delta Heritage Trail.

17.3 PHILLIPS COUNTY ROAD 464 – This dirt road heads west to provide access to miles of fields and several homes.

17.5 HOOP SPUR – Hoopspur (one word) was listed as a station on the Memphis, Helena & Louisiana Railway in March 1906, and Hoop Spur had a post office 1910-1912. Some sources just call the location Hoop. Today, there is little at Hoop except for a few houses in the area.

Hoop Spur was the location of the first public violence involving the 1919 Elaine Massacre, also known as the Elaine Race Massacres and the Phillips County War of 1919. At the time, a small number of white farmers and businessmen controlled the Phillips County cotton market. Most black farmers worked as tenants or sharecroppers, buying their seed and household goods from a series of company stores. Often they were paid on the low end for the cotton, with the buyers holding onto the cotton until prices were higher. In some cases, the sharecroppers weren't even paid until the cotton was finally sold into the market, but were still going further in debt through the company store and interest payments on unpaid bills.

In 1919, black sharecroppers were involved with two efforts to end these practices. One involved the use of a Little Rock law firm which was trying to work with the federal government on the legality of these practices. The second effort was led by the Progressive Farmers and Household Union of America, generally described as a union of African-American tenant farmers and sharecroppers created to get fair settlements from their white landlords in the Arkansas Delta. At the time, such unions were not looked upon favorably across much of the country due to several violent strikes and riots, support from groups calling for the overthrow of the United States government, the fear of socialism and communism, and the fear by those in charge of losing their power.

On September 30, 1919, the Progressive Farmers and Household Union of America was holding a meeting at a church at Hoop Spur, one of several that had been held over the previous few months. The union posted armed guards around the church, but an armed sheriff's deputy, a jail trustee, and private security officers stopped to investigate the meeting. Shots rang out, with both sides blaming the other. Several people were wounded, and Missouri Pacific Railroad Special Agent W. D. Adkins was killed.

Although the truth behind the shooting was never fully agreed upon, the killing of a railroad special agent attracted attention. Hundreds of white citizens poured into the area, fearing what some called an insurrection. Arkansas Governor Charles Brough had federal troops sent to Phillips County. Dozens, some say hundreds or even thousands, of black sharecroppers were jailed, lynched, shot, or convicted of murder. Again, the numbers involved and the events that happened vary by who is asked. Many records have disappeared, court trials took years with witnesses contradicting each other, those involved have all been dead for decades, and family oral traditions vary so much that there are almost no agreed-upon details about the events. However, all agree that the open violence, after years of quiet intimidation and individual attacks, was sparked at Hoop Spur.

The Railroad at Hoop Spur

Hoopspur was an early station on the Memphis, Helena & Louisiana, but there were never many facilities. A long spur track headed to the southeast from the mainline at Missouri Pacific Milepost 344.5, removed in August 1934. Railroad documents also show that there was an "Engines Stop Here" sign that was used to alert locomotive engineers as to where to stop to provide clearance for the spur track's switch.

17.7 **GOVAN SLOUGH BRIDGE** – This small timber pile trestle, once known as MH&L Bridge No. 30, now carries the Delta Heritage Trail across an eastern arm of Gavin Slough. This arm, like most streams in the area, has been channelized for both drainage and irrigation uses. This bridge was at Missouri Pacific Milepost 345.0.

18.7 **LORENZO SPUR** – Lorenzo is just north of the location where Arkansas Highway 44 makes a gentle S-curve, and the former railroad grade and Delta Heritage Trail cross over to the east side of the highway when heading south. Starting in the 1930s, the area became known as Morning Star after the Morning Star Church and School that developed here.

The switch for the Lorenzo Spur was at Missouri Pacific Milepost 346.0, and the track headed to the southeast. The track didn't last long as it was removed in early 1921. However, the location remained important for a while as it was the boundary between Track Section Gang 23 to the north, and Section Gang 24 to the south.

18.9 **ARKANSAS HIGHWAY 44** – The railroad once crossed the highway at a sharp angle. Today, the Delta Heritage Trail crosses straight across Arkansas Highway 44 for safety reasons. Be sure to watch for traffic on the state highway as well as Phillips County Road 468.

19.6 **MADRID** – Madrid was a spur track during the first half of the twentieth century that served the New Madrid Hoop and Lumber Company. In early 1915, the company filed their Missouri charter with the Arkansas Secretary of State and was granted permission to do business here. Immediately, the firm increased its stock from $12,000 to $20,000 to build the new sawmill and factory. The company was often cited as one of the four largest employers at Elaine, along with Howe Lumber, Chicago Mill & Lumber, and Acme Cooperage.

This grain elevator complex to the west of the Delta Heritage Trail marks the former location of Madrid.

Delta Heritage Trail: History Through the Miles

A track, located at Missouri Pacific Milepost 346.8, curved across Arkansas Highway 44 and headed to the northwest for many years, known as the Hoop Mill Spur as late as the 1950s. This track later served the grain elevator complex that still stands. Eventually, the station of Madrid was simply included in the series of tracks at Elaine.

20.0   ELAINE TRAILHEAD – On the east side of Elaine, along Arkansas Highway 44 and where the Missouri Pacific Railroad depot once stood, is the Elaine Trailhead of the Delta Heritage Trail. This location, the south end of the northern part of the finished trail in 2021, includes parking, a shaded area with a number of benches and history panels, a bike repair station, and restrooms. While parking is limited to a half-dozen vehicles, plenty of street parking is available throughout the area. For those visiting the Elaine trailhead, there is a small convenience store, a bank, several restaurants, and a few other businesses across Highway 44 to the west.

The Elaine Trailhead is well marked by highway signs like this one.

At one time, Elaine was a very busy place for the Missouri Pacific Railroad, located at Milepost 347.1. There were several sidings and numerous industry tracks, plus the connections to several logging lines. In 1926, southbound passenger train #343 departed Elaine at 2:58pm, while #344 departed at 12:57pm. The railroad station was also a telegraph station, with a passenger agency lasting to the end of passenger service. Many of the tracks at Elaine were removed when the industries shut down, but even during the 1960s, there were several sidings and at least four industry tracks. Track profiles from the mid-1960s show a 3441-foot, 65-car siding to the west, located north of the Main Street grade crossing. Off this siding there were three spur tracks that crossed Arkansas Highway 44 to reach various shippers about where Madrid was once located. This area is still busy with several farm-related businesses. At the Arkansas Highway 20 (Main Street) grade crossing, there was a 747-foot station track to the east that ran around the east side of the Elaine depot, which stood about where the Elaine Trailhead stands today. A few other spur tracks were also on the east side of the mainline, just north of the grade crossing.

Elaine was also the headquarters of Section Gang 24 for many years, and there were at least three bunk houses, a section house, and a number of tool houses and toilets. Because many track workers bounced from gang to gang based upon their union seniority, the railroad provided basic housing at many locations like Elaine. These track gangs were assigned a specific territory of the railroad which they patrolled, inspected and repaired. Until after World War II, this work was done by hand, and gangs of a foreman and a half-dozen men would use shovels to dig in new ties, wrenches and spike mauls to change rails, and track jacks and picks to level the track. They generally loaded their tools and materials on a pushcart, and patrolled their territory using a handcar – later a small gas-powered motorcar. Initially, these gangs were assigned about five miles of track, but the territories expanded as travel improved and larger gangs became popular to handle the larger projects. As this happened, section gangs were eliminated and many of the buildings were removed. Several of the Elaine buildings were removed during the late 1930s, while the last three bunk houses were retired in 1961. The section house at Milepost 347 Pole 3 was noted as being the location of a dispatcher telephone through the late 1950s. The section house was sold and removed in 1959.

The station area was also the home to a number of structures. Besides the depot, which was temporarily replaced by a covered shelter during the 1920s until a new 10' x 30' depot was built, there was a loading platform, cotton platform, an oil box, and a coal box. The depot featured a train order signal to alert train crews to any new orders that they needed to pick up. It wasn't removed until 1965. None of these buildings remain today.

Located at an elevation of 171 feet, the siding to the west remained until the early 1980s, shown as being shortened to 3019 feet, capable of holding 58 railcars. The former station track had one switch removed, leaving just a short spur track south of Arkansas Highway 20. The siding was removed during the 1980s as the line was rebuilt, leaving just the spur track by 1986.

Elaine, Arkansas

Like many of the communities along the Memphis, Helena & Louisiana Railway, Elaine came about because of the construction of the railroad. Much of this area was still swamp, but the land was covered with valuable timber. As was being discovered, once the trees were removed and drainage was improved, the soils were perfect for growing crops like cotton and corn. Therefore, those with the financial and planning abilities could profit by investing in these swamps of southern Phillips County.

Like at all trailheads, a number of information panels tell the local history. At Elaine, this includes the original creation of the town, the industry that developed, the Elaine Massacre, floods and other natural disasters that tried to destroy the town, and the decline due to the mechanization of farming in the Arkansas Delta. Information about the railroad that once passed through Elaine is also provided.

Besides the information at the Elaine Trailhead, the buildings of Elaine can also tell the community's history. This abandoned store features a mural that shows some of Elaine's history.

A key step was taken by John Casper Branner, appointed the State Geologist of the Geological Survey of Arkansas in 1887. Branner had studied around the world and had worked for several mining companies before taking the job. He felt that by exploring the state he would find many valuable riches. One of these was the discovery of bauxite in Central Arkansas, a material that was mined to produce aluminum for almost a century. He also went after a number of fraudulent mining claims across the state, especially claims about rich gold mines. Branner was also a supporter of the development of the Delta soils in places like Phillips County. One of the people that he spoke to was Harry E. Kelley, an important Fort Smith investor. Kelley's contributions to Fort Smith resulted in a park along the Arkansas River being named for him.

Kelley invested in railroads, natural gas wells, mining, electric power plants and Fort Smith's street railway. He was also a leader in establishing the Ozark and Ouachita National Forests. Meanwhile, in Phillips County, Kelley began buying land in 1892, soon controlling 35,000 acres. This land had first been acquired by Silas Craig and John Martin in 1850, using the Swamp and Overflow Act which had just been passed in Congress.

This law allowed federal lands to be transferred to various states. However, the lands had to be wet and unfit for cultivation, and the states had to make arrangements to drain the land and turn it into productive agricultural properties. In Arkansas, the plan was that developers could do the work and keep most of the property, soon paying taxes on their new farms. However, Craig and Martin couldn't make a living with the land and it passed through several owners due to unpaid taxes.

When the Memphis, Helena & Louisiana Railway was being built, Harry Kelley traded a right-of-way through his lands in return for a depot at the location of his choosing. First named Kelley, the name of the station was quickly changed because Kelley was already being used at another location. With this, the name Kelley was replaced by the name Elaine. The name Elaine came with multiple explanations. A number of sources state that it was named for Kelley's daughter. However, his only child was a son – Leigh Kelley – who served as a captain in World War I. So where did the name Elaine come from? According to one of Kelley's business partners, the name Elaine came from an actress who was greatly admired by Kelley. Possibly the most popular theory is that it came from the line "Elaine the fair, Elaine the loveable" in Alfred Lord Tennyson's poem *Lancelot and Elaine*.

As the town grew, a post office opened at Elaine in 1907. Much of this was due to Kelley selling standing oak and ash trees to John D. Crow and John Marvin Countiss. John Countiss started a sawmill town several miles to the south that took his name. By 1923, J. M. Countiss was shown as being at Ratio, Arkansas, another nearby lumber town. His family has worked in the area ever since, with J. M. Countiss, Jr., still farming at Elaine in the mid-1960s. John D. Crow stayed involved with the timber industry, but was also serving as the president of the Bank of Elaine by 1919. In March 1920, Crow was shown to be the vice-president of the new Delta Lumber Company.

With the area developing, Kelley began modernizing Elaine. Paved streets and sidewalks, electric lights, brick store buildings and a brick school, plus a 1600-foot water well were all built. Reflecting the times, Elaine was built with separate neighborhoods for white (to the south) and black (to the north) families. Hundreds of people worked in the sawmills and timber yards operated by Chicago Mill & Lumber, Howe Lumber, Gerard B. Lambert, New Madrid Hoop, H. W. Mosby, and Acme Cooperage. However, the town changed as the timber was cut, moving from loggers to farmers. This led to the construction of several churches and more businesses serving the needs of families. One thing that didn't change were the owners of much of the land as large farms and plantations were created on the cleared real estate.

Elaine was incorporated on April 23, 1919, and the first bank opened soon after. Crow's Delta Lumber Company opened at Elaine in 1920 and operated many miles of logging railroad in the surrounding woods. Much of this was likely earlier used by the Gerard B. Lambert Company.

Gerard B. Lambert Company

During the first part of the twentieth century, Elaine was the home of the Gerard B. Lambert Company, a lumber and farming company. The company acquired approximately 32 square miles of land west of town for $515,787. The plan of the company was to log the lands to the west, almost all the way to the White River, and then "put same under cultivation, mostly in cotton. The plans for towns, building, etc. have been carefully laid in advance and they will endeavor to establish a scientific up-to-date farming community," stated the company's owner in the January, 1916, issue of *Locomotive World* magazine.

Why a locomotive magazine? The Lambert Company was clearing the area using a logging railroad. Three Shay locomotives were used to haul the cut timber to Elaine, where a Chicago Mill & Lumber Company (Helena Southwestern Railroad) train would pick up the cars and haul them to their mill in West Helena.

Compared to many area logging railroads, the track of the Gerard B. Lambert Company was exceptional. Their mainline was more than ten miles long and Arkansas Highway 20 is built on much of the grade, which the railroad constructed using 18 inches of gravel to stabilize the line. The track was built to standard gauge and used rail weighing 60 pounds per yard. The company had logging spurs heading north and south from the main line every quarter of a mile. The two smaller Shay locomotives worked these logging lines while the larger Shay worked the mainline and brought the loads to Elaine.

Two of the Shay locomotives were built new for the Gerard B. Lambert Company. Lambert #1 was built in November 1912 (Shop Number 2616) as a 24-ton locomotive. By the 1910s it was owned by Birmingham Rail & Locomotive, and then at least four more logging companies, all in Louisiana, before being scrapped about 1934. Lambert #5 was a 42-ton Shay built in July 1913 (Shop Number 2667). It was sold to the Jonesboro, Lake City & Eastern Railroad as their #23 in April 1916, went to Lee Wilson & Company in late 1918, and then the Brown Paper Mill Company in West Monroe, Louisiana, in 1924. It was also scrapped. The third Shay was bought secondhand from the Arkansas Logging Company of Lorays, Arkansas. This was a 24-ton Shay (Shop Number 2608) built in October 1912. It went to Birmingham Rail, which sold it to a Texas lumber company by 1922. It then operated for several Louisiana lumber companies before being scrapped.

The lumber cut was almost all hardwood – 50% gum, 40% oak, 10% others – and all of it was contracted to the Chicago Mill & Lumber Company, which provided 150 steel flat cars for moving the logs. At its peak, Lambert was selling 48 million feet of timber each year. However, the logging didn't continue much longer and the last of the company's equipment was for sale by 1920.

Gerard Barnes Lambert was actually a resident of St. Louis, where he was president of the Lambert Pharmacal Company, the manufacturer of Listerine, which his father invented. Lambert served in World War I, was a leader of the Lambert and Feasley advertising firm, and president of the Gillette

Safety Razor Company. His daughter, Rachel Lambert 'Bunny' Mellon, created the Gerard B. Lambert Foundation to honor her father by funding libraries, children's hospitals, and the restoration of public gardens.

Lambert's primary partners in the Elaine project were Arthur H. Lowe, a director of the Equitable Life Assurance Company of New York, and E. M. Allen, a director of the Peoples Savings Bank & Trust Company of Helena. Its control by outside owners, and the use of sharecropper labor, made the firm unpopular with many in the Elaine area. Much of the farmland had been divided into 20-acre lots that were assigned to black farmers as sharecroppers. This was one of the primary issues that contributed to what became known as the 1919 Elaine Massacre, or the Phillips County War.

The 1919 Elaine Massacre

On September 30, 1919, the friction between different races and different economic classes exploded in the Elaine area. Although the first shot was fired at nearby Hoop Spur, the issues could be found through much of the Mississippi River Delta. Much of the land was controlled by a small number of large companies and white farmers, but most of the work was performed by black sharecroppers and tenant farmers. This created the first conflict – local workers versus strangers who often lived elsewhere. The image of cigar-smoking barons living off the sweat of workers could often be claimed as true, and some like George Lambert didn't help themselves with their flamboyant lifestyles.

A second conflict existed between small white farmers and the black sharecroppers. Many small white farmers couldn't find work or land to buy, while black sharecroppers worked for low or no wages. A number of plantation owners actually stated that they wouldn't use white workers because of their higher wages and lower production. This led some white farmers to attempt to run off black workers, helping to develop groups like the Ku Klux Klan.

A third conflict involved payment for the crops grown, and the forced use of the plantation company store. Many farm workers, both black and white, owed money to the owners of the large farms, and few could ever work their way out of debt. This was particularly hard on many black sharecroppers who could not read, or did not have the legal support to enforce agreements. Some farm owners admitted that their company stores were actually more profitable than growing crops, as there was often a good profit margin on what was sold. In addition, sharecroppers were required to buy their seed and other supplies from the plantation store to remain on the property. Since they weren't paid until after the crop was harvested, many tenant farmers couldn't even pay the interest on the items that they bought, much less the actual cost of the items. This kept the workers essentially as indentured servants or slaves, with no option of leaving. Furthermore, since the cotton market was controlled by a few large firms, they could buy at very low prices while selling at much higher prices. This led many tenant and sharecroppers to actually lose money on their harvests, forcing them to hold other jobs.

Another often-cited conflict is bolshevism and anarchism versus capitalism. For many, communism was the new menace to their way of life. Already in 1919, there had been violent protests in a number of large cities. In some cases, these efforts were through new unions and associations being created. A poster child for this concern was Big Bill Haywood, one of the founding leaders of the Industrial Workers of the World (IWW). Haywood also served on the executive committee of the Socialist Party of America, and he had called for a violent overthrow of the United States. Many of the same charges were made against Robert L. Hill, founder of the Progressive Farmers and Household Union of America, who was trying to organize local black sharecroppers. However, there is little to support the idea that Hill was planning a violent overthrow of society. Instead, he was an experienced railroad worker who wanted to apply the principles of the various railroad unions to farming. After his efforts here, Hill returned to railroading and continued to work for several railroads until his retirement in 1962.

An additional divide included one between landowners of small farms and the sharecroppers. Those owning their own farm had to produce enough to make it to the next year, and pay taxes. With widely fluctuating cotton prices during the 1910s, and the addition of thousands of new acres as land was being cleared, some existing farmers couldn't hold on to their farms. Finally, the typical city versus farm conflicts existed. Many who lived in the large towns of the area didn't have experience with the work required on the farm and just didn't understand those who did the work.

Whatever the final conflicts were, a Hoop Spur meeting of the Progressive Farmers and Household Union of America on September 30, 1919, ended in violence that lasted for weeks. What followed has been called a race riot, a massacre, an insurrection, an incident, and even a war. All of the personal conflicts, and conflicts between races and economic classes, exploded throughout the area. There are no clear details about the events that followed, but it is clear that there were murders, people illegally held for trial, and an ineffective law enforcement and military response. While many families – both black and white – fled the area, others poured in, often in response to wild reports in newspapers across the country. Hundreds of sharecroppers were held for trial, often with little true evidence or proper legal representation. One clear fact that came out of the terror is that the trials after the event led to a major ruling by the U.S. Supreme Court about a required due process for such cases and rules about complying with the Bill of Rights. This led to the release of most who had been charged with various crimes.

Especially over the last few years, a number of individuals and groups have tried to research the events that happened. However, with no living survivors and little written documentation, there is still conflict in the findings. What is known is that several hundred people were killed during the event. Also what is known is that discussing the event can be taboo to some, while many others have an opinion based upon family tradition. This makes it even more difficult to research exactly what happened. However, the Elaine Legacy Center is attempting to tell the story and help heal the wounds that still exist.

Today's Elaine

As Elaine moved through the 1920s and 1930s, the city followed many of the same patterns found elsewhere in the Mississippi River Delta region. Much of the timber business moved away as the final logs were cut, replaced by the J. S. Kimbro Lumber Company, a seller of lumber, mill work, sash, doors, and building materials. This firm was sold to Harrison Grady in 1922 and simply served as a lumberyard and hardware store. The Great Flood of 1927 covered much of the town, as it did for hundreds of miles along the Mississippi River. When the waters finally receded, many of the businesses remained closed, like the Bank of Elaine. Low cotton prices didn't help the economy, and much of the black neighborhood in Elaine was hit by a tornado in 1930. The Great Depression added to Elaine's misery, but the population continued to grow from the 377 residents in 1920 to 511 in 1930, and then 634 in 1940. Much of this growth came about thanks to highway transportation, with smaller towns nearby being replaced by the stores here.

After World War II, Elaine continued to grow, but segregated schools operated until the early 1960s, when the town's population reached almost 900 residents. Desegregation took place soon after, and today the Elaine High School sits empty at the south end of town as the Marvell-Elaine School District (created in 2006) has its schools at Marvell, almost twenty miles away. The population peaked at 1210 in 1970, just as machinery had really taken over most of the farm labor jobs in the area. Since then, the population of Elaine has dropped to about 500 residents, but the town holds on to a number of businesses along Arkansas Highway 44 and Main Street, including a recently built national discount chain store.

Like many Arkansas Delta towns, Elaine's Main Street is lined with brick storefronts, once busily serving local residents and area farmers. Also like many Arkansas Delta towns, most of these buildings now stand empty.

One point of pride at Elaine is that it was the birthplace of Levon Helm, drummer and singer for *The Band*. *The Band* started as a tour band, supporting Bob Dylan for several years, using the name *The Hawks*. Helm continued performing after the breakup of the group in late 1976. For many, he is more famous for his acting in more than twenty films. These included playing Loretta Lynn's father in *Coal Miner's Daughter*, Captain Jack Ridley in *The Right Stuff*, and the Tennessee gun expert in *Shooter*. As a child, he moved with his family to nearby Marvell where their house is preserved. The site now features a historical marker with the history of Levon Helm. Because of his connection to the region, U.S. Highway 49, which passes the Barton Trailhead, has been designated as the Levon Helm Memorial Highway between Marvell and Helena-West Helena.

Helena Junction to Elaine

Delta Heritage Trail: History Through the Miles

Map of future trail from Elaine to Watson. Map courtesy of the Delta Heritage Trail State Park.

Elaine to Watson –
Future Delta Heritage Trail

As of 2021, the north end of the Delta Heritage Trail starts at the Helena Junction Trailhead and ends at the Elaine Trailhead. Meanwhile, the south end of the Delta Heritage Trail starts at the Watson Trailhead and ends at the Arkansas City Trailhead. Information about the future route between Elaine and Watson is included here so that as the trail is expanded, information about the route is available. The milepost locations provided are based upon those currently assigned to Elaine and Watson, but they may be changed slightly as the trail is completed.

20.0 ELAINE TRAILHEAD – As of 2021, the Elaine Trailhead is the south end of the Delta Heritage Trail that starts near Lexa. However, planning is underway on extending the trail southward to Snow Lake and beyond. The description of the railroad grade is included for those that want to explore the route even before the trail is completed.

20.3 YELLOW BANK BAYOU BRIDGE – This three-span steel-beam open deck bridge was an improved structure built to replace a much older timber structure in 1935. The MH&L Bridge No. 33 was located at Missouri Pacific Milepost 347.4. Yellow Bank Bayou flows through the south side of Elaine, separating the old school from the rest of town.

21.1 RAGAN SPUR – At Ragan Spur, later known as simply Ragan, the tracks once crossed Phillips County Road 504. The *Bullinger's Postal and Shippers Guide for the United States and Canada* had Ragan listed in their 1922 edition. Some maps from the 1930s still show the location to be Ragan Spur. However, by the 1930s, the railroad had a station sign here using the name Ragan. The May 1, 1958, *Louisiana Division Special Instructions* showed that Ragan Spur was 15 cars long. As late as the early 1970s, a 797-foot spur track crossed Highway 44 at Missouri Pacific Milepost 348.2 to serve the old cotton gin, whose main building still stands.

Ragan Spur was another track that served a local cotton gin, which still stands to the west of the Delta Heritage Trail.

21.7 PHILLIPS COUNTY ROAD 507 – The railroad grade has turned to the southwest. From here, the county road heads south and then east before ending on the levee next to the Mississippi River, north of Fair Landing.

While there is no community there, Fair Landing, often simply called Fair, was the home of an American Washboard Company factory from 1905 to 1908. With the railroad being built several miles to the west, the community didn't last long and many of the settlers and businesses moved. The American Washboard Company moved to Helena and became the American Saw Mill Company.

22.7 COUNTISS – Countiss, located at Missouri Pacific Milepost 349.8, was another station along the railroad that was started due to the timber industry. J. M. Countiss had bought timber and land from Harry Kelley, and this small community was created as his home and base of operations. Besides timber and farming, Countiss also invested in other local business and helped to start the Bank of Elaine with John D. Crow.

In March 1906, the Memphis, Helena & Louisiana Railway announced the start of service, and Countiss was one of the stations listed. A post office opened here in 1907 due to the local investments by Countiss. Other logging companies that reportedly operated at Countiss included the J. H. Cammon Company, and J. Hammon of Vincennes, Indiana.

The logging railroad of J. H. Cammon & Company operated using a 20-ton Shay locomotive. This locomotive was built in 1889 (Shop Number 224) for D. A. & C. A. Goodyear of Tomah, Wisconsin. It then came to J. H. Cammon and was eventually scrapped. An Arkansas report from 1924 showed a population of 162 residents at Countiss, and the post office closed in 1925 as the last of the logging had ended.

In 1923, the carbody depot was removed and replaced by a shelter shed. The shelter didn't last long, and was removed during the summer of 1928 and moved to Mozart. The station sign was also removed, essentially ending Countiss as being a railroad location along the line. The spur track, which once curved across Arkansas Highway 44 to the southwest, was removed in 1932, leaving only the mainline track. However, Countiss was the home of a local track section gang for many years, and there were at least three 9' x 35' bunk houses (the size of railroad freight cars at the time), plus some toilets and tool sheds, located on the east side of the tracks.

This is farming country, and like many former railroad stations, Countiss is still marked by several farm buildings.

A short 6-car track was listed as being here again in the *Louisiana Division Special Instructions* of May 1, 1958. However, nothing remains here today except for a few buildings to the west and a large

Elaine to Watson

house to the east. Through this area, the grade of the Memphis, Helena & Louisiana is immediately to the east of Arkansas Highway 44, located on a higher fill than the highway.

22.9 ARKANSAS HIGHWAY 44 – Heading south, the railroad grade and the Delta Heritage Trail again cross Highway 44, moving from the east to the west side of the roadway. Watch for traffic as you cross the highway!

The work here was some of the very first on the entire Delta Heritage Trail. As has been seen to the north, the railroad grade was higher than the highway grade. This meant that the highway had a high hump here, required to cross the tracks. When the railroad was abandoned and the property transferred to the State of Arkansas, the Arkansas Highway and Transportation Department rebuilt the crossing area. The work removed the higher railroad grade, making the highway level and straighter. With plans already underway for the Delta Heritage Trail, a short stretch of the railroad grade was paved on each side of Arkansas Highway 44, and a crosswalk developed.

24.5 MARY – Mary, originally known as Mary Spur, was located at Missouri Pacific Milepost 351.6 where a farm road now crosses the former railroad. There was a siding on the east side of the mainline, and a spur track left its north end and headed to the southeast. The spur track was removed in late 1921, and the siding in late 1939.

In 1926, Mary was important enough for trains #343 and #344 to stop, at 3:06pm southbound and 12:47pm northbound. A station sign lasted here for

Delta Heritage Trail: History Through the Miles

many years, although no depot ever stood at Mary. The dividing line between Section Gangs 24 and 25 was north of here near the railroad's Milepost 351. During the 1960s, there was nothing here but a station sign, and now even that is gone.

25.0 WATERWAY BRIDGE – Missouri Pacific records show that this was MH&L Bridge No. 41, and that the timber pile structure is 37 feet long. Located at railroad Milepost 352.1, the stream it crosses was once much larger and shown as a slough. Today, thanks to farming and drainage practices, the bridge simply crosses a low channel that can fill during heavy rains.

To the east is a large Elaine Rural Water tower. There is little shade through this farmland, although some trees have started growing along the grade.

The Elaine Rural Water tower south of Mary is easy to see for miles.

25.8 RATIO – Ratio, an unincorporated community in Phillips County, can be found where Phillips County Road 517 crosses the former railroad grade at Missouri Pacific Milepost 352.9. The community features a few houses and several farm buildings. Early maps show that Allen's Lake and Gozlee Bayou marked the east side of the community, but both are gone today, replaced by what many maps show as a channelized Yellow Bank Bayou.

Ratio was one of the later logging communities, and the post office didn't open until 1916. The post office remained open until 1960, when it was replaced by the Ratio Rural Station until 1967. Ratio was named for the nearby Ratio Plantation. This 4700-acre farm was acquired by Joseph Levy Solomon, his brothers, and Amos Jarman in 1919. Solomon was a leading businessman of Helena, having a farm south of Helena and a significant office building in town. He also owned half a block of business property in Wabash, plus the 1400-acre Key-Ward property. He was vice-president of the Security Bank & Trust Company, the Citizens Ice Company, and the Forrest City Compress Company. He also served for almost two decades as the president of the Helena Board of Trade.

1919 was also the year when violence hit the region. Ratio was the site of one of the three lodges of the Progressive Farmers and Household Union of America (the others were at Hoop Spur and Elaine). This lodge was apparently the first to try to take legal action to end what was essentially bondage due to the way sharecroppers were being treated. Ulysses S. Bratton, a former assistant federal district attorney, was contracted through his Little Rock office. Earlier, Bratton had been involved with reports about illegal practices of white planters in the Mellwood area that essentially established a peonage system. The shooting at Hoop Spur and the regional violence apparently took place before Bratton could file suits against various landowners, but he was successful in a number of trials that overturned convictions of some of the members of the sharecropper union. However, reports show that several hundred were killed during the violence, with some reportedly lynched on the former railroad water tower at Ratio.

A system of railroad lines to the west of Ratio were shown as the "Ratio Tramway" on a map published by the Mississippi River Commission in 1939. The map showed that the Ratio Tramway headed north less than a mile and then turned west for two miles to a junction. An abandoned branch headed on west across Cypress Ditch, where several spur lines headed to the southwest. A second line that was shown to be in service headed southwest from the junction, staying to the east of Cypress Ditch.

In 1923, Missouri Pacific built a passenger and freight shelter that measured 8' x 28'. It sat on the east side of the tracks, just south of the spur track switch. There were several tracks to the southwest that served different buildings, and land was still being acquired as late as 1931 to build more rail lines. A mail crane was installed here in October 1925, and it was removed towards the end of passenger service during August 1955. As the sawmill and other industries closed, the tracks were removed. Up until the 1980s, there was still a 1697-foot spur track to the southwest that served the cotton gin, whose remains can still be seen. None of these railroad tracks and buildings remain today.

26.5 GOSLEE BAYOU BRIDGE – This 135-foot beam bridge at Missouri Pacific Milepost 353.6 is a 1935 replacement of the original timber trestle, known as Bridge No. 45. Four concrete piers hold up the five steel-beam spans. Some maps show the stream to be Yellow Bank Bayou, but a 1986 Union Pacific track chart shows it to be Goslee Bayou, with some earlier Missouri Pacific documents showing it to be Gozlee Bayou. Most modern spellings have it as Gauzley Bayou. Just south of this bridge at Milepost 353.8 was once Dugout Bayou, and the bridge was replaced by fill in 1943 as the stream was moved.

Heading south, the Delta Heritage Trail begins a long curve back to the south. The curve is more than a mile long, passing through several large farm fields.

26.6 PHILLIPS COUNTY ROAD 512 – This county road heads north and then west for several miles, connecting to a number of farm roads.

26.8 MINOT SPUR – Minot Spur was here for only a short time. Located at Missouri Pacific Milepost 353.9, *Bullinger's Postal and Shippers Guide for the United States and Canada* had Minot Spur listed in their 1922 edition, the same year that the track was removed.

27.6 PHILLIPS COUNTY ROAD 533 – This road heads west three miles and serves a house and several farms. It is near the south end of the long curve. Not far south of here there are concrete footings between the railroad grade and Arkansas Highway 44, once the location of a railroad water tower.

28.1 CATRON – Catron, a late addition to the railroad, was located just south of what was once called Si Young's Bayou, and was listed as Catron Spur in the 1922 *Bullinger's Postal and Shippers Guide for the United States and Canada*. Catron, or Catron Spur, was a 13-car spur track to the southwest that was in the Missouri Pacific timetable at Milepost 355.2 until at least 1980, but was gone by the 1986 Union Pacific timetable. Many switches and tracks were removed during the early 1980s as the line was rebuilt. Today, to the east is the Catron facility of Griffin Grain, a company based in Wabash, Arkansas. Phillips County Road 510 crosses the former railroad grade to reach part of a farm complex to the west.

These concrete footings mark the location of the former Catron railroad water tower.

Elaine to Watson

In 2020, this Griffin Grain facility was being repaired after a severe storm which damaged a number of the metal grain silos. Weather is just one of many risks that farmers deal with every year.

29.5 MELLWOOD – Although the Delta Heritage Trail has not been completed south of Elaine, Mellwood is a planned trailhead. Thanks to the station and house track that once were to the east of the tracks, there is plenty of room between the planned trail and Arkansas Highway 44.

Mellwood, often spelled Melwood during the early days, is a small unincorporated community in Phillips County that is about one mile west of the Mississippi River. Mellwood is apparently not the first name used for this location. In March 1906, the Memphis, Helena & Louisiana announced that the railroad would be serving a station named Curley near here. Other timetables showed a station with the name Gurley. However, by 1908, the station of Mellwood was shown in the timetables of the St. Louis, Iron Mountain & Southern Railway, and it featured telegraph service. A post office using the name Mellwood had opened in 1906. Early maps show that the original plat of the community was to the west of the tracks.

Just across Arkansas Highway 44 from the future Delta Heritage Trail at Mellwood is the local post office, first opened in 1906.

Within a few years, the Lundell Land and Lumber Company was operating a logging railroad from Mellwood. Records show that the logging operation was started in 1913 by the Archer Lumber Company, which bought a new Shay 24-ton locomotive (Shop Number 2620 that was built in November 1913). Archer and Lundell apparently had some joint operations since they were both owned by a corporation headquartered at Rockford, Illinois, and Lundell took over the logging and operated until about 1920, when the Shay was sold to A. M. Richardson Lumber of Helena. The locomotive eventually worked for several other companies, ending its career in Louisiana when it was scrapped.

J. V. Stimson Lumber Company operated a logging line at Mellwood during the 1910s, as did the Delta Logging Company, which was owned by Stimson Hardwood. The 1921 *Arkansas Marketing and Industrial Guide* listed the Delta Logging Company, Fitz Lumber Company, the Burk & Lucy Plantation, and the Blackburn Brothers cotton gin as major industries at Mellwood. The Mellwood Mercantile Company was listed as the dominant store in town in other sources.

During the 1920s, Mellwood was a telegraph station and a regular stop for the four passenger trains that operated over the line. With all of the mills and businesses in town, the trains handled a large number of people coming and going. The first passenger trains each day were #330 and #331, hauling sleepers and coaches between Memphis and Ferriday and scheduled to meet here at 1:02am. Next was #344, which headed north through Mellwood at 12:36pm. Finally, southbound #343 was scheduled to be here at 3:17pm.

On the east side of the mainline, south of downtown, the railroad once had a number of buildings. There were several section gang bunk houses, tool sheds, toilets, a cotton platform, and a dwelling for the station agent. Just north of town was a telephone booth, and a second railroad telephone was located in a section house. Because the station agent also handled orders for the train crews, there was a train order signal on the depot. There was also a water tower here until the late 1940s that was used by steam locomotives. Until the late 1950s, Mellwood also still had a passenger agency.

During the late 1960s, little remained of these Missouri Pacific Railroad facilities. There was still a

1528-foot house track to the east that looped around the depot, which had been built in 1907. The railroad also had a 16' x 32' section house at Mellwood, described as having a porch for recreation and relaxation. By the late 1980s, the Mellwood depot had been sold and moved to a nearby farm.

This photo from August 1986 shows the former Mellwood depot, at the time located on a nearby farm.

Until the railroad was abandoned, there was a spur track to the east, the remains of the house track at Missouri Pacific Milepost 356.6. The railroad is now gone, but Mellwood remains the home of a few hundred residents, several churches, and a few businesses. The Mellwood post office remains, and a small grocery store is still open along Arkansas Highway 44. Phillips County Road 518 crosses the former railroad downtown and heads west to the White River, serving several large farms. At the south end of town is the Mellwood elevator of Griffin Grain, which has several facilities in southern Phillips County.

Elaine to Watson

At the south end of Mellwood is an the old grain elevator complex.

31.5 LUNDELL – Heading south on the former Missouri Pacific right-of-way, Lundell, initially known as Lundell Spur, can be found because of the series of large warehouses to the east. There is also a "Lundell" sign on the adjacent Arkansas Highway 44. Lundell came about because of the Lundell Land and Lumber Company. The post office opened in 1914 using the name Lundell, a few years after the firm moved to the area. The lumber company operated a series of logging lines west of town, explaining the Missouri Pacific track that curved off to the southwest at Milepost 358.6. The main route of the logging line went straight west to near the White River, where the line split. A short spur went north, while a much longer line went south, crossed Bee Bayou, and connected with several other logging lines.

Lundell operated the logging lines with several Shay-type locomotives. One of these was a Shay locomotive that came from the Triangle Lumber Company at Clio, Arkansas. This Shay was built in January 1907 (Shop Number 1843) for the Bluff City Lumber Company at Clio, and it went through several owners at Clio. The 20-ton Shay became T. L. Shannon & Brothers #1 at Ferguson, Arkansas, during the mid-1920s and was eventually scrapped. The second Shay was former Archer Lumber Company #1, built in 1913 with Shop Number 2620. While Lundell Land and Archer Lumber both operated in the area, they were both owned by a company in Rockford, Illinois. The *American Lumberman* (November 27, 1920) reported on Archer Lumber being "succeeded by Lundell Land & Lumber Co." The firm also had a lumber mill here during the early 1920s.

Lundell Spur was shown to be a flag stop for trains during the early 1910s, but was never much more than that. The Lundell post office closed in 1972, and the railroad removed the last spur track about 1980. Today, besides the warehouses, a few other farm buildings still stand at Lundell.

31.9 BEE BAYOU BRIDGE – This was MH&L Bridge No. 57. Located at Missouri Pacific Milepost 359.0, this 109-foot timber pile trestle crosses Bee Bayou, another channelized stream now more of an irrigation and drainage ditch. The bridge once included 57 timber panels, but was shortened to nine in 1942.

Bee Bayou drains the west side of the Mississippi River levee system and then flows west to the White River. The adjacent bridge on Highway 44 has recently been replaced with a large concrete box culvert. Heading south, the future route of the Delta

Elaine to Watson

Heritage Trail is lined with trees, providing nice shade much of the day.

32.3 MOSBY SPUR – Look for the wooded community of a few houses and farm buildings where Phillips County Road 526 crosses the railroad grade. This location, known as Mosby or Mosby Spur, was once the location of H. W. Mosby's lumber company and the J. H. Woods plantation. It was listed in the 1922 *Bullinger's Postal and Shippers Guide for the United States and Canada*. The May 1, 1958, issue of the Louisiana Division Special Instructions stated that Mosby Spur had a 10-car capacity. Until the early 1980s, there was a 658-foot spur track to the southwest at Missouri Pacific Milepost 359.4. The track is gone, but parts of the large pecan groves in the area still stand.

Like at many places along the Delta Heritage Trail, the old cotton gin still stands, generally used as a garage for a local farmer.

Continental Gin Company

If you look at the remains of the cotton gin to the west you will see a sign with the lettering of the Continental Gin Company. This company was once the largest manufacturer of cotton gin equipment in the world. The company traces its history back to 1833 when Daniel Pratt of Birmingham, Alabama, began designing and building various types of mills, including cotton gins. In 1838, Pratt acquired land nearby at what became Prattville, Alabama, where he built grist, lumber and shingle mills. By 1844, Pratt had opened a cotton gin plant that produced many of the gins used in the south. Daniel Pratt expanded his manufacturing business, especially after the Civil War, and was producing the equipment for cotton gins, cotton spinning plants, foundries, sawmills, sash and door mills, and basically any type of mill that there was a demand for. However, the Daniel Pratt Cotton Gin Company was soon the heart of the business.

This sign on the old cotton gin at Mosby Spur shows that it once used machinery manufactured by the Continental Gin Company.

By the late 1880s, Pratt had competition from Robert S. Munger, who was building cotton gin equipment from his plant east of downtown Dallas, Texas. In an area that was called Deep Elm, but changed to Deep Ellum by the local pronunciation of the name, Munger built his first cotton gin in 1888, and was soon building cotton dryers, belt conveyors, and other heavy equipment.

In 1899, the operations of Pratt and Munger merged to create the Continental Gin Company, based in Prattville, Alabama. One of Munger's main contributions to the design was the use of steam engines as a power source, as most earlier mills relied upon water power. The company continued to modernize, adding diesel engines to replace steam power, and then electric motors as rural electrification took place. Marketing forces around the world led the firm to be the recognized international leader in cotton gin design and manufacturing. The demand kept production going in Texas until the early 1960s. The Munger facility near Dallas is now a series of loft apartments. By the 1970s, two firms dominated the production of cotton gin equipment – Continental Gin Company and Lummus Cotton Gin Company. Today, Continental Gin is a part of Continental Eagle, and production was moved overseas from Prattville in 2008.

Over the years, the equipment involved with ginning cotton has changed greatly. Initially, the gin simply removed the seeds from the cotton. Later, it helped to separate the strands and bundled it, requiring a compress to actually press the cotton into bales that could be shipped. Today, the ginning process typically starts with auxiliary cleaning machinery. The seed is then removed from the cotton. The gin now typically includes a press that turns out bales of uniform density and size. Much of this cotton is then graded automatically and bagging machines prepare the bales for shipment. Most of the cotton is then sold using computer markets that receive the grading reports straight from each cotton gin.

Ginning machinery. Jerome, Arkansas. This Russell Lee photo taken in 1939 shows the machinery of a cotton gin at Jerome, Arkansas, not far south of McGehee, Arkansas. Library of Congress, Prints & Photographs Division, Farm Security Administration, Office of War Information, Black-and-White Negatives. Russell Lee, Photographer. https://www.loc.gov/item/2017781890/.

34.0 RAVEN SPUR – About all that marks this location at former Missouri Pacific Milepost 361.1 is a single house to the east. *Bullinger's Postal and Shippers Guide for the United States and Canada* had Raven Spur listed in their 1922 edition, but it wasn't listed on the earliest timetables of the railroad. The spur

Elaine to Watson

track that headed off to the southwest was retired, along with its station sign, in early 1928.

Raven Spur also once marked the boundary between Section Gang 26 to the north, and Section Gang 27 to the south.

34.6 CRUMROD SPUR – This location was originally known as Struma Spur, which featured a track to the southwest. The track was removed in April 1925.

On October 29, 1940, the General Manager of Missouri Pacific Railroad issued a circular establishing Crumrod Spur at Milepost 361.7, just south of the former Struma Spur. Crumrod, or Crumrod Spur, was located about where Phillips County Road 528 crosses the grade. Like Struma Spur, the industry track headed to the southwest from the mainline. Crumrod is an unincorporated community in Phillips County that has had a post office since 1941, the year after the nearby Ferguson post office closed. The Crumrod post office is still open and located about where Ferguson once existed. The area of the two communities is made up of a scattering of houses and farm structures. The railroad had a 10-car spur track that went to the southwest until about 1980.

35.2 FERGUSON – Ferguson was located just south of the short curve in the railroad grade at Missouri Pacific Milepost 362.3, about where the Crumrod post office now stands. The town started as a Mississippi River town known as Ferguson Landing, located several miles to the east. A post office opened using the name Ferguson in 1899, and when the railroad was built, much of the town moved to the tracks and dropped the "Landing" part of its name. The Memphis, Helena & Louisiana listed Ferguson as a stop when passenger service over the line commenced. On March 7, 1919, the Helena-Ferguson Road Improvement District was created to build roads through 227,000 acres, or more than half of Phillips County. The purpose was to make more of the county accessible for farmers and industry.

The Crumrod post office marks the former location of Ferguson, basically the predecessor of Crumrod.

T. L. Shannon & Brothers, Inc., operated a logging railroad in the Ferguson area. Maps show that a logging line headed west at the county line less than two miles south of here. The company used former Lundell Land and Lumber Company Shay #8, obtained in 1924. It was scrapped when logging ended later that decade. The post office closed at Ferguson in 1940, and the area is now simply an unincorporated community.

For the Missouri Pacific Railroad, Ferguson was a busy place. A 20' x 50' depot was built in 1907 and had a 1206-foot siding that looped around the east side of the depot, which was located just north of the road crossing. Located north of the siding was a spur track to the southwest that was 1436 feet long.

Elaine to Watson

There was also once a railroad telephone booth at Ferguson.

Train #343 was here at 3:38pm and #344 at 12:35pm. Records show that the railroad depot was also served by Wells Fargo & Company. The depot was removed in early 1935. A section house, two bunk houses, and a tool house stood on the east side of the mainline. These were removed in early 1937. A mail crane was installed in October 1933, and retired in August 1955.

36.7 COUNTY LINE – At the former Missouri Pacific Milepost 363.8, **Phillips County** is to the north, while **Desha County** is to the south. The county line is clearly marked by signs on nearby Arkansas Highway 44. There is little else to mark the location except a single house and a small drainage ditch to the west. Several early maps show that a logging railroad once headed west from here, following Old Indian Bayou for several miles.

The county line between Phillips and Desha County is marked by signs on the adjacent highway.

Phillips County was created from land along the Mississippi River on May 1, 1820, making it the second oldest county in Arkansas. The county is part of the Arkansas Delta area, located where the St. Francis River flows into the Mississippi River. The county was named for Sylvannus Phillips, who arrived here from North Carolina by 1797 and is claimed to be the first white settler in today's county. He was also later a representative to the first Territorial Legislature of the Arkansas Territory. The county today is working to attract more tourism and industrial development, especially after the 1990 U.S. Census called Phillips County one of the sixteen poorest counties in the United States. The county seat is the combined city of Helena-West Helena.

Desha County was created on December 12, 1838, to deal with settlers cut off from their county seat (Arkansas Post) by the Arkansas River and the White River. To create the new county, land was taken from Arkansas County and Chicot County. However, this left some of the new county on each side of the river bottom lands, still an issue today as the county seat is at Arkansas City. Desha County was named for Captain Benjamin Desha, a veteran of the War of 1812. He made enough contacts to be selected by President James Monroe as the receiver of public moneys for the Arkansas Territory.

Desha County has actually had four different county seats as the county has developed. The first meetings were in the home of the Sexton family through 1841, when Bellville (later Red Fork) was chosen. Two years later, the river town of Napoleon was chosen, but it was mostly destroyed during the Civil War. Watson was chosen in 1874, but the county seat finally moved to Arkansas City in 1881, where it remains today. Because Desha County includes the junction of the Arkansas, White and Mississippi rivers, the longest levee in the United States is also reportedly in the county.

Desha County has had to deal with the Great Flood of 1927, and then drought and the Great Depression of the early 1930s. The biggest challenge has been the move to mechanical farming and the county's population has dropped to about 13,000 from the peak of 27,160 residents in 1940.

The Change to Mechanical Farming

The issue of mechanical farming cannot be overstated when looking at the population of this part of the country, and its impact on employment. When land was plowed using a mule, about an acre could be done in a day. The first tractors could plow almost ten acres in the same time. Today, the most modern tractors can plow as many as 150 acres in a day. Thus, one tractor and driver are doing the work of as many as 150 laborers and mules from a century ago.

When the land along the Delta Heritage Trail was first farmed, plowing was conducted using mules, getting about an acre worked a day.

Even when the first steam and gas tractors came along, large amounts of labor were still necessary. This farming demonstration shows that many plows required an operator for each plow blade, but allowed more acres to be plowed in a day.

As tractors and other machinery became available, the need for farm labor greatly decreased. This Farmall tractor is shown pulling a harvester and wagon, cutting corn on a demonstration farm.

Picking cotton was even worse. Up until World War II, cotton was picked by hand, using large bags that were drug along until filled. About 300 pounds could be picked in a day, and because the cotton matured at different times, fields had to be picked three or four times. It was estimated that it took 125 man-hours to fully pick an acre of cotton.

By the 1950s, new cotton varieties matured the cotton all at once. Additionally, cotton picking machines were invented that actually worked, with the first one reducing the time to pick an acre of cotton to 25 hours. Although pretty primitive, each two-row cotton combine and operator replaced about 80 sharecroppers, tenant farmers, and farm workers. The cotton pickers were improved, and by the 1960s, more than 95 percent of the cotton was picked using these machines. Today, a modern cotton harvest system can handle as many as eight acres per hour, what would have once taken one thousand man-hours to pick by hand.

Therefore, if you travel over the Delta Heritage Trail during planting or harvesting season, picture 150 men with a mule every time you see a tractor, and 1000 men, women and children picking cotton for every cotton picker that you see. Also note that rural schools generally didn't hold class during the planting and harvesting season since everyone, no matter their age, was working on the farm.

36.7 **BROLIN SPUR** – Immediately south of the county line was once Brolin Spur. A spur track headed to the southwest, but it was retired in December 1936. In 1911, a flag-stop station named Jarboe Spur was located near here.

37.5 **CYPRESS BAYOU BRIDGE** – A timber pile trestle measuring 108 feet long was used by the railroad to cross this stream, located at Missouri Pacific Milepost 364.6. The bridge was known as MH&L Bridge

No. 66. Many maps show the stream to be Little Cypress Bayou, and it flows west into one of several old channels of the White River.

37.6 LORAY – Also known as Lorays, this was not one of the original stations along the line. However, the Arkansas Logging Company was here by late 1912. *The Tradesman* of January 18, 1912, made the announcement about the project.

> MEMPHIS, TENN. – *A. Maas, of the Delta Land Co. has purchased 30,000 acres of timber land in Arkansas. The land lies in Phillips and Desha counties, along the Memphis, Helena and Louisiana railroad, and is studded with virgin growths of cottonwood, gum, oak and other hardwood timber. The deal involved $400,000 as a purchase price. It is proposed to log and market the timber, and for this purpose the Arkansas Logging Co., in the state of Arkansas, has been organized. T. W. Sofge, having his office at 52 South Front street, will have charge of the logging and marketing of the timber. In order to facilitate the handling of the logs, a tramway of eleven miles in length will be constructed through the property. Negotiations are now in progress for the construction of this road. The company also contemplates erecting another mill or two.*

More details on the project were reported in the July 10, 1912, issue of *Lumber World Review*. This report stated that no sawmills were being built, "but the timber is being gotten out as rapidly as possible and sold to other mills in the Mississippi Valley." The report also covered the long-term plans of the property. It stated that the "land is ultimately to go into cotton as the property of New England spinning interests."

The Arkansas Logging Company was a subsidiary of the Delta Land Company, which owned about 30,000 acres in Desha and Phillips County. The Delta Land Company was owned by A. Maas, a "prominent cotton man from Memphis," but the financing apparently came from other sources. The land company built the sawmill and railroad for the Arkansas Logging Company, but both were delayed by heavy rains and flooding in 1912. To move the timber, the company ordered a new 24-ton Shay locomotive for the railroad. The locomotive was built in October 1912 and carried Shop Number 2608. This locomotive was sold a few years later to Gerard B. Lambert at Elaine.

The logging railroad also had a log skidder manufactured by the Clyde Iron Works. This fact is clear due to a lawsuit based upon an accident that took place while the skidder was being tested. A Mr. Saltwick, an employee of Clyde Iron Works, was training employees of the Arkansas Logging Company when the skidder rolled over, trapping an employee under the machine. The court case determined that an "exhaust pipe burst, causing steam from the pipes to flow upon appellee's body and left leg – for about an hour and a half, during all of which time he was conscious and endured great pain and anguish." The Arkansas Supreme Court delivered a ruling in 1915 that the Arkansas Logging Company was the legally liable firm, despite the action taken by an employee of the Clyde Iron Works.

Things changed within a couple of years. First, the post office, which opened here in 1912 using the name Lorays, closed in 1914. Next, both *The St. Louis Lumberman* and the *Hardwood Record* reported in April 1914 that the Lorays Timber Company was founded at Lorays in Desha County. Like the Arkansas Logging Company and its capitalization of only $10,000, the capital stock of $5100 of the Lorays Timber Company does not appear to have been large enough to buy or build a new sawmill and a railroad, so it was obviously a part of the land development effort. Maps from the 1930s show that the logging railroads headed west across Little Cypress Creek and connected with several other logging railroads from as far away as Lundell.

There were two tracks that headed off from the Missouri Pacific mainline, both about Milepost 364.7. Just south of Cypress Bayou, a line headed to the southeast. This line was removed in June 1921. About 100 feet further south a line headed to the southwest. This line was abandoned in August 1936. Nothing exists here today to mark the location of Lorays except open farm fields, created by the loggers.

39.0 DEERFIELD – Deerfield had a 10-car railroad spur track until the early 1980s when many along this line were retired. The switch for the spur to the northwest was located just north of Desha County Road 611 (also known as Cane Ridge Road) at railroad Milepost 366.1. In the same area, but to the east, was the depot, made from a car body and installed in December 1920.

Desha County Road 611 provides access to East Moon Lake, a part of the Dale Bumpers White River National Wildlife Refuge. This sign on Arkansas Highway 44 points the way.

At one time, there was a small yard of five tracks to the west of the mainline, used to hold cars loaded with sand and fill material from a large borrow pit.. The pit track and the bunk car track were abandoned in July 1919. Most of the yard tracks were removed in July 1923. A bunk car was here for a number of years for track and bridge workers, and the tool house was destroyed by the 1927 flood. A cotton platform was built at Deerfield in 1932, but it didn't last through the 1950s. As at most stations, the mail crane was removed in August 1955 after railroad mail service ended.

Deerfield was in the middle of a mile-long curve of the railroad at an elevation of 162 feet. During the 1980s, the mainline of the railroad was rated at 60 miles per hour for most of its route, but this curve had a speed limit of 30 miles per hour. Heading south, the grade changes from heading south to heading southwest with this curve.

39.1 DEEP BAYOU BRIDGE – Deep Bayou is an old meander channel of the Mississippi River. Throughout this area are a number of such channels of both the Mississippi River and the White River. Changes in water levels, the development of sand bars, and other factors historically kept the rivers moving about. The railroad crosses Deep Bayou again just north of its crossing of the White River.

MH&L Bridge No. 68 used a 360-foot timber pile trestle at Missouri Pacific Milepost 366.2. Timber trestles were popular on this line as they are relatively cheap and fast to build. They consist of clusters of driven piles called a bent, installed at regular intervals, connected by timber stringers. The bridge deck is built on top of the stringers. Over the years, some were replaced by steel or concrete bridges to carry heavier loads, or when the original trestle was damaged or deteriorated.

South of here, the railroad enters a patch of heavy woods, then back into farmland.

39.7 SWAN LAKE CAUSEWAY – Swan Lake is today a chain of lakes that stretch east-west for more than a mile. However, it was once much larger, probably part of an old channel of the Mississippi River. The railroad grade used a high fill to cross the area, where there was once a long timber trestle.

40.3 ARM OF SWAN LAKE CAUSEWAY – Before the construction of the levee system, Swan Lake was larger and covered much of this area. This arm of the lake still remains. MH&L Bridge No. 70 was once here, but it was replaced by a concrete box culvert and a fill in 1932.

40.5 LACONIA CIRCLE LEVEE – The railroad climbed to an elevation of 170 feet to cross this levee, which is famous enough to have been included in *Ripley's Believe it or Not* syndicated newspaper publication. Construction began on the levee during the 1830s after Francis J. Keene and brothers-in-law Notley Maddox Flournoy and Thompson Breckinridge Flournoy moved to the area from New York. They had acquired more than 3000 acres and soon discovered that the area regularly flooded. Other plantation owners started building their own levees, and when combined, they encircled about 18,000 acres and more than a dozen plantation homes which became known as Laconia Circle. The name Laconia came from Laconia Landing, one of the most active steamboat landings on the Mississippi River at the time, as it was used to transfer shipments to boats operating on the White and Arkansas rivers.

The name Laconia Circle is still used in the area. This sign, having fallen off of its post, once marked the local road at Snow Lake, Arkansas.

In 1859, laws were passed that allowed the levee to become a publicly financed project. The first failure of the levee occurred in 1882, and the Laconia Circle Levee District was created in 1886, forming the northern part of the Desha County levee system. Additional laws were passed in 1893 and 1917 that allowed the District to issue taxes and bonds to pay for maintenance and improvements. By this time, the towns of Laconia and Snow Lake were located in the District and housed many of the local 2000 residents.

After having been breached again in 1890, 1897 and 1903, the Great Mississippi River Flood of 1927 was a major disaster for the Laconia Circle Levee District. Heavy rains early in 1927 led many families to leave the area, and the plantations to put their employees to work trying to save the levee system. The Corps of Engineers sent several boats to monitor the levee. A few minutes after midnight on March 30th, the levee system failed and the area was flooded until the fall season. Only two homes, the Keene-Thornton and the P. B. Martin homes, survived the high water. After the flood, the Laconia Circle Levee was rebuilt, and the U.S. Army Corps of Engineers has continued to make improvements to the system, helping to raise it to meet current height regulations.

The Great Mississippi River Flood of 1927

The Great Mississippi River Flood of 1927, also known as the Great Flood of 1927, or simply the Flood of 1927, was one of the most destructive floods in the history of the United States. South from Iowa and Illinois, the lower Mississippi River Valley was flooded, pushing floods up most of the streams that flowed into the Mississippi River. In this area, the Mississippi River was sixty miles wide.

After several months of heavy rain and an early snow melt along the northern part of the Mississippi River, large amounts of water moved south. Then it began to rain across Arkansas and Mississippi, filling the lower part of the river. With nowhere for the water to go, levees began to fail all along the Mississippi River, and eventually almost 25,000 square miles of land was flooded, almost one million people were left homeless, and about 250 people died. The federal government, the Red Cross, and many other groups established relief camps to feed and house the homeless.

In Arkansas, 6600 square miles was flooded and 350,000 people were affected. Arkansas was probably the most impacted state with the most people affected, requiring 80 of the 154 Red Cross camps, the second highest number of deaths (almost 100), the most farmland flooded (more than two million acres), and what is believed to be the largest financial loss. Fourteen percent of the state was covered with water, and the Red Cross relief camps operated until September 15th.

Missouri Pacific also suffered greatly, and the railroad was out of service for months, starting in late April. Only local service was possible out of Helena and McGehee. Railroad reports show that repairs were underway almost immediately, but lasted for several years.

The Drought of 1930-1931

The situation did not improve much after the Flood of 1927. Over the next several years, a series of tornadoes hit Arkansas, and then the stock market crashed in 1929. Starting early in 1930, a drought hit twenty-three states across the Mississippi and Ohio river valleys and further east. According to the weather data from the time, Arkansas was the state hit the hardest. The rainfall dropped by thirty-five percent (parts of Arkansas saw no rain for seventy-one days) while temperatures set records. Food was scarce, with the Arkansas Agricultural Extension Service reporting that only Benton County (out of seventy-five counties) had "sufficient food for its farm population and livestock feed to tide it over the winter."

The combination of the stock market failure and the drought was severe on the farming industry. Cotton prices dropped by more than half (16.79 cents a pound in 1929 to 5.66 cents a pound in 1931) while production per acre dropped by more than half (six bales per twenty acres in 1928 to two bales per twenty acres in 1930). This meant that it cost more to grow the cotton than it was worth.

Several changes came about because of the flooding and then the Drought of 1930-1931. With no way to grow crops, many sharecroppers headed north to factory jobs. Also, many of the plantations failed due to their inability to pay taxes, and for awhile small farms began to develop. For the first time for many in the area, jobs were not available and they had to rely upon government or private charity. This experience reportedly led many to support the New Deal projects of the 1930s. A final change often cited is that African-Americans began voting for Democrats and their New Deal policies, many the very same people whom they had fought against a decade earlier in the Elaine Massacre. This change reportedly came about due to promises of more programs that would help them recover from the flooding and drought.

40.8 ARKANSAS HIGHWAY 44 – The railroad once crossed Highway 44 just south of the Laconia Circle Levee. Arkansas Highway 44 is one of the initial highways created by the State of Arkansas in 1926. It connects Snow Lake with Arkansas Highway 20 just south of Helena, for a total of 66 miles.

41.6 SNOW LAKE – Snow Lake is the location of another planned trailhead on the Delta Heritage Trail. Snow Lake is at Missouri Pacific Milepost 368.7, located at the north end of the White and Arkansas river bottoms. Snow Lake, often known as Laconia at the time, was a small community during the late 1800s, one of several inside the Laconia Circle Levee system. The Desha County Historical Society stated that during the 1880s, the area around Snow Lake included a number of plantations and "50,000 acres of cleared alluvial land, second only to the Nile River land in productivity; cotton farming as a way of life; transportation by river; seven stores, two schools, two saloons and three or four doctors." When the Memphis, Helena & Louisiana built through the area, Snow Lake became the rail station for the region and grew quickly. Even before the railroad was completed, a post office opened in 1905. In March 1906, when the railroad announced its opening, Snow Lake was listed as an initial station on the line, and a 24' x 60' depot was built in 1907. The name Snow Lake reportedly came about because of a nearby shallow lake that was covered with blooming water lilies, making the lake look snow-covered, thus the name.

The railroad once had a number of tracks and facilities here. In fact, Snow Lake was very much a railroad town for the first part of the twentieth century. There was a siding to the west that was 5490 feet long and could hold 103 freight cars (listed as being 5068 feet and 97 cars long between mileposts 368.0-369.5 in 1969). The depot was located on the east side of the mainline just south of the grade crossing, with an 1169-foot house track looping around its east side. A spur track headed northeast off of the house track. Another track once headed to the southeast about a quarter-mile south of Snow Lake. Records indicate that this track connected to one of a number of private logging and farming operations in the area. The siding and part of the house track remained until the end of rail operations.

Even after the railroad was shut down in November 1986, Union Pacific continued to maintain the line for a limited number of train movements. On Monday, April 13, 1987, Union Pacific locomotive #1630 pulled a weed spray train northward past the cotton gin at Snow Lake, Arkansas.

In 2020, the cotton gin building still stands at Snow Lake, as shown on this September afternoon.

Snow Lake was also the home of more than thirty railroad buildings and a number of train, freight and passenger services. Besides the depot and train order signal – which were removed in December 1966 – there was an agent's house (known as Building No. 24). In 1922, the railroad installed seven bunk cars on pile foundations. These cars were used by the gangs working on the many bridges in the area, with much of the work involved with filling them with dirt and rock. These bunk cars were removed in 1930. A number of other bunk cars were also here, used by track forces. In 1936, five of these bunk cars, along with a bunk house and tool house, were removed. During the 1940s, at least three new bunk houses were built at Snow Lake, along with several tool houses. In 1924, the coaling platform and hoist was removed. In 1928, a part of the cotton platform on the east side of the tracks was converted into a vegetable platform, and was then extended. The southern end was retired in 1954. Just north of the south siding switch of Snow Lake was also once a watering station and a 9' x 36' bunk house. This was retired in September 1934. The pump house, coal bin and platform that originally supported the water tower was 1500 feet further south. It was retired in 1926 when another water source became available. Even in 1955, Snow Lake still had a station agent who handled selling tickets for the passenger train. The *Louisiana Division Special Instructions* (May 1, 1958) stated that there was a railroad telephone in the section house at Missouri Pacific Milepost 368 Pole 23.

An early plat of Snow Lake showed plans for a four-block community to the west of the tracks. In 1921, the C. M. Stevens cotton gin was operating at Snow Lake, and the railroad had a busy depot with telegraph service, plus a number of tracks to handle local freight business. Passenger train #343 was here at 3:45pm, while passenger train #344 arrived earlier at 12:10pm. Much of the prosperity of the area declined because of the Flood of 1927, the Stock Market Crash of 1929, and the Drought of 1930-1931. However, Snow Lake was also the savior of thousands of local residents during the flooding. The Missouri Pacific Railroad operated special passenger trains to Snow Lake to pick up refugees, hauling approximately 2000 people to camps in Helena and McGehee. For some time, many lived in boxcars provided by the railroad since there were not enough tents or other housing.

Today, Snow Lake is often called the most isolated community in the state. Only Arkansas Highway 44 reaches the town, and only from the north. Separated by the Arkansas and White rivers, to drive to the

Desha county seat at Arkansas City, it is 125 miles. With the railroad gone, the only route south is the old grade through the bottomlands. Snow Lake is an unincorporated community at an elevation of 159 feet. The community includes a house, a post office, a church, a closed cotton gin, and a number of farm buildings. This is very different from the dozens of homes and businesses that once stood here.

Snow Lake is at the end of Arkansas Highway 44, as this sign clearly indicates.

This church at Snow Lake shows that while the community is small, there are a number of farmhouses in the area, at least enough to support this congregation. Note that the soybeans are planted almost to the church building.

42.8 SNOW LAKE BRIDGE – This 12-span, 143-foot-long timber pile trestle crosses the remains of Snow Lake, the source of the name for the nearby community and railroad station. This was MH&L Bridge No. 73, located at Milepost 369.9, and was once 141 spans long. All but the very south end of the bridge was filled in during late 1939. Today, the levee system has allowed the lake to be drained to make the land available for farming. The railroad elevation here was 156 feet, the lowest north of the White River Bridge.

43.9 WHITE RIVER LEVEE ROAD – Located here is another part of the Laconia Circle Levee, and the land to the south is part of the floodplain of the White and Mississippi rivers. On top of the levee at an elevation of 167 feet is White River Levee Road, also known as Desha County Road 79. When the railroad was abandoned, the railroad cut through the levee was filled in, ending the need to close the gap with sandbags during high water conditions.

The railroad once had a High-Wide Detector here. This device would recognize anything on a train that was too tall or wide to safely pass through the White and Arkansas river bridges. Any train taking this route was measured when it was assembled, but loads could shift en route, so this device was a safety measure designed to keep trains from hitting a part of either bridge and knocking it down.

This was once the section line between Section Gang 28 to the north and Section Gang 29 to the south. Heading south, the railroad grade passes through heavy woods as far as Yancopin.

White River National Wildlife Refuge

Heading south, the railroad grade passes through the southern part of the White River National Wildlife Refuge. In fact, the railroad grade is the boundary of the property, which is to the northwest. A few small pieces of property are scattered to the southeast, generally donated or acquired through the failure to pay taxes. The refuge includes more than 160,000 acres with plans to increase it to more than 220,000 acres.

The White River National Wildlife Refuge was created in 1935 and follows about ninety miles of the lower White River. It is the permanent home of birds, fishes, and other animals, and wildlife are commonly seen throughout the refuge. Bald eagle, white-tailed deer, black bear, wild turkeys, river otters, eastern gray and fox squirrels, eastern cottontail and swamp rabbit, coyote, beaver, bobcat, and many other species can be seen here. In addition, migratory birds regularly use the refuge.

In 2014, the refuge was officially renamed the "Dale Bumpers White River National Wildlife Refuge" to honor Dale Bumpers, former Arkansas Governor and Senator.

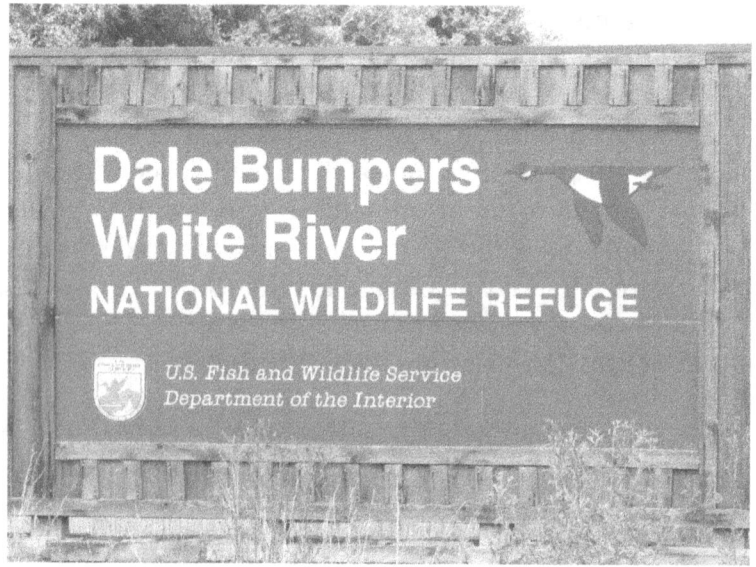

Signs like this mark many of the entrances to the Dale Bumpers White River National Wildlife Refuge, but future users of the Delta Heritage Trail will have their own access to the southern part of the refuge.

44.1 LACONIA CIRCLE LEVEE – If you look around, you don't find a substantial levee guarding the farms, fields and communities of the area. However, this was where the levee was in 1927, just before it was washed out in the floods of that year. After the floods, standards were created for the Mississippi River levee system and a new levee was built to the north, the one that still stands today.

44.7 FIFTH PRINCIPAL MERIDIAN – You won't see anything here, but the north-south survey line that passes through this location was made in 1815 to provide a reference line for land claims in the Public Land Survey System. This important survey line started at the confluence of the Arkansas and Mississippi Rivers, and headed north. It is the only principal meridian used in Arkansas, Iowa, Missouri and North Dakota. In Minnesota, it is used west of the Mississippi River. In South Dakota, it is used in the eastern half of the state.

What is so important about this? Simply stated, most or all land surveys in these states are based upon this line that started just a short distance to the south in these deep woods and bottomlands. Two lines were actually surveyed. Starting on October 27, 1815, Prospect K. Robbins started surveying northward, creating the Fifth Principal Meridian. On the same day, Joseph C. Brown started surveying west from the confluence of the St. Francis and Mississippi rivers, creating what was called the Base Line. On November 10th, the two lines crossed in the middle of a cypress swamp. All measurements in the involved states get their townships and ranges from this point.

The location was eventually forgotten about until 1921 when Helena surveyors Tom Jacks and Eldridge Douglas were hired to locate and mark the county line between Lee and Phillips counties. During this work, the point was identified as it serves as the corner point for three Arkansas counties (Lee, Monroe, and Phillips). To their surprise, the original bearing trees with the markings made by Robbins were found. Bearing trees are trees that are marked or blazed as part of a survey, and were historically one of the primary methods used to determine specific positions. In 1926, the L'Aguille Chapter of the Daughters of the American Revolution (DAR) placed a granite monument called "The Louisiana Purchase Monument" at the location where the Fifth Principal Meridian crossed the Base Line.

> THIS STONE MARKS THE BASE ESTABLISHED NOV. 10, 1815 FROM WHICH THE LANDS OF THE LOUISIANA PURCHASE WERE SURVEYED BY UNITED STATES ENGINEERS, THE FIRST SURVEY FROM THIS POINT WAS MADE TO SATISFY THE CLAIMS OF SOLDIERS OF THE WAR OF 1812 WITH LAND BOUNTIES. ERECTED BY THE DAUGHTERS OF THE AMERICAN REVOLUTION SPONSORED BY THE L'ANGUILLE CHAPTER

Today, the location where the two survey lines crossed is the **Louisiana Purchase State Park**, authorized by the Arkansas legislature in 1961. The park covers 37.5 acres and the DAR monument was listed on the National Register of Historic Places on February 23, 1972. In 1977, the Arkansas Natural Heritage Commission added the park to the Registry of Arkansas Natural Areas. At the same time, a 950-foot boardwalk was constructed from the swamp's edge to the monument. In June 1981, the boardwalk was designated a National Recreation Trail by the U.S. Interior Department, and the National Park Service designated the point a National Historic Landmark on April 19, 1993.

Elaine to Watson

The Fifth Principal Meridian ties together the Delta Heritage Trail State Park and the nearby Louisiana Purchase State Park.

45.0 **BRIDGE NO. 76** – At one time, there was a 74-span timber pile trestle here, at Missouri Pacific Milepost 372.1. This bridge was rebuilt by the railroad in 1928 to handle heavier trains, but it was eventually filled in as flooding was controlled throughout the area. Many trestles and bridges along this line, built quickly to get the railroad in service, were filled over the years to create a solid roadbed.

45.2 **DEEP BAYOU BRIDGE** – This 32-span timber pile trestle measures 364 feet long. It crosses Deep Bayou just north of where the stream flows into Scrubgrass Bend of the Mississippi River. This bend is now a horseshoe lake, cut off from the river except during high water conditions. Deep Bayou is itself an old channel of the Mississippi River.

This was known as MH&L Bridge No. 77, located at Missouri Pacific Milepost 372.3. It was rebuilt in late 1928 as the railroad was increasing the size and weight of its trains.

During January 1943, a 6' x 7' guard house was built at the north end of the Deep Bayou Bridge. This small building allowed a patrol employee to monitor the various bridges in the area and help protect them from flooding, fire, and even World War II enemy espionage.

45.3 STIMSON SPUR – Look for the grade crossing with Stimson Road, generally called Stimson Crossing by railroad employees. Stimson Spur, or more simply Stimson, is another location along the Memphis, Helena & Louisiana Railway created by the timber industry, located at Missouri Pacific Milepost 372.4. During the early 1900s, the brothers of the Stimson family started buying timber in Arkansas using several different companies, and even built some sawmills across the state. Initially based in Huntingburg, Indiana, the firms soon were based in Memphis and Helena.

The first lumber company was the J. V. Stimson Lumber Company, which built a sawmill at Earle, Arkansas. Not long after the Memphis, Helena & Louisiana was built, the firm was operating mills and logging railroads at Mellwood, using the name J. V. Stimson Hardwood Company. Jacob V. Stimson had long specialized in hardwood timber, cutting lumber for the furniture and interior finish trade, but using lower grades of timber for car and structural timbers, switch ties, fence posts, piling, and other commercial uses. J. V. Stimson Lumber was based in Helena.

Another Stimson firm was the Stimson Veneer & Lumber Company, of which R. C. Stimson was secretary-treasurer. This firm was based in Memphis, and often bought products from the J. V. Stimson

Lumber Company. Both firms cut and bought timber throughout the region. The veneer company eventually became the parent company, but both names were used through the 1920s. During the late 1910s and early 1920s, Stimson bought standing timber when possible, and land when necessary. During September 1923, the J. V. Stimson Hardwood Company bought 13,000 acres of virgin hardwood in Desha County from Taylor & Crate of Buffalo, New York. Just the previous year, it had been announced that the company's sawmill at Helena was shut down due to a shortage of log supply.

The announcement about the land purchase included the statement that the company would erect a plant and build a rail line to the timber. Maps show that a logging railroad was built to the west and then north on the east side of Scrubgrass Bayou (often spelled Scrub Grass), once a part of the Arkansas and White rivers. The line stayed west of Deep Bayou all the way to north of Snow Lake. The lumber company eventually abandoned their railroad and moved to truck logging, with the land becoming part of the Stimson Veneer Lumber Trust.

A track was built here in early 1919 to connect to the company's operations, and the location became known as Stimson Spur on the railroad. Even after regular logging ended, the spur track remained to handle any local business, such as farm products, occasional timber shipments, and railroad materials. The track also provided a location for track forces to get off the mainline to allow trains to pass. Missouri Pacific Railroad records show that Stimson Spur was finally removed in December 1962.

The land between Deep Bayou and Scrubgrass Bayou became the subject of a court case immediately after World War II. The Laconia Levee District brought action against the Stimson Veneer Lumber Trust because it had not paid taxes for the years 1943, 1944, and 1945. The lumber trust said that it had not paid taxes because "all of said lands are located outside or on the river side of the levees of the Laconia Levee District and receive no benefit or protection whatever from the District or its levees, and that to collect tax from said land would be unauthorized and illegal."

However, the boundaries of the Laconia Levee District were established by Arkansas General Assembly Act 463 of 1917, and the "western boundary of the District was fixed as Scrub Grass Bayou, the northern line being the county line between Phillips County and Desha County, and the eastern and southern line being the Mississippi River Levee, and comprising some 30,000 acres of land." This left the lands of the Stimson Veneer Lumber Trust east of the Scrub Grass Bayou and west of the levee of the Laconia Levee District, subject to backwater overflow of the Mississippi River and White River, but it also placed the property within the taxing levee district. An earlier ruling involving much of the same property dealt with the White River Lumber Company. In this case, the same argument was made and the ruling was that certain lands were benefitted and could be taxed.

Much of the land is still owned by a Stimson firm, now the Stimson Lake Land & Timber Company. Adjacent is the Anderson-Tully Company. The Anderson-Tully Company owns about 42,000 acres in the area that is used for timber production. A unique part of this logging is that the firm occasionally uses a barge on the Arkansas River to move the cut timber. This can require that the turn span be opened on the Arkansas River bridge. The two firms own the land around Stimson Lake, as well as a three-mile river chute called Stimson Chute. The chute connects Stimson Lake to the Mississippi River during high water conditions.

These channels keep changing as the rivers move. During the 1800s and early 1900s, the Mississippi River migrated westward. Following the Flood of 1927 and the Drought of 1930-1931, the river moved eastward, creating Stimson Lake and Stimson Chute. Because of this, there have been many issues involving land ownership, what is a navigable waterway, and what is private and public access to the area.

45.9 SCRUB GRASS BAYOU BRIDGE – This bridge is more than one thousand feet long and crosses the lowlands created by a former channel of the Arkansas River, known as the 1844 Meander Line. These meanders are closely followed as many land surveys and property ownerships use them in their descriptions. From the north, this bridge includes 302 feet of timber pile trestle, a 21-foot deck plate girder span, 75 feet of beam spans, and then 652 feet of timber pile trestle. The railroad knew this as MH&L Bridge No. 78, located at Milepost 373.0.

The bridge has a number of timber spans, several of which on the north end burned after the line was abandoned. The bridge then crosses a farm access road using several I-beam spans. The north concrete pier that supports the beam spans has a 1946 date stamped into it. To the east, the access road, shown as Lake Lane or Stimpson Road on various maps, is used to reach the Mozart Hunting Club and several houses along the bank of Stimson Lake to the south. The lake was once Scrubgrass Bend of the Mississippi River. The bridge then crosses the remains of Scrub Grass Bayou, which consists of a channel of the Arkansas River used during the 1830s and 1840s. Thanks to levee construction and drainage ditches, this area is now a mix of timber and farmland. There are also several small communities in this area, generally used for hunting and fishing.

While the concrete pier may be below your feet when the Delta Heritage Trail is completed, the 1946 construction date was clearly visible in 2020. This photo also shows the end of the steel spans, made possible by the fire that burned the timber spans to the north.

46.4 WATERWAY BRIDGE – This short 109-foot timber pile trestle crosses another small stream that was once part of the Arkansas River channel, and later a bayou that helped to drain the area. This was MH&L Bridge No. 79, and it was strengthened in late 1929 as part of a project to increase the capacity along the railroad. This short bridge, located at Missouri Pacific Milepost 373.5, remains to allow water to flow during the wet season.

47.5 WATERWAY BRIDGE – Because of the need to build the Memphis, Helena & Louisiana Railway above the floodwaters that often are found in this area, the railroad was built on almost continuous timber trestle through this area. As time and money became available, parts of the trestle were filled in to provide a solid footing for the line. This bridge consists of 537 feet of timber pile trestles and was known as MH&L Bridge No. 80. Located at Missouri Pacific Milepost 374.6, this bridge was shortened from 75 timber spans to 47 in 1932, with only the center of the bridge remaining.

During the last days of the railroad, it was not uncommon for a train to meet a small four-wheeler all-terrain vehicle (ATV) using one of these bridges during high water conditions. Most of the houses and cabins through this area are raised up on stilts, so they are not impacted by normal flooding. However, many of the roads can become impassable due to the water, so the higher railroad grade became a popular route to travel. Because of this, there were several reports of riders diving off of their ATVs just before a train would hit them and knock the vehicle into the stream below.

47.7 16 MILE BAYOU BRIDGE – Union Pacific Railroad documents use this name, but the name doesn't show on most maps. The bridge includes fourteen timber spans, forming a 168-foot timber pile trestle. This was MH&L Bridge No. 81 (Milepost 374.8). It was once a two-track bridge because of a short 581-

foot spur track to the east, part of the complex of tracks at Mozart. This spur track, once the north end of a siding, and the bridge that it used (Bridge No. 81A) were removed in September 1937. On the east side of the mainline was a shelter shed that was moved here from Countiss in July 1928.

48.0 MOZART – The Mozart area is relatively easy to find due to the cabins and houses just southeast of the railroad grade. This is the Mozart Hunting Club, a private membership club that owns about 5500 acres in the area. This area was once a station (Missouri Pacific Milepost 375.1) that connected to a logging line that headed to the northwest to Paradise Bayou. There was never a post office here, but the *ABC Pathfinder Shipping and Mailing Guide* listed the station by 1915, and *Bullinger's Postal and Shippers Guide for the United States and Canada* had it listed in 1922.

Mozart was a busy place, with a telephone booth, station sign, and several tracks to the east. Most of these tracks were removed in early 1921. A carbody depot was installed on the east side of the mainline at the south end of the spur tracks in April 1918. The depot was equipped with a train order signal which was removed in September 1921.

During the 1920s, Mozart had a train station that also served as a telegraph station. In 1926, passenger trains #343 and #344 both stopped here. The northbound train stopped at 11:55am, while southbound #343 stopped at 4:03pm. After the logging ended, the station was replaced with a shelter measuring 8'x 28', located on the west side of the mainline. Just to the south, there was a spur track that came off the mainline heading north that then curved to the west. A spur track remained in service until the railroad was rebuilt during the early 1980s.

There is no defining record of how the location got the name of Mozart. One story is that a train with a number of railroad officials stopped in the area so the line could be inspected. The wife of one of the railroad officials stepped outside and was amazed by the sound of all of the birds. She reportedly stated that it was as pretty as the music of Mozart, and the name stuck.

48.9 HOLE IN WALL LAKE BRIDGE – Hole in Wall is another lake created from an old bend of one of the rivers that used to flow through the area. The lake is shown to be 51 acres in size, but it can vary greatly based upon area rainfall.

The railroad passed right over the center of the lake on a 1341-foot bridge. The northern 988 feet across the lake consisted of a timber pile trestle. The south end of the bridge had been replaced by concrete pile trestle spans. The timber trestle, like almost all trestles on the line, was built as an open deck structure. This means that the deck was simply made up of the bridge ties that the rails attached to. The concrete pile trestle used a ballast deck design. This means that there was a solid deck that was full of railroad ballast (rock). Normal railroad ties were placed in the ballast to hold the rails.

Open deck bridges are typically lighter, and allow more air to flow through them to reduce standing water. This slows the rot of the timber components. Ballast deck bridges are typically heavier, but are easier to work on to make the ride smoother for the train traffic. The same processes are used as on regular ballasted track.

This bridge, MH&L No. 82B at Milepost 376.0, originally consisted of 114 timber pile panels. In 1962, the south end of the bridge was rebuilt with the concrete ballast deck spans. A 6' x 7' guard house was installed at the south end of the bridge in January 1943.

49.9 **WATERWAY BRIDGE** – This long 1380-foot timber pile trestle was built to cross the south end of Paradise Bayou, another former channel of the Arkansas and then the White River. It was originally part of the 1.2-mile-long trestle off the north end of the White River Bridge. In 1933, much of the 258-panel trestle was filled, leaving just this structure. With the work, this became Bridge No. 82C, located at Missouri Pacific Milepost 377.0.

The project to fill in this trestle was underway when Union Pacific stopped operating the railroad. While most of the project was near completion, about two dozen of the 115 spans were not completely filled. This part of the timber pile trestle was burned by parties unknown after the plans for the trail were announced.

50.1 **DISTANT SIGNAL** – In September 1936, the railroad installed a distant signal at Milepost 377.2 to alert southbound trains about the status of the lift span on the White River Bridge. It was located at the south end of Bridge No. 82C.

50.3 **VESTAL SPUR** – To the west is the former Vestal spur track and railroad yard. It was located just north of the approach to the White River Benzal Bridge at Missouri Pacific Milepost 377.4. The May 1, 1958, *Louisiana Division Special Instructions* stated that there was a 25-car spur track at Vestal, plus what was known as Log Spur. The switch and one or two tracks were still used by maintenance forces who were working on area bridges when the line was shut down.

There was a four-track yard on the Vestal Spur, with the yard tracks measuring 1000 to 2500 feet long. The yard was modified several times, including during the mid-1930s and early 1960s. Originally, the tracks led to a four-panel pile trestle that formed a pier over the White River. Later, they led to a rotary car dump. This type of device could turn a railroad car upside down to pour out its load. The purpose of this operation was to transfer rip rap (large rock) from railcars to barges to use on the Arkansas and White River navigation projects. A small slackwater and concrete dock were located alongside the river as a part of this operation.

This photo from the 1980s features the rotary car dump at Vestal Spur. It shows how the rock was dumped out of railcars and then moved to barges on the White River.

Delta Heritage Trail: History Through the Miles

A strange part of this project was that when it was finished, a small railroad locomotive was abandoned on Vestal Spur. The locomotive is still there, heavily covered with vegetation. The locomotive was built as Tennessee Valley Authority #3 in April 1942. The manufacturer, General Electric, classified it as a 45-ton centercab locomotive, and assigned it GE builders number 15243. During the mid-1980s, the locomotive was derailed with the north axles of both trucks still on the rail. Soils had been pushed up against the engine during a recent construction project in the area. The engine had also been used for target practice by local hunters, the motor had been half stripped, and the controls had been damaged.

Tennessee Valley Authority #3 can still be found in the brush at Vestal. This small locomotive was last visible in 1986 as Union Pacific used Vestal Spur as part of the rebuild of the Wynne Subdivision.

50.6 WATERWAY BRIDGE – This was another of the series of timber pile trestles, once including 63 spans for a total of 752 feet. It provided more area for the White River to move water during high water levels. In 1930, Missouri Pacific reported that they spent $292,000 on "renewal and filling portion of north trestle approach Bridge 83."

With the work on the approach trestles, this became MH&L Bridge No. 82D, located at Milepost 377.7. Immediately off the south end was a short stretch of fill before the White River Bridge began. In this area were a number of railroad facilities, including a telephone booth, a 6' x 7' guard house (installed January 1943), a 28' x 28' bridge tender house and toilet (installed November 1940), and a home signal. The home signal informed the train crews if they could cross the White River Bridge or not. They could only pass this signal if the bridge was open for railroad traffic. The bridge tender house was used by the railroad employee who had the responsibility of opening and closing the bridge.

50.7 WHITE RIVER BENZAL BRIDGE – After the decision was made to build the Memphis, Helena & Louisiana, the major crossings of the White River and Arkansas River required the approval of the federal government. On February 24, 1902, Congress passed acts that allowed the Memphis, Helena & Louisiana Railway Company to build the two bridges. Each act included the statement: "Said bridge shall be constructed to provide for the passage of railway trains, and, at the option of said railway company, may be used for the passage of wagons and vehicles of all kinds and for the transit of animals and for foot passengers, for such reasonable rates of toll as may be fixed by said railway company and approved by the Secretary of War." The Secretary of War approved the design of both bridges on August 14, 1902. Following this, *The Railway Age* of February 13, 1903, reported on the construction plans.

> *The Missouri Pacific Railway Company has let contracts for the construction of bridges across the Arkansas and White rivers, about 30 miles north of Arkansas City, Ark. The two bridges are for the use of the Memphis, Helena & Louisiana, and are about two and one-half miles apart, with five miles of trestle. The bridges proper will be steel structures, consisting of two 300-foot and two 200-foot fixed spans, and one 440 and one 370-foot draw span, with foundations of concrete. The Missouri Valley Bridge & Iron Works have the contract for the substructure, and the contract for the superstructure has been let to the American Bridge Company. H. Rohwer, chief engineer for the road.*

During the 1980s, this bridge (MH&L Bridge No. 83 at Milepost 377.8) was described as being approximately 4300 feet long. From the north, it included 500 feet of timber pile trestle, 149 feet of concrete pile trestle, a 200-foot through truss span, a 24-foot through truss lift bridge tower, a 313-foot lift span, a 24-foot through truss lift bridge tower, a 200-foot through truss, and then 2888 feet of deck plate girder (DPG) spans. The deck plate girder spans on the south end were of four different lengths. Thirty-four of them were 55 feet long, sixteen were 54 feet long, two were 51 feet long, and there was one DPG that was 52 feet long. All of the DPG spans were set on concrete frame bents, which replaced the timber trestle that once was here.

This plate shows that Waddell and Hedrick were the consulting engineers who designed the White River Bridge. Based in Kansas City, the firm was busy across the Midwest and as far east as Eastern Tennessee.

The 313-foot lift span is not original to the bridge. Instead, it and the two short lift bridge tower spans on either side replaced a 370-foot turn span that was once in the center of the river. This project was conducted as a part of the McClellan–Kerr Arkansas River Navigation System. The construction plans stated that the center turn span and pier were going to be removed, and two large piers and one long lift span would be installed. The lift span was to be built elsewhere and floated to the site on barges, and then lifted and set on the new piers. The original plan was to start installing the lift span in early July 1973.

However, there were delays that set the work back to mid-August. It was estimated that it would take 72 hours to install the span, and then it would take five months to make the lift span operational. When the bridge was not in service, trains were diverted through North Little Rock.

This photo shows the complex arrangement at the north end of the lift span, all required as part of the reconstruction of the bridge for the McClellan–Kerr Arkansas River Navigation System.

The delays in completing the bridge resulted in a series of lawsuits. Missouri Pacific Railroad and the federal government reached an agreement on June 19, 1967, to install the lift span on the Benzal Bridge. A bid from San Ore-Gardner was accepted on November 5, 1968. Construction was originally to take 660 days, and then it was extended to March 5, 1972, a total of 1122 days. San Ore-Gardner didn't finish the work until July 18, 1974. San Ore-Gardner admitted to a year's delay in completing the substructure work, but Missouri Pacific also caused delays by failing to send reports on to the Corps of Engineers for approval. Missouri Pacific also held back $70,000 "for noise in the bearings of the lift mechanism." Despite proof that most of the delay was caused by the contractor, the Eighth Circuit Court ruled that any act contributing to the failure to meet contractual deadlines by Missouri Pacific made it entirely responsible, despite previous Arkansas law.

Today, boats operating on both the Arkansas and White rivers pass under the Benzal Bridge as part of the McClellan–Kerr Navigation System. The elevation of the bridge's deck is 177 feet, with the tracks off each end being 168 feet. In 1969, the turn span was shown to be a manual interlocking, requiring an operator or train employee to turn it so that a train could pass. What is an interlocking? It is essentially a series of interconnected signals that control the movement of trains. A manual interlocking is controlled by an employee who lines the switches and sets the signals locally. In this case, it was a bridge tender who operated the signals and opened and closed the bridge. At one time, a bridge tender's house was located on the east side of the mainline at the north end of the bridge. This house provided a place for the bridge tender to eat and sleep while off-duty. Later, the new lift span was automated. An automated interlocking has the work done by a computer or electrical system, and the bridge tender's job was eliminated.

Lift Bridge Operations

Initially, the new lift bridge was operated manually, with a bridge tender operating the controls. During the early 1980s, signals were installed along much of the Wynne Subdivision, and the lift span on the Benzal Bridge became an automatic interlocking, meaning that the dispatcher and train signal system could operate it. However, controls to lower and raise the bridge could still be operated manually. Since the railroad closed the line, the lift span has been raised and has remained in this position except for periods of work on the structure or right-of-way. A presentation at the 1990 American Railway Bridge & Building Association explained the bridge's operations after it was made an automatic interlocking.

The presentation stated that the lift span stayed in the raised position. When "an approaching train is within approximately ten miles, the signals system activates the bridge controls." This included an announcement on the marine radio that the bridge was to be lowered, the activation of microwave boat detectors to look for boats on the river, the flashing of lights on the bridge, and the sounding of a horn. If no boat was detected in ten minutes, the bridge was automatically lowered for the train. If a barge was detected, it was allowed to pass and the train received a red signal, telling it to stop.

If while the bridge was being lowered a barge was seen, the bridge would then return to its raised position. Once the boat passed, the span would then be lowered. Once the bridge was down and a green signal given to the train, the bridge stayed down and red signals warned any river traffic. The author of this book crossed the bridge many times during the late 1980s, and almost always had to manually operate it. There were numerous times where boats were in the area and the use of the railroad had to wait until they cleared the area. It should be noted that many smaller boats could pass under the bridge even when it was down for trains. Only the larger barge loads and tow boats required the lift span to be up.

McClellan-Kerr Arkansas River Navigation System

The improvements on the bridge in 1973 came about because of the navigation improvements on the Arkansas River. This project was designed to provide regular barge service between the Mississippi River and the Tulsa Port of Catoosa in Oklahoma. Small boats had operated on the Arkansas River since the first settlements were made in Arkansas, but many operated only during high water conditions. For almost one hundred years, sternwheelers provided freight and passenger service up and down the river, and along many of its tributaries. By the 1920s, there were proposals to improve the river system to allow larger boats to operate all year long.

The first major step forward took place with the passage of the Rivers and Harbors Act on July 24, 1946. This Act authorized the Arkansas-Verdigris Waterway, but provided little funding for the Catoosa to Mississippi River route. However, it did specify that the project would provide navigation, hydropower, flood control, and recreation along the route. After several more small fundings, major construction began in 1958 with the Lake Dardanelle Lock and Dam, the route's largest. On October 4, 1968, navigation with the nine-foot-deep channel opened to Little Rock, and the rest of the system opened on December 30, 1970. Additional projects continued for years, but when finished, the renamed McClellan-Kerr Arkansas River Navigation System was 445 miles long and included eighteen locks and dams. It climbs 420 feet along its length.

During the construction, the project was renamed for its two largest supporters – Senator Robert S. Kerr of Oklahoma, and Senator John L. McClellan of Arkansas. An official dedication ceremony took place on June 5, 1971, with President Richard M. Nixon attending. The waterway is operated by the Army Corps of Engineers, and was the largest civil works project undertaken by the U.S. Army Corps of Engineers to that time.

While the McClellan-Kerr Arkansas River Navigation System covers the Arkansas River, it includes a few miles on the Verdigris River in Oklahoma, and the White River in Arkansas. In this area, the White River is straighter than the Arkansas River, thus was the preferred waterway route. The Arkansas Post Canal was built to connect the White and Arkansas rivers, and still allow access to the White River for navigation. The Montgomery Point Lock and Dam (Lock 99) was the last structure built (in 2004) and is located at Navigation Mile 0.5 on the White River. The Benzal Bridge, as the Memphis, Helena & Louisiana bridge is often known, is at Navigation Mile

7.6. The Norrell Lock and Dam (Lock 1) is located at Navigation Mile 10.3 on the Arkansas Post Canal.

The White River

The White River starts as several branches in the Ozark/Boston Mountains in northwest Arkansas. It flows north into Missouri, and then east and southeast back into Arkansas. In this area, it is a clear mountain river. Leaving the Ozark Mountains, it becomes a Delta river, wider and muddier. It eventually flows into the Mississippi River south of Helena, across from Rosedale, Mississippi, making it about 725 miles long.

The earliest recorded steamboat movement on the upper White River was in 1831, and there were efforts for decades to clear the river of debris and to dredge the sandbars and shallow areas to make the river navigable. Today, the White River is navigable from the Mississippi River as far upstream as Batesville, Arkansas, but Newport is as far as the eight-foot-deep channel is maintained. At one time, Locks #1, #2, and #3 in the Batesville area allowed barge movements even further upstream, but in May 1952, Lock and Dam #1 was leased to the City of Batesville for recreation and hydroelectric purposes. On June 20, 1952, the lock gates at dams #2 and #3 were made inoperative by securing them closed. During April 1957, Lock #1 was heavily damaged by flooding and the lower gate was destroyed, ending any ability to navigate further upstream. Since 1935, much of the lower part of the river has been included in the White River National Wildlife Refuge.

County Line

The north bank of the White River serves as the border between **Desha County** (to the north) and **Arkansas County** (to the south). The railroad is in Arkansas County only between the White River and the Arkansas River bridges.

Desha County was created on December 12, 1838, to deal with settlers cut off from their county seat by the Arkansas River and the White River. To create the new county, land was taken from Arkansas County and Chicot County. However, this left some of the new county on each side of the river bottom lands, still an issue today as the county seat is at Arkansas City. Desha County was named for Captain Benjamin Desha, a veteran of the War of 1812. He made enough contacts to be selected by President James Monroe as the receiver of public moneys for the Arkansas Territory.

Desha County has actually had four different county seats as the county has developed. The first meetings were in the home of the Sexton family through 1841, when Bellville (later Red Fork) was chosen. Two years later, the river town of Napoleon was chosen, but it was mostly destroyed during the Civil War. Watson was chosen in 1874, but the county seat finally moved to Arkansas City in 1881, where it remains today. Because Desha County includes the junction of the Arkansas, White and Mississippi rivers, the longest levee in the United States is also reportedly in the county.

Desha County has had to deal with the Great Flood of 1927, and then drought and Great Depression of the early 1930s. The biggest challenge has been the move to mechanical farming and the county's population has dropped to about 13,000 from the peak of 27,160 residents in 1940.

Arkansas County was the first of 75 counties formed in Arkansas, being created by the Missouri Territorial Legislature on December 31, 1813, from part of New Madrid County. The county was huge, with the southern border being Louisiana, the eastern border being the Mississippi River, the northern border being New Madrid County in today's Missouri, and the western border being the Indian Boundary Line. More than half of today's counties in Arkansas were formed from the original Arkansas County.

The county was named after the Arkansas River, which took its name from the Arkansas tribe, the name the French used for the Quapaw. The first county seat was at Arkansas Post, but it moved to DeWitt during October 1855. Today, DeWitt serves as the county seat of the southern district of Arkansas County, while Stuttgart serves as the county seat of the northern district. The population of Arkansas County peaked in 1940 with 24,437 residents. The population stayed steady through the early 1980s, but has since dropped to about 17,500.

Trivia time: Arkansas County is one of seven counties in the United States that shares its name with its state, along with Hawaii County, Idaho County, Iowa County, New York County, Oklahoma County, and Utah County.

50.9 BENZAL – What is a benzal? In the scientific world, it is a transparent crystalline substance. For the White River, it is a former shantyboat community. For the Missouri Pacific Railroad, it was the Memphis, Helena & Louisiana bridge across the White

River. For the railroad it was also a station name for a 4.5' x 14.5' Type "F" Shelter on the south end of the river bridge at Milepost 378.0. A large elevated deck was part of the bridge at Benzal, which included the shelter, a 4' x 6' coal bin (installed December 1922), a telephone booth, and a fish loading dock. A home signal for northbound trains was also located here in September 1936. This deck was so busy that it was extended 55 feet in 1941.

This view shows the large elevated concrete deck that once supported the various railroad facilities at Benzal, Arkansas.

The area developed as a river community during the 1870s. Calvin Tichenor operated a floating store in the area and reported on the community, consisting mostly of fishermen living on their boats. From 1928 until at least 1931, the Bureau of Fisheries operated a buffalofish hatchery at Benzal. The first year, the hatchery hatched and stocked 8,392,000 buffalofish, far under the planned 50 million. By 1931, the hatchery was producing more than 11 million fry a year. The purpose of the hatchery was to restore a depleted supply of commercial fish in the area. During the 1930s, an estimated 500 people lived around Benzal, many on boats. By 1999, when the federal government gave notice that riverboats could no longer tie up here, only a half-dozen remained at the shantyboat town.

Benzal seems to be an isolated location in the White River bottomlands. However, there is a road under the bridge at this location, improved with the construction of the Montgomery Point Lock and Dam. To reach the Benzal area by road, take U.S. Highway 165 south from DeWitt toward Gillett for 10 miles. Turn east on Highway 44 to Tichnor. At Tichnor, take the paved county road (Tichnor Blacktop Road) south 10 miles toward Lock and Dams 1 and 2 and Merrisach Lake. Note that there are signs along the route. Upon reaching the Lock and Dam and Merrisach Lake turn-off, continue south across the Post Canal Bridge at Lock 2. Immediately over the bridge, turn left on Benzal Road and go several miles. Some maps show that Benzal Road is also known as Big Island Road. Some maps also show a primitive campground that is located just east of the bridge at Benzal. Benzal Road continues on southeast and provides access to the Montgomery Point

Lock and Dam. Note that during high water levels, the road can be flooded.

Trusten Holder State Wildlife Management Area

Heading south, the railroad grade passes through parts of the Trusten Holder State Wildlife Management Area. According to the Arkansas Game and Fish Commission (AGFC), this "area is a typical overflow bottomland hardwood area with overcup oak, Nuttall oak, sugarberry, ash and persimmon being the dominate species." The area was bought in 1973 "for the purpose of protecting prime bottomland hardwood tracts which had been dwindling in eastern Arkansas in the early 1970s because of increased farming activities."

The area, named after Trusten Holder, a biologist and Federal Aid Coordinator for the AGFC in the 1950s, is managed to protect both the bottomland, but also the wildlife that inhabits the area. Selective timber harvest is done to create wildlife openings, and controlled burns are also conducted. A number of food plots have been created and planted with soybeans, cowpeas, millett, sorghum and winter wheat. Hunting is also allowed, during specific seasons, for deer, quail, rabbit, squirrel, waterfowl, alligator, bear, and turkey.

51.3   MARDI GRAS LAKE – The south end of the Benzal Bridge, Milepost 378.4, consisting of deck plate girder spans set on concrete frame bents, crosses Mardi Gras Lake. Most maps actually show this to be La Grues Lake, but the Missouri Pacific name is more interesting. This is another former river channel that has been cut off except during flooding. The lake is also called a wetlands, a swamp, and a floodplain.

At the south end of the bridge at Milepost 378.6 was a northbound distant signal for the Benzal Bridge, installed in September 1936.

51.6 **WHITE RIVER SPUR** – Until February 1921, there was a track that headed northwest at Missouri Pacific Milepost 378.7. In this area, the railroad had an easement to acquire borrow material, used to fill in the many trestles along the line.

51.8 **SATTERFIELD** – A switch was installed here about 1913 to allow the Helena Southwestern to reach its private logging railroad to the southwest. In late 1913, the Chicago Mill & Lumber Company chartered the Helena Southwestern Railroad, and it soon obtained trackage rights across the Memphis, Helena & Louisiana route to haul timber from various logging operations.

The switch at Satterfield (Milepost 378.9) was based upon an agreement with the Helena Southwestern that guaranteed traffic to the MH&L. Satterfield was listed in the 1922 *Bullinger's Postal and Shippers Guide for the United States and Canada*. After the timber was cut and the logging railroad was abandoned, the switch was removed during October 1923.

The name Satterfield honors W. R. Satterfield, a director of the Helena Southwestern when it was chartered. Satterfield was also a director of the Chicago Mill & Lumber Company, and an active attorney in Helena, Arkansas.

52.2 WATERWAY BRIDGE – This 540-foot timber pile trestle crosses another old river channel. This was MH&L Bridge No. 84 at Milepost 379.3. Like many of the bridges along the line, it was strengthened during the 1920s and 1930s, this time in October 1933.

53.0 WATERWAY BRIDGE – This former river channel is crossed using a 2205-foot timber pile trestle. The solid fill between this and the previous bridge was one of many projects during the early 1900s to replace various timber trestle spans with solid earth fills. The trestle once included 259 timber spans, but by 1933 it was rebuilt. Forty-five panels on the north end and 53 panels on the south end were retired and filled, while the middle part was strengthened. This bridge was known as MH&L Bridge No. 85 and was later shown to be at Missouri Pacific Milepost 380.1.

The work on Bridge No. 85 actually took several years to complete. For example, in 1930, the Missouri Pacific Railroad reported that it spent $148,000 on renewal of Bridge 85 at Medina. If you look closely, you can see the ponds created from the borrow (bar) pits used to fill in parts of the various trestles in this area,

54.0 MEDINA – Until the end of the railroad, Medina was a short 4123-foot siding on the east side of the mainline at Milepost 381.1. The length of the siding was limited by the bridges on each end. In 1943, the siding was extended 763 feet to these bridges, especially to Bridge No. 85 which had been shortened. In January of that year, a 6' x 7' guard house was installed at the south end of Bridge No. 85 where the north Medina switch was soon located. A telephone booth was located at Missouri Pacific Milepost 381 Pole 4. By 1987, the siding was often used to store excess railroad freight cars.

After the railroad was shut down in late 1986, the siding at Medina was used to store unneeded railcars. During late January 1987, the Cypress Bend Local (LAI73) with Missouri Pacific locomotive 2149 was at Medina to return these cars to the yard at McGehee, Arkansas.

R. F. Scott of Memphis, Tennessee, reportedly operated a logging railroad near Medina during the early 1920s. At one time, Medina was considered to be an unincorporated community, but now it is little more than a spot in the woods. However, a number of hunting cabins are now located alongside the railroad grade.

54.3 **KRAGEN** – The station of Kragen was located at Missouri Pacific Milepost 381.4, on the very north end of the Arkansas River Bridge. Other records show that Kragen was at Milepost 381.8 before the Yancopin Bridge was extended northward. A spur track once headed off the mainline to the southwest to connect to a private rail operation. After the switch was moved, it was actually north of the south switch of Medina. Later, the siding and spur track were often used by maintenance forces working on the nearby Arkansas River Bridge.

Union Pacific train LAI73 (Cypress Bend Local) is heading north off the end of the Arkansas River Bridge in January 1987. The train operated over the line to collect railcars that were stored on tracks in the area.

54.9 ARKANSAS RIVER YANCOPIN BRIDGE – The Arkansas River is a 1469-mile tributary of the Mississippi River, flowing from Lake County, Colorado, near Leadville, southeast across Kansas, Oklahoma and Arkansas until entering the Mississippi River near what was once Napoleon, Arkansas. The river is the second-longest tributary of the Mississippi-Missouri River system, the sixth-longest river in the country, and the 45th longest river in the world. The Arkansas River was once part of the border between the United States and Mexico, as created by the Adams–Onís Treaty of 1821. The treaty established the western border of the United States as being the Sabine, Red, and Arkansas Rivers to the Rocky Mountains, then west along the 42nd parallel to the Pacific Ocean. This ended with the Annexation of Texas (1845) and the Treaty of Guadalupe Hidalgo (Treaty of Peace, Friendship, Limits and Settlement between the United States of America and the Mexican Republic – 1848), which ended the Mexican-American War.

The Arkansas River is now used by the McClellan-Kerr Arkansas River Navigation System. The commercial river system was named for Senators John L. McClellan of Arkansas, and Robert S. Kerr of Oklahoma. The work by the U.S. Corps of Engineers has made the river navigable from the Mississippi River as far west as the Tulsa Port of Catoosa. However, in this area, commercial ships use the nearby White River since the Arkansas River is blocked just a few miles upstream by the Wilbur D. Mills Dam and Hydropower Generating Station. Construction on the hydropower plant began in 1994 and was completed in 1999. It is now known as the Electric Cooperatives of Arkansas Hydropower Generating Station and has a generating capacity of 102.6 megawatts. However, even with the dam blocking the channel, logging barges still use this part of the Arkansas River and the bridge's turn span must be opened every few years to allow logging along the river's banks.

Building and Rebuilding the Bridge

The Memphis, Helena & Louisiana Railway Company received authority to build the bridge from Congress on February 24, 1902, through *An Act Au-*

thorizing the Memphis, Helena and Louisiana Railway Company to construct and maintain a Bridge across the Arkansas River, in the State of Arkansas. The Act included a sentence about the purpose of the bridge and the final approval requirements.

> Said bridge shall be constructed to provide for the passage of railway trains, and, at the option of said railway company, may be used for the passage of wagons and vehicles of all kinds and for the transit of animals and for foot passengers, for such reasonable rates of toll as may be fixed by said railway company and approved by the Secretary of War.

The Secretary of War approved the bridge on August 14, 1902. Despite the option of adding a toll road, the bridge was designed to only carry trains.

The Arkansas River Bridge was built as a joint project with the White River Bridge. The superstructure was built by the American Bridge Company. The American Bridge Company was formed in April 1900 as a J. P. Morgan & Company engineered merger of 28 steel companies. The firm has dominated the industry since. The Missouri Valley Bridge & Iron Works was awarded the contract for the substructure. The firm changed its name to the Missouri Valley Bridge & Iron Company in 1904. Missouri Valley Bridge was based in Leavenworth, Kansas, and built bridges across the country, often buying the superstructure from other firms and then installing it themselves.

Building the bridge, which soon was called the Yancopin Bridge, was a challenge for the contractors and the railroad. After the bridge piers were built, the river changed its course. In December 1904, the railroad and its contractors had to work to reroute the river back under the proposed location of the drawspan. This effort delayed the construction of the steel work. The river moved again in 1905, this time as much as a mile, leaving the bridge standing over an abandoned river channel. This moving of the Arkansas River has remained a challenge. Today, the lift span generally stands over dry land while the river sometimes is centered under the through truss swing span.

In late 1908, the north end of the Arkansas River Bridge washed out several times. These were due to flooding upstream on the Arkansas River, and a low water condition on the Mississippi River. This led the water to flow very quickly through the area. After the first flood, Pier 5 was washed out, but held. During the second flood, the pier failed. The engineering report became a part of a series of articles on river bank erosion in the April 8, 1909, issue of *Engineering News*.

At the time, the bridge consisted of two through truss spans on the south end, sitting on Piers 1 through 3. The north end of the bridge consisted of the double ended draw which revolved on a center pier, known as Pier 4. Pier 5 was at the north end of the drawspan. The rest of the bridge consisted of long timber pile trestles off each end. A study of the situation stated that the bridge was poorly located in what was known as a caving bend. Apparently, this was discovered as the original bridge construction started, but the railroad grade had been built from either end and the railroad felt that it was too late to change the bridge's location. Over the decades since, the river has continued to move back and forth, requiring the installation of additional bridge spans.

The railroad kept fighting the Arkansas River, and in early 1914, it contracted A. W. Farney of Kansas City, Missouri, to install 3000 feet of revetment (rock lining along a shoreline) and conduct other shore protection work to protect "the Memphis, Helena and Louisiana bridge across the Arkansas river." In January 1917, the railroad received approval to make changes in the bridge's design, and the September 1, 1917, issue of *Railway Review* reported that the Missouri Pacific had let a contract to the Missouri Valley Bridge & Iron Company to install a lift type draw span over the new river channel. As described by the railroad's A.F.E. (Authorizations For Expenditure) #261414, the work was to convert a through truss span into a lift span and the turn span into a fixed span.

The late 1940s was another period of significant work on the bridge. In 1946, the Corps of Engineers dredged an older channel of the Arkansas River, known as Garland Lake, to move it further east as an effort to stabilize the river's meanderings. This required the railroad to install large amounts of rip-rap stone, as well as thousands of feet of fascine mattress. A fascine mattress is a large pad made of fabric, brush or even concrete that can be placed on a river embankment to help hold it in place and protect it from strong currents.

Work continued for decades, and there were several public works appropriations to do work along the river that would protect the bridge. For example, in 1957, the federal government planned and funded a project to protect the Missouri Pacific Railroad bridge at Yancopin. The study stated that caving of the river bank north of the bridge was threatening the bridge's revetment (rock-lined embankment) on the south abutment, causing a misalignment of the channel under the bridge. Because of the continuous work on the bridge, railroad officials often stated that it was the most expensive bridge on the entire Missouri Pacific system.

This view from the south end of the Arkansas River Bridge shows the turn span and the lift span, further to the north. The Arkansas River is not the main channel of the McClellan-Kerr Arkansas River Navigation System, but the turn span is still opened every few years for barges moving logs that are cut nearby.

During the late 1980s, Union Pacific described the bridge, located at Milepost 382.0, as being 6020 feet long, with a bridge deck elevation of 177 feet. The north end started with 1515 feet of concrete pile trestle. Next, there was 355 feet of timber pile trestle, and then two 300-foot through truss spans. There was then a 208-foot through truss and then the 300-foot lift span. To the south was a 440-foot through truss turn span, a 300-foot through truss span, a 71-foot through plate girder span, and then 2231 feet of beam spans. For many years, a 9' x 14' tool house and a stop sign were located just north of the lift span. A bridge tender's house was installed as part of the project to rebuild the south approach to the bridge. Railroad notes indicate that the house came from Wynne, Arkansas, in 1934.

The south end of the bridge can be accessed from Watson, Arkansas, via Desha County Road 41. Take Wood Street to the north end of town and then County Road 41, also known as Yancopin Road, north to the levee at Yancopin. Turn left onto the levee. The road will soon turn north (right) to the Arkansas River and Missouri Pacific's Yancopin Bridge.

County Line

At this location, the Arkansas River is the county line between **Arkansas County**, to the north, and **Desha County**, to the south. **Arkansas County** was the first of 75 counties formed in Arkansas, being created by the Missouri Territorial Legislature on December 31, 1813, from part of New Madrid County. The county was huge, with the southern border being Louisiana, the eastern border being the Mississippi River, the northern border being New Madrid County in today's Missouri, and the western border being the Indian Boundary Line. More than half of today's counties in Arkansas were formed from the original Arkansas County.

The county was named after the Arkansas River, which took its name from the Arkansas tribe. The first county seat was at Arkansas Post, but it moved to DeWitt during October 1855. Today, DeWitt serves as the county seat of the southern district of Arkansas County, while Stuttgart serves as the county seat of the northern district. The population of Arkansas County peaked in 1940 with 24,437 residents. The population stayed steady through the early 1980s, but has since dropped to about 17,500.

Trivia time: Arkansas County is one of seven counties in the United States that shares its name with its state, along with Hawaii County, Idaho County, Iowa County, New York County, Oklahoma County, and Utah County.

Desha County was created on December 12, 1838, to deal with settlers cut off from their county seat by the Arkansas River and the White River. To create the new county, land was taken from Arkansas County and Chicot County. However, this left some of the new county on each side of the river bottom lands, still an issue today as the county seat is at Arkansas City. Desha County was named for Captain Benjamin Desha, a veteran of the War of 1812. He made enough contacts to be selected by President James Monroe as the receiver of public moneys for the Arkansas Territory.

Desha County has actually had four different county seats as the county has developed. The first meetings were in the home of the Sexton family through 1841, when Bellville (later Red Fork) was chosen. Two years later, the river town of Napoleon was chosen, but it was mostly destroyed during the Civil War. Watson was chosen in 1874, but the county seat finally moved to Arkansas City in 1881, where it remains today. Because Desha County includes the junction of the Arkansas, White and Mississippi rivers, the longest levee in the United States is reportedly in the county.

Desha County has had to deal with the Great Flood of 1927, and then drought and Great Depression of the early 1930s. The biggest challenge has been the move to mechanical farming and the county's population has dropped to about 13,000 from the peak of 27,160 residents in 1940.

55.7   **SCHATZ SPUR** – Located at Missouri Pacific Milepost 382.8, there was a spur track to the northwest to the Arkansas River, first shown in a General Manager circular in June 1936. The *Louisiana Division Special Instructions* (May 1, 1958) reported that there was a 40-car spur track at Schatz, as well as what was called Log Spur. The tracks were gone by 1980. In this area, a distant signal was installed in early 1959 to alert northbound trains about the status of the Arkansas River Bridge. Another signal had been installed earlier in 1936, located closer to the river.

The name Schatz is somewhat unique in the area. However, S. W. Schatz was active in eastern Arkansas for many years, promoting water transportation. At one time, he was president of the Port Harbor Commission of Helena, Arkansas.

The more likely source of the Schatz name was Frederick W. Schatz, a director of the Chicago Mill and Lumber Company. Chicago Mill and Lumber obtained timber throughout the region, using their Helena Southwestern Railroad which had trackage rights across the Missouri Pacific line. Schatz was later the vice-president and general manager of Chicago Mill and Lumber.

55.8   **SANDY BAYOU BRIDGE** – This 29-span, 320-foot timber pile trestle, located at Missouri Pacific Milepost 382.9, crosses a small lake that is part of a

Elaine to Watson

former channel of the Arkansas River. Everywhere you look through this area is another former river channel – some dry and some still wet, often based upon the weather and river conditions.

56.1 DESHA COUNTY ROAD 43 BRIDGE – At Milepost 383.2, the railroad crossed the Arkansas River Levee protecting the land to the south, and then County Road 43. The bridge over the county road is a 42-foot timber pile trestle. County Road 43 is generally located on top of the levee through this area. Immediately to the south of the levee was the community of Yancopin.

During July 1988, Union Pacific Railroad sent their Cypress Bend Local (LAI73) to Medina to pick up stored railcars. Here the train, pulled by Missouri Pacific locomotive #2086, heads north past the general store at Yancopin.

56.1 YANCOPIN – By the 1870s, the Desha County seat of Napoleon had washed into the Mississippi River. A new town was platted here called New Napoleon, but it was never developed. Instead, the town remained the site of several plantations and a steamboat landing on the Arkansas River.

As the Memphis, Helena & Louisiana Railway was building through the area, the railroad based much of their construction here. Reportedly, many of the workers lived in railroad bunk cars. This led to the development of Yancopin, which received a post office in 1905. Additionally, there was a railroad station, two churches, three stores, a post office, a cotton gin, and a small school for white children. Black students attended school in a local church. In 1921, E. F. Massey and Huddleton & Taylor operated cotton gins at Yancopin. However, Yancopin never incorporated. As Watson became the primary town in the area, Yancopin shrank back to being a farm and river community. As farming ended its use of labor and replaced it with machinery, even more residents left the community. The post office, located in the store building that still stands at Yancopin, closed in 1958. The store building opened about 1900 and closed in 1972. Today, the area is owned by the Arkansas Department of Parks and Tourism and there are few residents.

The milepost used by Missouri Pacific for Yancopin was 383.2. Yancopin was the first community south of the Arkansas River, so the railroad built some facilities here. At least one spur track was here, shown as being 10 cars long in 1958, but gone by 1970. The original railroad station was replaced in late 1918 by a shelter which included a freight room (8' x 11') and a passenger room (5' x 17'). There was also a 9' x 14' tool house and a section house, removed in November 1940. A bridge watchman for the nearby Arkansas River Bridge had a railroad company house nearby. The house, a water tank, and a toilet were all retired in 1956.

A major feature of Yancopin is the former store building, now owned by the Arkansas Department of Parks and Tourism.

Besides the community, the nearby Arkansas River bridge acquired the name Yancopin. There is no clear explanation of the name. One version is that the word comes from a Quapaw Indian word for water lily – chinquapin – but pronounced with the accent used by early settlers. The second explanation of the name says that a Confederate base was here that held Union prisoners. This version says that the term Yankee Pen was shortened to Yancopin. The Quapaw explanation seems the most likely.

The name Yancopin is also used as the name of a series of soils in the western lowlands of the Lower Mississippi River Valley. The soil is described as "very deep, somewhat poorly drained, moderately slowly permeable soils that formed in silty alluvium." The term seems to be very local and is not used anywhere else.

Heading south, the railroad right-of-way is immediately to the west of Desha County Road 41. It is generally shaded, even when passing through farmland, thanks to the trees along the edge of the property.

Ernest Hemingway and Yancopin

Yes, Ernest Hemingway has a direct tie to the Yancopin area. In May 1927, Hemingway married Pauline Pfeiffer, whose parents, Paul and Mary Pfeiffer, lived in Piggott, Arkansas. The Pfeiffer family owned more than 60,000 acres of farmland, and Pauline Pfeiffer was a writer for *Vogue* magazine, working in Paris when she met Hemingway.

Ernest Hemingway began visiting Arkansas almost immediately, partaking in numerous quail hunts. During December 1932, he and a few friends and family members came to the Yancopin area to duck hunt and fish. Notes from various members of the hunt covered the trip and included comments about the country and people still being like they were in the days of Mark Twain. There were also numerous comments about drinking corn whiskey on houseboats at Benzal Bridge. The community and general store at Yancopin were mentioned several times as this was the source of many of their supplies.

Today, the Paul Pfeiffer house on West Cherry Street in Piggott is now the Hemingway-Pfeiffer Museum and Educational Center, owned by Arkansas State University since 1997.

Red Fork

An early name for this area was Red Fork, and it is still used for the township which includes Yancopin and Watson. The early community of Red Fork was several miles to the west of Yancopin on County Road 43, and was located near today's Red Fork Lake. An article in the January 29, 1905, *Arkansas Gazette*, reported that the Arkansas River railroad bridge near Red Fork, Arkansas, would be completed within a few days, with operations to begin in a few weeks.

57.4 **WATERWAY BRIDGE** – This 37-foot timber pile trestle, known as MH&L Bridge No. 91, crosses part of a former horseshoe bend of the Arkansas River. The area to the west is Carter Slough. The railroad used Milepost 384.5 for its location.

57.6 **ECCLES SPUR** – Eccles Spur was shown to be at Missouri Pacific Milepost 384.7. While *Bullinger's Postal and Shippers Guide for the United States and Canada* had Eccles Spur listed in their 1922 edition, railroad records show that the spur track to the southeast was removed September 1920.

57.8 **WATERWAY BRIDGE** – This is a 69-foot timber pile trestle that crosses another former river channel. Some maps show this to be Carter Bayou. To the southeast is Mound Lake, created in one of many old river channels.

The Missouri Pacific Railroad showed this bridge to be at Milepost 384.9, and it was listed as MH&L Bridge No. 92. Like many of the timber bridges on the line, it was strengthened during the 1920s and 1930s. In this case, the bridge was rebuilt from being a four-panel bridge to having six panels to increase its capacity, needed for the heavier trains being operated over the line.

58.2 LACY SPUR – Look for the farm road crossing that connects with Robertson Loop (Desha County Road 226) to the east. Like much of East Arkansas, this area was initially covered with timber, but now it is farmland. Lacy Spur, Missouri Pacific Milepost 385.3, was listed in the *ABC Pathfinder Shipping and Mailing Guide* (January 1915) and *Bullinger's Postal and Shippers Guide for the United States and Canada* (1922). Until it was removed in January 1928, there was a spur track on the west side of the mainline. The switch was located just north of the grade crossing, and the spur track then headed southwards.

The name Lacy came from the Lacy Brothers, partners in a number of companies across Desha County. The firm was based in Arkansas City, but dealt with construction, farming, and lumber. For construction – the Lacy Brothers were awarded a contract during the early 1900s to build a number of drainage ditches across the county. For farming – the Lacy Brothers & Kimball Company was a noted cotton firm. For lumber – there was the Kimball-Lacy Lumber Company, which had a large mill at Arkansas City. The firm was operating several logging lines in the county by 1910, using a small 13-ton Shay (built January 1906 as Shop Number 1629) which later switched the sawmill before being scrapped.

In October 1914, the firm had a large fire at its Arkansas City mill, losing about half of its stock of lumber. A month later, Kimball-Lacy Lumber announced that it was opening an office in the Railway Exchange Building in Chicago with plans to become a national dealer in lumber.

The Lacy Brothers weren't the only ones who operated in the Lacy Spur area. The Perkins Land & Lumber Company had a sawmill at Lacy Spur from 1909 until at least 1911. The firm moved to Kelso, Arkansas, in late 1911.

58.4 BONHAM – Bonham was a station on the Memphis, Helena & Louisiana during the line's construction, but the name seems to not have been used anywhere else. Railroad reports stated that the location was about 3.5 miles south of Arkansas River Bridge. The 1904 *Missouri Pacific Annual Report* stated that the Memphis, Helena & Louisiana had completed 22.39 miles of track from McGehee to Bonham by August 1904. The railroad would not go much further until early 1906 due to delays building the Arkansas River Bridge.

Note that the railroad grade is again passing through miles of open farmland, but that the right-of-way is lined with large trees providing lots of shade.

59.2 CANAL NUMBER 67 BRIDGE – Located at Missouri Pacific Milepost 386.3 is this 60-foot, five-span timber pile trestle. It crosses a canal which drains the area to the west and takes the water to the southeast into a series of canals which drain the dry side of the Mississippi River Levee system. Most of the water will wind up in Boggy Bayou, which the Delta Heritage Trail crosses at Rohwer.

Railroad records show that there was once a short spur track just north of this bridge on the east side of the mainline.

59.9 WATSON TRAILHEAD – The Watson Trailhead is the south end of the undeveloped part of the Delta Heritage Trail. The trail has been completed from here south to Arkansas City.

Welcome to Watson - population 211!

Elaine to Watson

Delta Heritage Trail: History Through the Miles

Trail map from Watson Trailhead to Rohwer Trailhead. Map courtesy of the Delta Heritage Trail State Park.

Watson Trailhead to Rohwer Trailhead –
Active Delta Heritage Trail

59.9 WATSON TRAILHEAD – The Watson Trailhead for the Delta Heritage Trail includes parking, restrooms, a picnic area, and a shaded area with benches and information panels. Watson is a good location for the trail as some facilities are located here. At Watson, the post office is still open, located near the north end of town. There is a small convenience store (don't let the liquor sign fool you) downtown, located just west of the railroad grade along Arkansas Highway 1.

Downtown, it is easy to find where the railroad once had its tracks and station. Arkansas Highway 1, locally known as Main Street, crosses the grade at Missouri Pacific Milepost 387.1. Clayton Street crosses the old railroad at Milepost 387.3. Heading on south, the Delta Heritage Trail exits the river bottomlands and heads straight south through farmland. While much of the route passes through fields of cotton, soybeans and corn, the right-of-way is typically lined with trees, providing shade.

The economy of Desha County is still heavily based upon farming. In 2016, corn (45,000 acres), cotton (15,000 acres), and soybeans (130,000 acres) all ranked in the top ten for county production in the state. Other crops like rice (20,000 acres), sorghum (1000 acres), and wheat (750 acres) are also grown. Most or all of these will be seen along the Delta Heritage Trail between Watson and Arkansas City.

Watson is the first significant town south of the Arkansas and White river bottoms, and thus once featured a number of businesses. The remains of the cotton gin can still be found near the Watson Trailhead.

The Railroad at Watson

Watson was the first significant community south of the Arkansas and White river bottoms. Because of this, there were several tracks, a large station, and a number of maintenance-of-way facilities, officially located at Milepost 387.0. The depot served as a telegraph station, and in 1926, four passenger trains stopped here daily. Southbound #343 was scheduled to be here at 4:40pm and northbound #344 was to be here at 11:25am.

The railroad had a siding to the east that could hold 90 freight cars. There was a short siding off of the main siding, located south of the Main Street grade crossing. Just north of the crossing there was a spur track that once connected with a logging line. The 24' x 60' depot and train order signal were on the west side of the mainline, just south of the Main Street grade crossing, and an agent was still here in 1955. There was a 1301-foot house track that looped around the back side of the depot. The May 1, 1958, issue of the *Louisiana Division Special Instructions* stated that there was a telephone in the section house at Watson. A Howe Lumber Company track was still listed. The document also stated that the train order device at Watson was located 60 feet north of the train order signal because of the sharp curve near the train station.

Watson was also the home of a section gang, and a number of bunk houses were scattered throughout town. Two carbody bunk houses and a tool house were installed on the north side of town in March 1927, but were removed in March 1939. There were two more 14' x 22' bunk houses near the depot, plus several toilets, tool houses, an oil house and a coal shed. Many of these were removed during the 1930s. Two tool houses and the last section house were retired in late 1962. In 1970, Watson was still the home of a foreman and four trackmen, the only track gang based between Helena Junction and McGehee. However, it was supported by similar gangs at Helena and Forrest City.

Stock pens were built at Watson in 1921, but they were retired and removed in 1946. A 16' x 24' water tower was here. It, a water column, and two pump houses were retired in December 1954 as the railroad was changing from steam to diesel locomotives. Missouri Pacific converted entirely to diesel in 1955.

When the line was rebuilt during the 1980s, the siding was on the east side of the mainline and measured 6946 feet long. The track basically was squeezed between the bridges at Mileposts 386.3 and 387.8. The short house track remained to the west. This track was retired in the last days of the railroad.

On July 25, 1988, Missouri Pacific locomotive #2089 is pulling a train of covered hoppers southward through Watson. These cars had been stored on the line, but it was time to move them back to McGehee as they were needed by shippers.

The Community of Watson Switch

Watson had been a popular camping spot for the Quapaw tribe, early explorers, traders and settlers. While it was somewhat isolated from other communities, it was close to the Arkansas River and its fish and game, and later trade goods that moved on steamboats. Like most towns in the area, it has gone through the cycle of heavy logging and then farming. Also like others, it has fought flooding, drought, changes in crop prices, the mechanizing of farming, and the closure of the railroad.

On January 9, 1839, the Arkansas General Assembly granted a charter to build a railroad from Little Rock to Napoleon, and another from Little Rock to Memphis. A great deal of competition for the land grants soon developed, especially since both lines were after the Mississippi River traffic to Little Rock. Construction on the **Little Rock & Napoleon Railroad** started during the late 1850s, but no track was built before the Civil War ended all construction. A lack of money after the war kept the line from being completed, and in July 1869, the rights to the route were sold to the **Little Rock, Pine Bluff & New Orleans Railroad**.

Lewis W. Watson was an early settler of the area, eventually developing a successful plantation. With the grade and then the railroad being built through the Watson Plantation, the community took the name Watson Switch. By 1872, the Little Rock, Pine Bluff & New Orleans Railroad was in financial trouble with about 65 miles of track completed between Chicot and Pine Bluff.

On November 11, 1873, the Little Rock, Pine Bluff & New Orleans merged with the Mississippi, Ouachita & Red River Railroad Company to create the **Texas, Mississippi & Northwestern Railroad Company** (TM&NW). More change came quickly and the TM&NW was sold at foreclosure to the bondholders on December 16, 1875, and then to the **Little Rock, Mississippi River & Texas Railway** on December 18, 1875. The new company received permission to build a straighter line from Varner to McGehee, and about 1878, moved the rail service to the new line and abandoned the route through Watson.

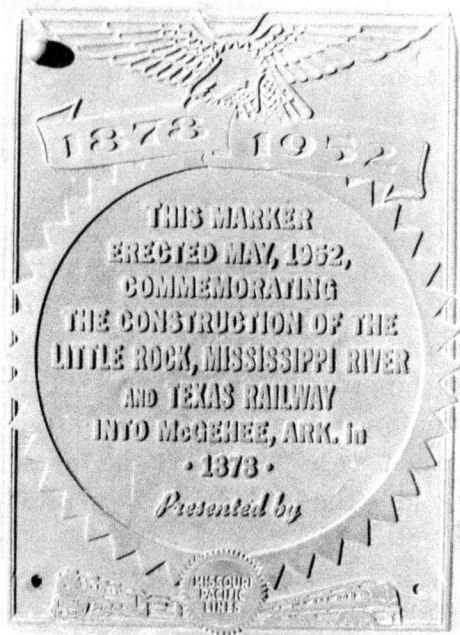

This historical marker is located on the McGehee depot, and celebrates the completion of the new route of the Little Rock, Mississippi River & Texas Railway, which built a shorter route south of Varner to McGehee, and then abandoned its line through Watson.

The construction of a series of levees during the 1870s attempted to protect Watson from the flood waters of the Arkansas and Mississippi Rivers. With a railroad at Watson, the property became more popular after the Desha County Seat at Napoleon washed away. In 1874, the county seat moved here, a post office opened using the name Watson's, and the town started growing as Watson, Arkansas. However, the county seat moved to Arkansas City in 1881 after the railroad was abandoned and things slowed down. In 1882, the post office changed its name from Watson's to simply Watson.

This marker near the Watson Trailhead discusses Watson and its short history as a county seat.

Watson stayed a simple farming and logging community for the next twenty years, but with the announcement of the construction of the Memphis, Helena & Louisiana Railway, Watson was again going to be a railroad station. The Memphis, Helena & Louisiana completed a 20.84-mile line from McGehee to Watson by September 1, 1904, and the town was used as a base for building the nearby Arkansas River and White River bridges. Watson was significant enough to be one of the stations listed in the March 1906 announcement about the start of St. Louis to Ferriday, Louisiana, train service.

Watson and the Timber Industry

Once the railroad was built, the timber industry showed up at Watson almost immediately. Numerous sawmills soon opened, dominated by the Perkins Land & Lumber Company. Like many lumber companies during the era, Perkins acquired land, logged it off, and then used the cleared land for farming, or sold it. Perkins Land & Lumber arrived at Watson by 1909, and operated for several years. The company was a partnership between the George C. Brown Lumber Company and H. E. and E. C. Perkins, and it moved to nearby Kelso during August 1911. During this time, logging lines reached deep into the river bottoms both east and west, some using the grade of the Texas, Mississippi & Northwestern Railroad.

With the growth of Watson, it incorporated on December 2, 1907. In 1910, the population of Watson was recorded as being 139, but it was 254 in 1920. By then, the timber industry was represented by the Brock Lumber Company and the Pine Bluff Heading Company and its cooperage operation. Cotton farming had also become important, and C. R. McKennon (cotton gin) and the Planters Gin Company both had operations here.

The Flood of 1927 greatly impacted the Watson area, and the sawmills didn't reopen since most of the timber had been cut. However, farms started on the cut-over lands, and after the drought of the early 1930s, many began to grow and hire more workers. As the cotton demand returned during the late 1930s due to the start of World War II, the population stabilized between 200 and 300 residents.

The population dipped to 209 in 1950 as the need for farm labor was replaced by machinery. However, Watson started to grow as it became a rural bedroom community for jobs in neighboring towns. In 1970, Watson's population had reached 371, and the public school had almost 400 students thanks to the number of families living across the township. The local schools merged with the school at Rohwer in 1972, and then McGehee in 2004. The school is now closed at Watson and students are bused to McGehee, twenty-five miles away.

Watson's population peaked at 433 residents in 1980, and has dropped ever since, with 211 residents in 2010. The economy of Watson is still based on local farming and the industry in nearby cities. Hunting, fishing, and other outdoor recreation like the Delta Heritage Trail are also having some impact on the community. The annual Watson Fish Fry, held on the third Saturday in March, attracts more than one thousand people and is a popular reunion event. Besides the food, there is an auction and many other events.

60.5 UNDINE SPUR – This location was once near the south end of the Watson siding, just north of Red Fork Bayou. Multiple newspaper reports covered the activities of the Undine family, who lived at Watson during the first part of the twentieth century. The location was listed in both the *ABC Pathfinder Shipping and Mailing Guide* (January 1915) and *Bullinger's Postal and Shippers Guide for the United States and Canada* (1922).

Missouri Pacific General Manager Circular No. 391, published on November 2, 1921, officially listed the station at Milepost 387.6, even though it was apparently in existence earlier. The track, which once headed to the southwest, was removed in April 1936.

60.7 RED FORK BAYOU BRIDGE – When the Delta Heritage Trail was opened in 2018, the timber pile trestle was replaced by a modern metal arch span. The railroad crossed this stream using a 132-foot timber pile trestle, known as MH&L Bridge No. 94, and located at Milepost 387.8. The south switch of the Watson siding was just north of this 11-panel timber pile trestle. Undine Spur was also once located just north of this bridge.

The stream has long been a transportation route through the area. When the first European explorers reached the area, an Indian trail ran along the east side of the bayou. The bayou was also used as a shortcut between the Arkansas River and the Mississippi River when water levels were high. Today, Mankin Loop and Red Fork Bayou Road follow the same route. Both ends of Red Fork Bayou are now blocked by the levee system around Desha County.

61.4 WATERWAY BRIDGE – Look for the short concrete bridge that replaced the 49-foot timber pile trestle that was once at Missouri Pacific Milepost 388.5. This bridge has never been long and crosses a small drainage canal that empties the fields to the east. The bridge was rebuilt in December 1944, but was in too poor of condition to be used for the Delta Heritage Trail. This was a common issue on the bridges south of Watson. The grade and bridges had sat unused for three decades, and even though the bridges were worked on during the 1980s, there were too many repairs needed to use them for the trail.

61.9 DESHA COUNTY ROAD 38 – Also known as Blythe Road, Desha County Road 38 heads west several miles to Cypress Creek. In this area, the railroad grade is very noticeable as it is often the highest location available.

The railroad once had a High-Wide Detector here. This device would recognize anything on a train that was too tall or wide to safely pass through the White and Arkansas river bridges. Any train taking this route was measured when it was assembled, but loads could shift en route, so this device was a safety measure designed to keep trains from hitting a part of the bridge and knocking it down.

62.2 LITTLE SPUR – This location was shown in *Bullinger's Postal and Shippers Guide for the United States and Canada* (1922). The track headed to the southeast from Milepost 389.3, and it was retired during July 1931. Across the road to the east is a large farm complex, likely the goal of Little Spur during the 1920s.

62.4 DESHA COUNTY ROAD 263 – This dirt county road heads west a short distance before becoming a farm road. Immediately to the east is Arkansas Highway 1. This highway is an original Arkansas Highway from 1926. It is 160 miles long and goes from McGehee northward all the way to Missouri. It generally follows the Delta Heritage Trail from McGehee to Watson, and then today's Union Pacific northward from Helena Junction.

62.7 CYPRESS CREEK BRIDGE – The railroad had two bridges here that are used to cross the old channel of Cypress Creek, and the newer Canal No. 81. The canal basically replaced Cypress Creek in this area, which drained 430 square miles in the northern part of Desha County, eventually flowing into the Mississippi River north of Cypress Bend. A small community named Cypress Creek was located several miles east of here during the late 1800s.

The north bridge was located at Milepost 389.8 and was MH&L Bridge No. 96. It was a 132-foot timber pile trestle, consisting of eleven spans. It had been shortened by 27 panels in 1923, creating Bridge No. 96A to the south. The south bridge over the canal was at Milepost 389.9 and was known as MH&L Bridge No. 96A. It was a 97-foot timber pile trestle using eight timber spans. Both of these bridges were replaced by steel spans as part of the construction of the Delta Heritage Trail.

The Delta Heritage Trail uses modern steel and concrete spans to cross Cypress Creek and Canal No. 81, replacing the deteriorated timber spans that once carried trains across the streams.

Watson to Rohwer

About a half-mile south of here, Gould Road heads east into the farmland. Whether it is a coincidence or not, the Gould family was involved with the Memphis, Helena & Louisiana Railway through their Missouri Pacific Railway and the St. Louis, Iron Mountain & Southern Railway. However, this Gould is probably James Gould, Secretary of the Delta Land Company during the late 1910s and early 1920s. James Gould had an office at nearby Watson and sold area land for the Delta Land Company.

Gould is a name tied closely to the railroad, but Gould Road was probably named for James Gould, a local land salesman.

64.1 KURDO SPUR – There is nothing to mark the location of Kurdo Spur except for the grade crossing with Desha County Road 51, also known as Experiment Station Loop (Expy. Station Loop on the road signs). Kurdo was shown in *Bullinger's Postal and Shippers Guide for the United States and Canada* (1922). At one time, a logging railroad headed northeast from here, used to cut the timber that was southwest of Cypress Creek. The last track at Kurdo Spur, located at Missouri Pacific Milepost 391.3, headed to the northwest and was retired in August 1941.

64.3 **HALLSTEAD SPUR** – This is another spur track that served local timber and farming interests. Located at Milepost 391.5, this track headed to the northwest and was retired in April 1939.

64.5 **KURDO LANE** – Also known as Desha County Road 398, this road curves west around the south side of Amos Bayou.

64.9 **LEVEE** – A levee once stretched north-south here. However, it was abandoned after the improved Mississippi River levees were built.

65.5 **ZELLNER SPUR** – East of here is Zellner Brake, a location once described as full of sloughs, bayous and ravines, and wholly unfit for cultivation. Work by the Cypress Creek Drainage District made the land available for farming, and the Zellner family eventually farmed in the area. This area is now a series of drainage ditches and farmland.

A logging railroad spur once headed east to near Zellner Brake. A brake is a thicket of various grasses and brush that is almost impossible to pass through. Building the railroad took a great deal of labor to cut the route. The railroad headed east and crossed Red Fork Bayou. East of Red Fork Bayou, a series of rail lines headed north. This route was eventually blocked by other logging lines coming in from the north. A second route continued east, crossing Lake Cheatham. It then turned south and through Dead Lake, reaching the timber to the north of the Mississippi River levee. As far east as Red Fork Bayou, this route is now Zellner Road. Further east, much of the grade is used as private farm roads.

According to railroad records, a track was built at Zellner Spur (Milepost 392.7) in July 1920, and it was retired during May 1930.

65.7 AMOS BAYOU BRIDGE – This was once a 133-foot, 11-panel timber pile trestle in a heavy patch of woods. In 1928, the trestle was shortened with the north end filled. It was rebuilt and strengthened again in 1949. Located at Missouri Pacific Milepost 392.9, this bridge has been replaced by a steel and concrete bridge for the Delta Heritage Trail.

Amos Bayou is another stream that is now crossed by the Delta Heritage Trail using a modern steel and concrete span.

Amos Bayou is a series of channels that start west of Dumas, Arkansas, and wind their way to the southeast. After passing under the railroad grade and Arkansas Highway 1 at this location, the bayou continues south and east. While it once flowed into the Mississippi River, many of its connections with other streams still exist, creating a new route for the waterway.

Amos Bayou was the location of a small Civil War battle in 1863. A historical marker at the Kelso Cemetery on Arkansas Highway 1 explains the action at what became known as the Skirmish at Amos Bayou.

> In mid-February 1863, Confederate troops at Cypress Bend fired on Union transports on the Mississippi River. On Feb. 19, a force of Union cavalry and mule-mounted infantry set out in pursuit. The Union troops drove off enemy pickets before encountering Confederate artillery at Amos Bayou. The combatants traded fire until Union canister forced the Confederates back. The U.S. soldiers crossed the bayou on home-made rafts, but darkness halted their pursuit. The next day, they found a 12-pound howitzer the Confederates had to leave behind.

65.8 DESHA COUNTY ROAD 51 – The Delta Heritage Trail again crosses Desha County Road 51, also known as Experiment Station Loop (Expy. Station Loop on the road signs). Not far to the west at 140 Experiment Station Loop is the Rohwer Research Station, established in 1957 as the Southeast Branch Experiment Station. Through gift and purchase, the facility obtained 634 acres that are used to test innovations in crop practices, machinery, and various technologies as they apply to southeast Arkansas.

Part of the research is conducted on land that was once part of the Rohwer Relocation Camp.

> **Southeast Research and Extension Center**
> **ROHWER DIVISION**
> UNIVERSITY OF ARKANSAS
> DIVISION OF AGRICULTURE

To the west of the Delta Heritage Trail at Desha County Road 51 is the Southeast Research and Extension Center – Rohwer Division, as indicated by this sign next to the trail.

Serving the needs of area farmers places a research emphasis on row crops like cotton, corn, rice, soybeans, grain sorghum, wheat, and bio-energy crops. About 175 field trials are conducted each year, and since 1977, the Rohwer Research Station has been a division of the Southeast Research & Extension Center at Monticello. This changed in 2018 when it became an independent part of the Arkansas Agricultural Experiment Station.

Immediately to the south of Desha County Road 51 were once two spur tracks to the east. The northernmost track was removed in September 1920, while the southern track was removed in October 1931. Apparently, the railroad had plans for more here as the company bought an 80' x 425' plot of land on the west side of the mainline just south of the grade crossing. This was an area known as New Kelso in the May 1, 1958, copy of the *Louisiana Division Special Instructions*. At that time, there was one 14-car spur track.

66.5 KELSO SPUR – Kelso was started due to the construction of the railroad, grew and prospered thanks to the timber industry, and settled into a daily routine because of farming. The area was settled by the Civil War, when a number of residents who lived along the Mississippi River moved inland to escape shelling by union gunboats.

The Memphis, Helena & Louisiana built through here in 1903, and some sources state that the community took its name from George Kelso, a railroad contractor, engineer and surveyor. The town must have grown quickly as a post office opened in 1903. Rail service was operating as far north as Watson by 1904, but through passenger service didn't start until March 1906. When the service was announced, Kelso was one of the stations listed in the railroad timetable, and was shown later to be at an elevation of 153 feet.

For the railroad, Kelso Spur was at Milepost 393.8. It was a fairly typical station location with a depot, a carbody bunk house, and several tracks. The station apparently was originally in a retired railroad car, and a new depot, oil box and coal box was built in October 1923. The depot was on the east side of the mainline and just south of the main grade crossing. It was removed in April 1934. South of Kelso Spur were a section house, two bunk houses, and a tool house. The tool house was removed in 1935 while the rest of the buildings were removed in 1936. The first track removal apparently took place in 1919, an 8-car spur track remained in 1958, and all were gone by the 1960s.

Perkins Land & Lumber Company

The timber industry immediately moved to Kelso after the railroad arrived. *The Lumber Trade Journal* of September 15, 1911, reported that the Perkins Land & Lumber Company had purchased timber land at Kelso, and was going to build a sawmill and establish a company town. Perkins was a major lumber company in the region, and had operations at Lacy, Watson, Kelso, Arkansas City, and Helena.

The company started as the Perkins Land & Lumber Company in 1909 with an operation at Watson, Arkansas. The company was actually a partnership between the Perkins brothers (H. E. Perkins and E. C. Perkins) and the George C. Brown Lumber Company. The firm moved about as the timber was cut and land holdings were sold, a common practice for the industry. In 1913, the George C. Brown Lumber Company withdrew from the partnership and the firm was reorganized as Perkins Brothers. At the time, Perkins Brothers owned about 6000 acres around Kelso.

By the early 1920s, the firm had built a new sawmill at Helena, Arkansas, but was still operating at Kelso. An article in *Southern Lumberman* (December 23, 1922) reported on the new Helena mill, and provided a history of the company. It stated that a standard 8-foot Allis band mill with a 250-HP power plant was built at Helena. Additionally, the company's main office was moved to Helena to manage all lumber manufacturing and product sales. At Kelso, the company still had an operation. *Southern Lumberman* stated that the "mills at Kelso are used to work up the small and inferior timber into ties, dimension stock and handle blanks." At the time, company advertising clearly stated that the company's Kelso mills were located on the Iron Mountain Railroad.

The Town of Kelso

Kelso was incorporated during February 1913, but no real action was ever taken and it is now considered to be an unincorporated community. The population peaked in 1920 at 231 residents, and the Cook Brothers cotton gin showed that farming was becoming important to the community. The railroad station was listed in 1922 by *Bullinger's Postal and Shippers Guide for the United States and Canada*.

Records show that at the community's peak, there were two sawmills, a few stores, and a small school. The Flood of 1927 shut down all logging in the area, and with the timber almost cut, the mills closed for good. Where thick bottomland timber once stood, fields of corn, cotton and soybeans now exist. Today, the post office is long gone, but Kelso is a small wooded community in the middle of miles of farms.

66.7 ARKANSAS HIGHWAY 138 – At the south end of Kelso, Arkansas Highway 138 crosses the former railroad and heads northwest and west to Winchester and on to Monticello, Arkansas. The road is a total of 37 miles long. The road started in 1930, but has had its route changed and extended many times since then.

Signs for Arkansas Highway 138 and the Delta Heritage Trail stand near each other just east of the trail at the Highway 138 grade crossing.

To the east of the Delta Heritage Trail is this marker about the "Old Town of Napoleon."

67.6 DUCE – This was a 1588-foot spur track to the southeast until the 1970s, located at Missouri Pacific Milepost 394.9. However, for many years, it was much busier, and had other names. The location was originally called Kelso Pit, and then W. F. Siding. It was changed to Duce in August 1939. A track once curved off to the east, with a small four-track yard to the south of the mainline switch, all located off of railroad property. The railroad showed that their removed in 1924 was unauthorized. Further south on railroad property, also to the east, were two more tracks that were also removed in early 1924. At the same time, two water tanks were removed from just north of town.

The community is now a large patch of woods and a few houses alongside Amos Bayou. The Kelso Cemetery is located just east of the community on Desha County Road 201, also known as Kelso Road. Not far south is Bailey Lane, which forms the north boundary of the former Rohwer Relocation Camp site.

Through this area, the Delta Heritage Trail is generally lined with a thin row of tall trees, providing shade most of the day. For those looking for a cool drink or a snack, there is a small grocery store along the east side of Arkansas Highway 1.

68.0 DESHA COUNTY ROAD 220 – This road, also known as Delta Lane, and on some records as Eye Street, heads west a short distance through the north end of the Rohwer Relocation Camp. A number of information and audio kiosks, interpretive panels, and memorials can be viewed while touring the remains of the relocation camp.

A siding was built along a roadway just north of Eye Street in November 1943, and was removed in June 1948. Railroad records from World War II called the area west of the tracks "Jap Camp."

68.2 WATERWAY BRIDGE – This small three-panel timber pile trestle was at Missouri Pacific Milepost 395.5. For years, it carried the designation MH&L Bridge No. 103, and was shown to be 37 feet long. It was rebuilt in November 1943 to handle the heavier train loads required by World War II. When the railroad was removed and used for the Delta Heritage Trail, the trestle was replaced by a new concrete span.

68.9 ROAD TO ROHWER HISTORICAL SITE CEMETERY – To the west is a dirt road that heads to the Rohwer Relocation Center cemetery. This road marks the south end of the main housing camp and is marked by large brown highway signs for the "Rohwer War Relocation Center National Historic Landmark." An information display is located just west of the tracks at a miniature guard tower. The short walk, and a visit to the cemetery, is certainly worth the time and effort.

Just to the west of the Delta Heritage Trail is the Rohwer War Relocation Center National Historic Landmark, certainly a stop worth the time.

Rohwer Relocation Camp

Following the attack on Pearl Harbor by Japan, and accusations that some Japanese-Americans had assisted with the attack by spying on the site, there were demands that action be taken. On February 19, 1942, President Franklin Delano Roosevelt signed Executive Order 9066, authorizing the Secretary of War, Henry L. Stimson, to establish military zones where certain groups could be excluded. Military Zone One was established along the west coast, allowing the removal of Japanese-American citizens and Japanese immigrants. To handle the movements, Roosevelt issued Executive Order 9102 to establish the War Relocation Authority (WRA) to build and operate a series of ten relocation camps.

Most of these relocation camps were west of the Rocky Mountains, but two were built in Arkansas. Located at Rohwer and Jerome, Arkansas, the idea was that many Japanese were farmers and would fit into the environment. Other requirements for the camp locations included remote locations but with access to rail transportation for the movement of the internees. The Rohwer Relocation Center was located on more than 10,000 acres of undeveloped Farm Security Administration lands, plus some privately-owned farmland. Most of the land had been acquired by the Farm Security Administration from tax-delinquent landowners in the 1930s.

Ray D. Johnston was appointed by Milton Eisenhower, the first director of the WRA, as Director of the Rohwer facility, and construction started on July 31, 1942. The U.S. Army Corps of Engineers prepared and built most of the site, with a number of structures built by local contractors. The first group of Japanese-Americans – 250 volunteer inmates – arrived on September 17, 1942, to help complete the center. The next group arrived within a week, and by October 31, 1942, the population peaked at 8475 inhabitants.

The Rohwer Relocation Center was large. There were about 500 acres of 20' x 120' barracks, each divided into six apartments with different sizes based upon the size of the families. Each block also featured a mess hall, a laundry, and a combination bath/toilet building. The northeast part of the complex housed the various administrative buildings, and there was a hospital to the north, marked by its tall smokestack. Several school buildings, a firehouse, a school shop complex, and several open areas were also inside the fenced area lined with guard towers. A cemetery, originally not part of the facility, was soon built at the south end of the complex. Reportedly only three of the relocation centers had a formal cemetery, and the one at Rohwer is the largest and includes two large monuments. One is dedicated to those who died at the camp – there are 24 burial sites in the cemetery. This monument features a request for the Arkansas people.

> "May the people of Arkansas keep in beauty and reverence forever this ground where our bodies sleep."

The second monument honors those Japanese-American war dead from the camp. 581 men from the Rohwer Relocation Center fought for the United States during World War II. Many of these joined the 100th Infantry Battalion, the 442nd Regimental Combat Team, and the Military Intelligence Service. These units were some of the most honored in the history of the United States and they fought across Europe. Members of the Military Intelligence Service served with combat units from a number of countries, handling translation, interpretation, and interrogation services across the Pacific campaign.

About 2000 students attended the camp's school. Most adults worked at various jobs at the camp, or performed local agricultural work outside the camp. The camp also grew much of its own food, producing more than 100 agricultural products. An interesting observation from many is that there were few problems between those held at the camp and the farmers that they worked for. However, there were some concerns that the low wages hurt local laborers. There were also the issues about different languages, religions and customs. The biggest problem seemed to be jealousy about the conditions that the Japanese-Americans were living under. The camp had running water, plumbing, electricity, heat, schools, and a steady source of abundant food, things many local residents didn't have.

Among the memorials at the Rohwer Relocation Center Cemetery is this one, dedicated to the Japanese-American war dead from the camp.

Delta Heritage Trail: History Through the Miles

A large number of information signs, located near the Delta Heritage Trail and around the cemetery, explain the story of the Rohwer Relocation Center. This one explains the confusion of many in the camp since they were multi-generational American citizens.

As internees were approved for other work or released, some camps were closed, including the nearby Jerome center. This facility was not looked upon as favorably as the Rohwer facility by the internees, and in June 1944, a large number of former Jerome internees were transferred to Rohwer. The Rohwer Relocation Center was one of the two last relocation camps, and finally closed on November 30, 1945. Today, building foundations, walkways, culverts and other improvements are still visible and some are still in use by the local residents. Parts of the high school gymnasium and auditorium remain, as well as the smokestack from the hospital incinerator. The camp site was listed on the National Register of Historic Places in 1974, and was listed as a National

Historic Landmark in 1992. Some of the property is now used by the Rohwer Research Station.

A number of famous people were internees at the Rohwer Relocation Center. Some of these include Takayo Fischer (American stage, film and TV actress), Aiko Herzig-Yoshinaga (political activist), Taitetsu Unno (Buddhist scholar, lecturer, and author), and George Takei (author and actor best known as Hikaru Sulu of *Star Trek*). George Takei in particular has worked to preserve the history of Rohwer.

69.1 ROHWER – The town of Rohwer was named for Henry Rohwer, who as chief engineer of the Missouri Pacific Railway was in charge of the construction of the Memphis, Helena & Louisiana Railway. It was not uncommon to honor railroad officials and investors with a town named after them. According to his obituary in the May 31, 1916, issue of *Engineering and Contracting*, Henry Rohwer was "one of the best known railway construction engineers in the country." Rohwer was born on October 17, 1849, educated in Germany, and came to the United States in 1869. He started as a topographer with the Burlington & Missouri Railroad, and then became their engineer in charge of location and construction. He next was the resident engineer for the Omaha & Southwestern Railway, and then the chief engineer of the Burlington & Missouri River Railroad. He entered private practice in 1875, and then became the city engineer for Omaha, Nebraska, in 1877. He went to work for the Oregon Short Line (Union Pacific) in 1881 as their engineer in charge of location and construction. Rohwer went back to private practice in 1884 to build brick kilns, and then was back working as engineer in charge of location and construction for the Omaha Belt Railway and the Missouri Pacific. He became chief engineer for Missouri Pacific in 1901 and handled 550 miles of line improvements, 700 miles of new lines, served as chairman of the board of engineers for the Thebes bridge project (joint St. Louis Southwestern and Missouri Pacific bridge across the Mississippi River near Cape Girardeau), and was a member of the board of chief engineers for the Kansas City Union Depot terminals. He went back into private consulting in 1906, working with railroads, city water works, power plants, and many other major projects. Henry Rohwer passed away on May 4th, 1916.

In 1902, the Memphis, Helena & Louisiana Railway was incorporated, and construction soon began. Timber was harvested in the area and shipped out on the railroad. One of the first companies was the Emigh Land & Lumber Company, which operated out of the Rohwer and McArthur area by 1907. The company had a narrow gauge (3'-6") logging railroad shown to be 1.25 miles long with four cars to haul logs. Reports show that the company had its headquarters at Rohwer, but it was later based at McGehee. The August 1, 1911, issue of *The St. Louis Lumberman* reported that the "Emigh Land & Lumber Company of Rohwer, Desha County, has surrendered its charter."

A post office opened here in 1904 (other sources state 1901 and 1907). Apparently the first suggested name was Harding, but the name was rejected because there was already a Harding, Arkansas. The name Rohwer was then chosen. The town was incorporated on February 25, 1913, but little action was taken using the incorporation and it was eventually withdrawn. An early plat of the community showed four blocks to the west of the tracks and two to the east. There were several stores that served the local loggers, farmers and mill workers. In 1921, there was also the J. G. Morton cotton gin.

Rohwer's population increased by about 10,000 during World War II due to the Rohwer Relocation Center, an internment camp for Japanese-Americans, but the community returned to being a small farm town soon after the war ended. The Rohwer school system, Desha Central School, consolidated with the schools at Watson in 1972 and became the Delta Special School District. The school was located at Rohwer, using some of the property and facilities of the Rohwer Relocation Center. In 2004, the school system merged with the schools in McGehee. In 1973, the town's population was so small that the post office closed, becoming the Rohwer Rural Station. A number of homes and several churches still mark the unincorporated community of Rohwer.

The Railroad at Rohwer

When rail service began on the Memphis, Helena & Louisiana, Rohwer was an initial station served by the railroad, later located at Missouri Pacific Milepost 396.5. For the first few decades, there were several tracks to handle the logging and lumber business. At the north end of town was a track to the northwest that was removed in January 1923. A second track, located at the south end of town, also headed to the northwest. In town, there was a siding to the east that later was converted into a house track.

On the spur track was a 16' x 32' cotton platform, built in 1925. Nearby was the depot and train order signal, removed in 1957. Several tool houses and bunk houses were at Rohwer, and a section house and three bunk houses were removed during the summer of 1960. A telephone booth was installed in 1933 in one of the section houses, and a new 8' x 14' tool house replaced an older building the same year.

Train #343 stopped at Rohwer at 5:02pm while #344 stopped at 11:04am. During World War II, several additional tracks were installed to handle the freight business for the Rohwer Relocation Center. However, by the 1960s, all there was at Rohwer was a short 832-foot-long spur track to the east. This track remained until the late-1980s when the line was abandoned.

Rohwer features the Kemp Cotton Gin Historic District, a cotton gin built in 1950 by O. O. Kemp. Kemp built the cotton gin, as well as a pump house, scale house, and office, after the Rohwer War Relocation Center closed. Much of the land became available for farming and other uses, and Kemp used some of the land next to the Missouri Pacific tracks. The gin building is now the only remaining cotton gin complex in the area. The Kemp Cotton Gin Historic District was placed on the National Register of Historic Places in 2005.

To the west of the Delta Heritage Trail is this yellow building, once the Kemp Cotton Gin.

Along with the cotton gin, there was also once the Kemp Mercantile at Rohwer, located across the highway to the east.

69.2 ROHWER TRAILHEAD – Rohwer is also the location of the Rohwer Trailhead of the Delta Heritage Trail. There is parking, information panels, shaded benches, restrooms, a bicycle repair station, and a picnic area at the trailhead. All of this is located at the Landers Lane grade crossing at the south end of town. This is the main grade crossing at Rohwer and the road heads west several blocks, passing by the closed Kemp Cotton Gin. The Rohwer depot was once located not far south of here.

The Rohwer Trailhead, like all trailheads, features information signs and other facilities. The Rohwer Trailhead includes restrooms, located in the small building that resembles a railroad tool house or section gang office. Rohwer also has this track bumper, manufactured by Wasco Supply Company of Chicago, Illinois. These devices were used to keep cars from rolling off the end of a track, appropriate for the end of the rail-trail section of the Delta Heritage Trail.

By 2020, Rohwer was part of the southern corridor of the trail, almost 24 miles of trail on a former railroad grade and Mississippi River levees. Watson to Rohwer was on the former grade of the Memphis, Helena & Louisiana Railway. From Rohwer to Arkansas City, the trail turns east and uses roads built to inspect and maintain the Mississippi River levee system.

The Railroad South to McGehee, Arkansas

The Delta Heritage Trail turns east at Rohwer to follow a series of levees to Arkansas City. The Memphis, Helena & Louisiana Railway (Missouri Pacific Railroad) once headed on south to the large rail terminal at McGehee, Arkansas. The line has been abandoned as far as Cypress Bend at Milepost 399.7. Here, a former industrial lead heads east to reach the former Potlatch paper mill (now Clearwater Paper), which the Delta Heritage Trail passes. This line was built in the 1970s, and now is essentially the mainline for the railroad.

South of Cypress Bend, the railroad is still in service due to the paper mill. Several stations were once on the line including Bogota Spur (Milepost 401.9) and McArthur (Milepost 402.5). McArthur was a community that predated the railroad, and then briefly boomed due to logging. Several more spur tracks existed on south (Bester Spur at Milepost 404.4 and Marrs Spur at Milepost 406.5) before the junction at McGehee (Milepost 408.1) with the Union Pacific mainline between Little Rock, Arkansas, and Monroe, Louisiana. McGehee has a large railyard, and the former depot and Van Noy eating house buildings still stand in downtown. The author of this guide was once based at McGehee when he worked for Union Pacific, and his office in the depot is now part of the visitor center and the WWII Japanese American Internment Museum.

McGehee once featured a railroad roundhouse and many other facilities. However, it wasn't on the route of the first railroad built in the area. When the Arkansas General Assembly approved a railroad route from Little Rock to Napoleon on January 9, 1839, the initial surveys bypassed the area. However, during the 1870s, the route was changed by the Little Rock, Mississippi River & Texas Railway and the McGehee location was suddenly on a railroad.

The location was on property owned by Abner McGehee, and he operated a sawmill to make railroad ties. Abner McGehee also handled the station agent job when the railroad opened. In 1879, he submitted an application for a post office at Holly Glade in Chicot County, but it was McGehee in Desha County by the time it was approved and he was named postmaster on March 8, 1879. With this, he created a town, a general store, commissary, and a boarding house at the site, which took the name McGehee Station, or simply McGehee.

To assist with the development of McGehee, Abner McGehee gave 51 acres of land east of the Iron Mountain mainline to be turned into a railyard and shops complex. It also made land available for the southern terminal of the Memphis, Helena & Louisiana Railway. Construction on the yard and shops was underway by early 1905. Several plats of the new town were filed in 1904 and 1905, and a petition for the incorporation of McGehee was filed on January 15, 1906, and approved March 5, 1906,

For the next eighty years, McGehee was an important railroad town with lines in multiple directions. Train crews and shop forces were based here. Besides the roundhouse and car shops, there was a re-icing station to keep fruits and vegetables cool, plus a series of feeding yards for cattle in transit. However, by the late 1980s, the shops were mostly closed and train crews were no longer being changed here. Today, Union Pacific trains pass straight through town while several shortline railroads handle the business on the local branch lines. The town has approximately 4000 residents, a number of stores and gas stations, and several hotels.

The railroad depot at McGehee was once a busy place with rail lines coming in from four directions. The station area was crowded in 1986 with the cars of station employees and train crews.

Today, the former Missouri Pacific depot at McGehee serves as the Jerome-Rohwer Interpretive Museum and Visitor Center.

Rohwer to Arkansas City –
The History of the Levee Route of the Delta Heritage Trail

Rohwer marks a change of trail characteristics. Heading north to near Helena, the trail uses the railroad grade donated by Union Pacific Railroad. Heading south to Arkansas City, the trail uses county and local roads, most of them on top of the Mississippi River levee system.

The levee system is a story that involves the draining of the lands across much of Desha County, and the farming that followed. Flooding was historically almost a yearly event in this part of the country, especially with the snow melt to the north, and the heavy winter rains locally. This meant that crops couldn't be planted many springs, and houses were often destroyed. To protect their properties, individuals began building their own levees, often connecting to those of their neighbors. By 1844, there were levees on the west bank of the Mississippi River from the mouth of the Arkansas River all the way to 20 miles below New Orleans.

By 1858, the levee system was even longer, going from 45 miles south of New Orleans to the Arkansas River, and then intermittently to just opposite Cairo, Illinois. Much of this expansion came about due to the efforts of various states. For example, in 1859, Arkansas laws were passed that allowed some of the levees to become a publicly financed project, and more work was accomplished. The Civil War ended much of this construction, but it began again by the late 1860s.

Building levees to protect dry land was and still is a challenge for this region. The watershed of the Mississippi River is huge, covering more than 1,245,000 square miles and all or parts of 31 states and two Canadian provinces. It drains 41 percent of the continental United States, stretching from Montana and Canada to western New York.

In 1879, the federal government took some action by creating the Mississippi River Commission, but its powers were very limited and most dealt with aiding navigation. High water in 1882 caused the failure of a number of Arkansas levees, and more state laws were quickly passed that allowed the creation of levee districts. The problem was that they required the local citizens to fund them, but there was not a great deal of wealth in the area. Similar laws were passed in other states, and soon a series of levees were built from the junction of the Mississippi and Ohio rivers at Cairo, Illinois, to below New Orleans, Louisiana. However, the lack of cooperation and common standards often led to the districts competing against each other, with failures common at certain locations that impacted many others.

> *"One who knows the Mississippi will promptly aver—not aloud, but to himself—that ten thousand River Commissions, with the mines of the world at their back, cannot tame that lawless stream, cannot curb it or confine it, cannot say to it, Go here, or Go there, and make it obey; cannot save a shore which it has sentenced; cannot bar its path with an obstruction which it will not tear down, dance over, and laugh at."*
>
> *Mark Twain, Life on the Mississippi (1883)*

Additional Arkansas laws were passed in 1893 and 1917 that allowed drainage and levee districts to issue taxes and bonds to pay for maintenance and improvements. Another action was the creation of the Southeast Arkansas Levee District by General Assembly Act 83 of 1917. The levee district covered all of Chicot and Desha Counties, and that part of Lincoln County east of Bayou Bartholomew.

At the same time, Congress was studying the need for federal coordination of the Mississippi River levees. On March 1, 1917, Congress passed an act that made $60 million available to control flood waters along the Mississippi River. Another act was passed on March 4, 1923, that provided additional funding, but only with matching local monies. This again led to the rich districts getting additional protection while the poorer districts were ignored.

The Flood of 1927 showed the problems with this plan as the weaker levees failed, often allowing water to flow around and behind the stronger levees, meaning that millions of acres were flooded. This situation led to the passage of the *Flood Control Act of 1928*, that required a comprehensive plan for all of the levee districts. The existing Mississippi River Commission was given the assistance of the United States Army Corps of Engineers to create these plans and to coordinate the construction of the required levees, drainage systems, ports, and other features along the river.

One of the first actions taken to comply with the *Flood Control Act of 1928* was the Jadwin Plan, named for Major General Edgar Jadwin, Chief of Engineers from 1926 until 1929. Jadwin was a U.S. Army officer who served as district engineer during the expansion of the ports of Los Angeles and Galveston, as an assistant in the construction of the Panama Canal, and who fought in the Spanish-American War and World War I. He was an advocate for the new levee designs and the use of floodways to provide Mississippi River flood control.

As a part of the *Flood Control Act of 1928*, local communities were required to perform post-construction operation and maintenance for the flood-control levees. Another provision was that the federal government could not be held liable for damage from floods. The *Flood Control Act of 1936* took the next step by stating that the federal government should protect people and property from flooding. It authorized the Corps of Engineers and other agencies to construct flood-control structures like levees and floodwalls, and make channel improvements.

During the late 1930s and early 1940s, a number of major projects were completed along the river, including in Desha County and around Arkansas City. This created what is considered to be the longest levee in the United States. A congressional hearing and report in 1948 broke the Arkansas levee system into three parts. The first was from Missouri to the St. Francis River near Helena. The second part was the various levees north of the Arkansas River to the St. Francis River, as well as the various White River levee districts. The third part included the levees in southeast Arkansas "beginning south of the city of Pine Bluff, Jefferson County, Ark., and along the south bank of the Arkansas River and thence down the Mississippi River to the Louisiana line. This district comprises 139 miles of levee." The report stated that there was a total of 397.3 miles of front line levees in Arkansas at the time.

These levees are large, and have grown larger over the years. In 1882, a typical Mississippi River levee near Arkansas City stood eight feet high and contained approximately 31,500 cubic yards of material per mile. In 1927, that same levee was 22 feet high and contained 421,000 cubic yards of material per mile. After more floods and engineering work, a typical mainline Mississippi River levee near here now stands 30 feet tall and contains 907,000 cubic yards of material per mile.

One issue with the levee designs became evident during the Flood of 1937. During this high water event, access to the levees often became difficult since roads for motorized vehicles were generally prohibited on the levees by the Mississippi River Commission (MRC). This changed in 1938 when the MRC passed a resolution that directed the various districts to begin building gravel roads on the levee crowns. These roads are still used today, including by the Delta Heritage Trail.

Another key design feature of the new levee system was to move many of them away from the river. This was done for several reasons. One was to reduce the erosion at the foot of the levee from the regular flow of the river. Inspections often found levees being weakened even during regular water levels. The second reason was to provide a wider floodplain, putting less stress on the levees during most flood conditions. This means that while walking the Delta Heritage Trail on the levees, views of the Mississippi River will be somewhat rare. Instead, views towards the river will feature woods, oxbow lakes, and large ponds that were once borrow pits for the levee's construction. Views away from the river will generally feature open fields, planted during the summer with soybeans, cotton and corn.

Delta Heritage Trail: History Through the Miles

Trail map from Rohwer to Arkansas City. Map courtesy of the Delta Heritage Trail State Park.

Rohwer Trailhead to Arkansas City Trailhead –
The Guide to the Levee Route of the Delta Heritage Trail

This part of the Delta Heritage Trail makes a loop east to follow the Mississippi River and then south to Arkansas City along the river levee system. Like the rail-to-trail part of the Delta Heritage Trail, the directions of north-south will generally be used for the route's direction, but real directions will also be used when appropriate.

The levees being used by the trail were generally built in the early 1930s as part of a response to the Flood of 1927, and after a master plan for the entire river system was created. Because this route was never a transportation corridor like the railroad to the north, there were not a series of communities whose history must be covered. However, a few historic locations do exist along the route, and the Mississippi River certainly has a history of its own. Some of the highlights of any trip over this part of the trail are the terrific views down onto the many farms, out onto the floodplain of the Mississippi River, and the wildlife that seems to be around every bend.

69.2 ROHWER TRAILHEAD – Located near Landers Lane alongside Arkansas Highway 1 is the Rohwer Trailhead. This is a typical trailhead along the Delta Heritage Trail and features parking, information panels, shaded benches, restrooms, a bicycle repair station, and a picnic area. Nearby is the Kemp Cotton Gin Historic District, the remains of a cotton gin built in 1950 by O. O. Kemp. Also nearby are the remains of the Rohwer Relocation Center, a World War II internment camp for Japanese-Americans.

The trail turns east to follow Rohwer Road toward the Mississippi River. Be careful crossing Arkansas Highway 1, as it is the main roadway in this area. Arkansas Highway 1 is 160 miles long, and connects U.S. Highway 278 at McGehee with Supplemental Route BB at the Missouri state line. Along this route it parallels the former Memphis, Helena & Louisiana Railway between McGehee and Watson, and from Walnut Corner northward. Highway 1 is one of the original state highways created by Arkansas in 1926, and its route has changed little in the almost one hundred years since.

This sign, located just east of the Rohwer Trailhead, points the way down Rohwer Road and on to the Mississippi River levee.

69.3 JUNCTION WITH DESHA COUNTY ROAD 55 – Look for the bicycle emblems painted on the road, plus the numerous signs. The Delta Heritage Trail continues east (straight) on Rohwer Lane, also shown as Desha County Road 64 on many maps. Do not be fooled by the paved Desha County Road 55 to the north, which follows Boggy Bayou for several miles.

69.5 BOGGY BAYOU BRIDGE – According to many maps, the road changes from Rohwer Lane to Desha County Road 64 at the bridge. Boggy Bayou is an original stream in the area, but is today part of the local drainage system. Several of the drainage canals and streams that the Delta Heritage Trail crossed north of Rohwer flow east into Boggy Bayou. From here, it flows to the south, often in a channelized ditch, and passes west of Arkansas City. It eventually turns east and flows into the Mississippi River near Yellow Bend, Arkansas.

Heading east, Desha County Road 64 and the Delta Heritage Trail pass through some patches of woods and tree plantations, as well as open farmland, for a bit more than a mile.

70.8 LEVEE ROAD – Whether you are heading north or south on the Delta Heritage Trail, be sure to follow the signs here. **Heading south**, Desha County Road 64 climbs the levee to an intersection with Levee Road. Turn right (south) and follow the paved levee road. **Heading north**, turn left (west) when the levee road turns to gravel and follow the signs and Desha County Road 64 to Rohwer.

The junction of Desha County Road 64 and Levee Road is on top of a levee built to protect the farmlands to the west from the flood waters of the Mississippi River to the east. The elevation of the top of the levee is approximately 170 feet, while the land on each side is about 140 feet. This means that the Delta Heritage Trail provides terrific views of the surrounding country. However, it also means that there is generally little shade along the route.

Heading south, the road is paved and the levee loops to the west and around a small lake. In this area, Cypress Creek flows alongside the Mississippi River levee. Cypress Creek was a major stream in the area and drained 430 square miles of northern Desha County. This made the stream a major source of flooding, especially when the Mississippi River was also experiencing high water conditions. This created what was called the Cypress Creek Gap, a stretch of the Mississippi River that was not contained by levees. It was not until 1920 that the gap was closed and a diversion route for Cypress Creek was built. Several million dollars were spent by local residents and drainage districts to move the water, but the project was still not finished by the 1950s. At least the levee was built with the help of the federal government.

71.6 SOUTH END OF LAKE LOOP – The levee and Delta Heritage Trail now turn ninety degrees to the south-southeast. Cypress Creek is to the east and the levee is built on its western shore.

Just south of here are views of several beautiful bald cypress swamps. These trees can live up to 600 years or more, and are usually found near streams, rivers, and swamps with slow moving water. If you are here in winter, don't be concerned. Bald cypress trees lose their needles each winter and grow a new set during the spring. Bald cypress are also known for their cypress knees, a part of their massive buttressed base that helps stabilize them and provides support in the soft, mushy ground.

Throughout this area, there are a number of views of the backwaters of the Mississippi River. Many of these feature thick stands of cypress trees.

Bald cypress, known by some as gopher wood, can grow to be more than 150 feet tall, and some claim that it was used in building Noah's Ark. Hollow cypress logs, due to their slow rot, were used as water pipes by the late 1700s. Cypress was one of the tree species that were heavily cut by the logging companies during the early 1900s, and even today its lumber is widely used for homes and businesses. Because of its natural oil base, cypress lumber will repel pests and insects, and the oil protects the wood from decay and corrosion.

72.3 CATTLE GUARD – Watch out for the cattle guard as it can be a bit rough if you are on a bicycle. There are eight cattle guards on the levee road, so keep your eyes open for them.

This sign says it all. Bicyclists should take care crossing the eight cattle guards located on the Mississippi River levee section of the Delta Heritage Trail.

Just north of this cattle guard is a dirt road that heads east off of the levee that provides access to areas that are sometimes logged or farmed. This large space is designed to provide an area to hold water during flooding on the Mississippi River.

Just to the south, a road heads off the west side of the levee to reach a small farm complex that includes a house and a large barn. The levee begins to curve to the southeast.

72.6 FARM ROAD – This is another road down to the farm complex to the west. About all that can be seen to the west are large farm fields, with different crops often based upon the current commodity prices. To the east are a number of sloughs and horseshoe lakes created by the Mississippi River. The ponds are often full of white egrets (Great Egret and Cattle Egret) and Great Blue Herons. During winter, many different types of ducks and geese also will be found here.

73.6 KEMPCAMP ROAD – To the east at a small S-curve of the levee is a dirt road into a private lake cabin, with a gate sign calling it Kempcamp. Much of the land on either side of the levee is owned by the Kemp Land Company.

73.8 OPOSSUM FORK – At this location, the trail crosses a **cattle guard** and then makes a ninety-degree turn to the southwest. This is the second of eight cattle guards from the north. The cattle guards are here for a reason, so look out for cows on the road.

Just to the south is a sharp curve to the right (west). There is then a dirt road to a lake to the east used by fishermen, and a dirt road to the farm fields to the west. In this area, Cypress Creek curves to the east and eventually flows into the Mississippi River. The lake immediately east of the levee is Opossum Fork, basically a short-cut for Cypress Creek waters to reach the Mississippi River.

74.4 LUCCA LANDING JUNCTION – The Delta Heritage Trail turns to the southwest at Lucca Landing Junction, and continues on the main Mississippi River levee using Levee Road. Straight ahead was once the site of Lucca Landing, and a dirt road still heads that way on an arm of the levee. For many years, Lucca Landing was a major port in the area where steamboats would land to drop off and pick up shipments, and to pick up wood for their boilers. Lucca Landing was listed as being active in the *Report on Transportation Business in The United States at the Eleventh Census: 1890*. There was enough activity at Lucca Landing that a small cemetery was created on a local Indian mound.

During the late 1880s, a series of levees were raised in this area in response to flooding in 1882. A government report described the work as follows. "During this period the grade was raised from Amos Bayou to Lucca Landing 3 feet, and from Lucca Landing to Arkansas City 2.5 feet above high water of 1882; from Arkansas City to Linwood 5 feet, and Linwood to Louisiana State line 3 and 4 feet above high water of 1888."

Steamboat landings like this moved around as the river channels changed. Today, the Mississippi River has moved about three-quarters of a mile away from Lucca Landing. Another landing in the area was Richland Landing, which was the home of the Richland post office 1894-1913.

74.6 FARM ACCESS ROAD – A dirt road heads off the west side of the levee to several farm buildings.

74.8 LILY PONDS – To the east are several large ponds almost covered with water lilies. These plants are famous for their large green leaves and white flowers.

Rohwer to Arkansas City

There are several large ponds covered with water lilies along the Delta Heritage Trail around trail milepost 75.

75.5 CLEARWATER PAPER CORPORATION – West of the levee is the large Clearwater Paper paperboard mill, generally known simply as Cypress Bend for its location. The plant is the reason that the railroad still exists out of McGehee and up to the Cypress Bend railroad station south of Rohwer. A four-mile industrial lead connects the railroad's mainline with the paper mill.

The pulp and paperboard facility was built in 1977 by the Potlatch Corporation to use local timber from their forest properties, and the sawmill waste from their nearby sawmills. The construction of the mill created a small population boom in the area and a number of well-paying jobs. During the late 1980s, the board mill was upgraded with new machines as part of a modernization plan to "produce better quality products with fewer pollutants." Further improvements were made in 2000 to improve the surface quality and printability of its products as part of a plan to gain a larger market share of high-end packaging, particularly for drugs and cosmetics.

While tall trees grow throughout the area, there are several clear views of the Clearwater Paper Company facility at Cypress Bend. This paperboard plant explains why the railroad was preserved north of McGehee, and many of the trucks that you see in the area hauling logs.

On December 9, 2008, Potlatch established the Clearwater Paper Company and assigned its pulp-based businesses to the new independent company. This plant still produces bleached paperboard, mostly for the packaging industry. It also produces slush pulp (excess or waste pulp) that is sent to the company's consumer products operations. Clearwater is known as the primary manufacturer of grocery store brand bathroom tissue, paper towels, facial tissue and napkins, made at other plants across the country.

75.8 CATTLE GUARD – This cattle guard is easy to find thanks to the abandoned crane just to its north. A bit further north is an access road into the back side of the Clearwater Paper Company site.

This crane can be seen to the east of the Delta Heritage Trail near the cattle guard at trail milepost 75.8. The crane was manufactured by Northwest Engineering Company, founded in 1917 and the second largest seller of excavators by 1927. It was acquired in 1983 by Terex Corporation and closed in 1990.

75.9 BUNGE ROAD – At the southeast corner of the Clearwater facility is a levee extension that goes south to Bunge North America, a barge and grain facility located on the Mississippi River. Bunge North America is an agribusiness and food ingredient company that was founded in 1818. The firm has "more than 350 port terminals, oilseed processing plants, grain facilities, and food and ingredient production and packaging facilities around the world." This facility is known as their DeSoto Landing terminal, named for the river landing that has been here for one hundred years.

This grain elevator complex is operated by Bunge North America, and is used to load local crops onto barges for movement to customers around the world.

DeSoto Landing was named for the historic Hernando de Soto, a Spanish explorer and conquistador who hunted for gold and other wealth throughout South America, and then along the lower Mississippi River. He died in 1542 somewhere in the area, with Lake Village, Arkansas, and Ferriday, Louisiana, the two most cited locations. A rock from the area is part of the Tribune Tower (Chicago) collection of stones from historic locations that have been built into the exterior of the building.

This area is the Cypress Bend of the Mississippi River, named for the Cypress Creek which flowed in to the large river near here. A community was in this area before the Civil War, with a post office first opening in 1837. The number of river landings in the area led to a string of small but successful communities. Most were abandoned during the Civil War due to cannon fire from Union gunboats. Floods during the late 1800s also forced many of the towns to move, and then the construction of the levee system cut others off from the river. A better regional railroad system, and then a highway system, finally ended most of the need for the riverboat landings in the area.

The Delta Heritage Trail stays on Levee Road, turning to the southwest at the junction. Watch the roadway traffic in this area as the road is used by large trucks to and from Bunge North America.

76.5 JUNCTION – At this location, be sure to follow the trail signs and stay on the paved road on top of the levee. While the trail and levee turn directly south, a road continues straight west and connects with Arkansas Highway 4 in one-tenth of a mile. This road is used by grain trucks from across the county to reach the Mississippi River port operated by Bunge North America.

If you are heading south on the Delta Heritage Trail, this sign to the McCallie Access on the Mississippi River helps point the way at the junction at Milepost 76.5, near Bunge North America and the Clearwater Paper Company.

77.6 CHICORA LANDING – Chicora was a legendary Native American kingdom or tribe that the Spanish and French searched for during the early 1500s. The legend about this rich tribe dates back to Spanish slavers Pedro de Quexo and Francisco Gordillo, who in 1521 captured about 60 Indians from today's South Carolina area. Quexo and Gordillo then reported to the Spanish king on this land of abundant wealth and natural resources and requested the right to conquer and settle the land. Apparently, the wealth of the territory grew with each new petition and telling of the story. A number of Spanish and French explorers searched throughout the southeastern part of today's United States hunting for the treasures, including Hernando de Soto, who searched all the way from Florida to Arkansas.

Chicora Landing doesn't exist today, another casualty of the moving Mississippi River and the changes in transportation. In a 1931 Secretary of War report, Chicora Landing was listed as a Mississippi River port and was shown to be 541.8 miles north of New Orleans, and 427.0 miles south of Cairo, Illinois.

78.0 ROAD TO CHICORA LANDING – Continuing south on Levee Road, there is another access road off of the levee. On the river side of the levee, a road heads down to the river that provides access to the site of the old Chicora Landing. It also reaches a few small fields plus the timber that is cut. Several large patches of commercial timber have been cut during the past few years, showing that some of the Desha County timber industry is still active.

Part of the road near the Mississippi River uses an old levee, abandoned when the larger and more modern levee was built in the 1930s. Other work was also done to try to control the river. Along the west bank of the Mississippi River is the Cypress Bend Revetment, a long stretch of the bank that was lined with stone and heavy concrete matting. This revetment stretches around almost the entire Cypress Bend and is designed to keep the river in its channel, preventing it from cutting a new channel west of Arkansas City. An older river channel once existed along this route, showing that the river has moved about a great deal. Across the river in Mississippi is Catfish Point, once also known as Island No. 77. Near here, the Mississippi River cut through

Caulk Neck, leaving part of Desha County on the east side of the river. This has happened quite a few times, and the river no longer marks the state line in a number of places.

To the west, the base of the levee is lined with recently planted trees. Tree farming is back in style in the area, particularly on smaller plots of land. Also to the west, marked by the small stand of trees next to Arkansas Highway 4, is a private home.

Heading south, the levee and the Delta Heritage Trail make several small turns to head southeast. Along these next several miles, the trail moves away from Arkansas Highway 4. Wildlife become more common, and in the fall and winter, the bar pits to the east can be full of migrating birds.

Bar Pits

Along the levee to the east can be seen a number of small lakes. These lakes were made when the levee was built, as this is where much of the material came from. Before the levees were built, soils were tested in the area to find the right types that could be used to make the levees, and that would hold back the water. These materials were immediately adjacent to the new levee location, so the soils were simply scooped up and moved to where they were needed. This left behind these large holes, which today have formed a chain of lakes.

During the 1930s, heavy work was conducted on the levees in this area, with some improved and others replaced. This was in response to the Flood of 1927, and several new laws passed to control flooding and making the Mississippi River more reliably navigable. With the introduction of new machinery,

Rohwer to Arkansas City

the Corps of Engineers experimented with many new methods of moving dirt. Besides the larger draglines and cranes with buckets, they used overhead cable systems to drag large scrapers. The tall towers were erected on crawlers that could move slowly as the work was completed. Crawlers (bulldozers without blades) were used to pull large dump wagons. Even trucks with large pneumatic tires were used. Mechanized tractors and dozers were used to move the dirt and prepare the levee. However, mules and plows were still used, and much of the grass was planted by hand. Fortunately, film exists of some of this construction, made by the U.S. Army Corps of Engineers, and it has been released by the U.S. National Archives. Look online for the video "Levee Construction, Mississippi River, Vicinity Arkansas City, September 10-11, 1936."

So where did the term "bar pit" come from? A bar pit is actually a borrow pit. It received the shorter name typically in the southern and southwestern parts of the United States, where it is often pronounced that way. It also became a way to shorten the time taken to make notes and document the movement of materials, so it is even written "bar pit" in many cases, and has grown to be used across the country.

78.7 **CATTLE GUARD** – This is another recently installed cattle guard. To the east are a number of bar pits, used to build the levee that you are traveling on.

79.3 **CATTLE GUARD** – This is the fifth cattle guard from north. The large bar pits are still to the east.

A number of new cattle guards were installed when the Levee Road was paved, all designed to separate the pastureland of different farmers in this area.

79.7 CURVE – The levee and trail curves to the southeast. To the west is a tree farm, using small patches of land that are too small for the large crop production common in the area.

80.0 CATTLE GUARD – The bar pits are still to the east and cattle still roam the levee, so watch out for this cattle guard. The lakes that formed out of the bar pits are often the homes of hundreds of egrets.

80.8 DESHA COUNTY ROAD 335 – At this location, the Delta Heritage Trail turns back south to follow Levee Road and the main levee. To the northeast,

Desha County Road 335 heads to the Mississippi River at the former location of Chicot Landing. This was once an active landing that had an employee of the Mississippi River Commission based here in 1895, being paid $2 per day for his work monitoring the trade. The landing was still listed in a 1931 Secretary of War report. It was shown to be 539.0 miles north of New Orleans and 429.8 miles south of Cairo, Illinois.

At one time, this area was part of Chicot County, but the county line was redrawn and it became part of Desha County. While the commercial landing is gone, there is still a boat ramp and parking there, part of McCallie Access. The road also provides access to the area for timber cutting and farming.

80.9 CATTLE GUARD – Located not far south of the intersection with Desha County Road 335 is another cattle guard.

81.1 FARM ROADS – There are two roads that head to the west and reach a home and a farm complex. To the east is John's Bayou. This waterway is an old riverbend, and is located just east of the levee system. The levee cut off part of the old bayou, making it dependent upon floodwaters for much of its source of water.

81.3 FARM ROADS – Two more roads head to the west to connect to a private home and farm complex. This farm features a corral complex, once common on most farms in the area as most early farming was done with a simple mule and plow. This practice lasted until World War II in this area, when higher crop prices and lower machinery costs allowed farmers to buy tractors and harvesting equipment.

81.4 CATTLE GUARD – Just south of the south farm road is the southern-most cattle guard on the levee trail.

If you are heading north on the Delta Heritage Trail, this sign warns you about the livestock that you might find on the trail.

81.6 FARM ROAD – A farm road heads west and down off the levee to reach the farm fields. Several farm ponds are further to the west. The raising of catfish, minnows, and other fish has been taken up by a number of farmers in the Mississippi River Delta region.

82.5 WHITE HILL ROAD – This is another junction of several local roadways. Levee Road has stayed on top of the Mississippi River levee. To the northeast is Desha County Road 351, which provides access to a number of farm fields and timber for logging. To the southwest is White Hill Road (County Road 351), which heads to the north side of Arkansas City.

Mound Cemetery

To the south along White Hill Road is Mound Cemetery. The cemetery features a Mississippian culture mound built between 1200 and 1600 AD. Being the highest ground in the area, it was used as a cemetery by early settlers. When the first settler remains were buried, artifacts and older human remains were reportedly discovered. While settlers and slaves were buried here before the Civil War, the oldest dated grave is for Rachel Horton, who died March 15, 1866. About eighty early marked graves exist today, and the cemetery is still used for burials, meaning that there are more than 120 total marked graves throughout the property.

At one time, there were hundreds of these mounds across the region, but time and the efforts of farmers removed most of them. The mounds are believed to have also been built over a number of generations. According to the National Register of Historic Places, the "Mississippian people would build up the earth and raise a building of importance. After the building burned either as an accident or an intentional burn as part of a cleansing ceremony, the people would bring basket loads of soil to cover the mound. Often these cleansing burns would take place after a leader or well-to-do member of the community died and so the person would be buried in the mound."

This marker notes the history of Arkansas City's Mound Cemetery, located not far from the Delta Heritage Trail.

Many of the grave markers at Mound Cemetery carry markings of organizations such as the Mosaic Templars, Knights and Daughters of Tabor, the Royal Circle of Friends, and Woodmen of the World. Several stones honor World War I and World War II veterans. On top of the mound is the grave of Oscar Bowles, surrounded by an iron fence. Oscar Bowles worked for John R. Campbell, founder of Arkansas City. Bowles cleared the lands for Campbell, and later bought his own plantation, which included the land that the mound sits on. When he drowned in the 1874 flood, he was buried on top of the mound. Because of the historic nature of the cemetery, it was placed on the National Register of Historic Places in 2008.

Rohwer to Arkansas City

Many of the graves in Mound Cemetery are marked with various organizations, such as this one for J. H. Inman, provided by Woodmen of the World.

82.9 MORNING STAR AVENUE AT ARKANSAS CITY – This access road heads to the southwest to connect with Morning Star Avenue in Arkansas City. This part of town is primarily residential in nature.

Delta Heritage Trail: History Through the Miles

This view of the Delta Heritage Trail near Milepost 83 shows the paved road, grassy levee, and open farmland that is typical of this part of the route.

Signs like this one identify the Delta Heritage Trail milepost locations along the levee.

83.1 DESHA COUNTY ROAD 69 – This junction is on the east side of Arkansas City. County Road 69, also known as Kate Adams Avenue, crosses the Delta Heritage Trail here. County Road 69 heads east to what was once the site of Chicot Landing, identified as being 473 miles south of Cairo, Illinois, in an 1894 listing of Mississippi River landings. Today, the U.S. Army Corps of Engineers shows it to be at river milepost 565.0. County Road 69 also provides access to the northeast parts of the Freddie Black Choctaw Island Wildlife Management Area and Deer Research Area East Unit, including Old River Lake, the Old River Lake Trail, and one of four primitive campsites.

The name Chicot means teeth in the French language. Early French explorers saw that the river's snags looked like ugly blackened broken teeth, and started using the term Chicot for the area. In this area today is the McCallie Access to the Mississippi River. Expanded in 2019, this small park provides two boat ramps and parking areas to accommodate boaters and anglers. Heading west into Arkansas City, Kate Adams Avenue passes through downtown.

83.7 PRESIDENT STREET/THANE ROAD – To the north is President Street, also known as DeSoto Levee Drive. This street passes the Arkansas City High School, built in 1910 and listed on the National Register of Historic Places in 1984. In 2004, a new school was built on the northwest side of town, and the building became the Desha County Courthouse Annex.

Arkansas City is basically oriented southwest to northeast, with the levee along the northeast and southeast sides of the community. A block northeast of President Street was once Park Street. Where the woods stand today, several different industries operated. The St. Louis & Arkansas Lumber and Manufacturing Company had a large sawmill here by 1903. The mill was important to town as its artesian well served as the source of the community's water. The well was later acquired by the Lambe DeMarke Company, which operated a water works and power plant. By 1917, the Whitehill cotton gin was also located here. The old water tower marks the location.

This old water tower marks the location of the St. Louis & Arkansas Lumber and Manufacturing Company, and the several industries that later used the same property.

Freddie Black Choctaw Island Wildlife Management Area

To the south, the road becomes Thane Road, the main access road to the Freddie Black Choctaw Island Wildlife Management Area and Deer Research Area East Unit. The Wildlife Management Area includes 7500 acres and supports more than 400 species of wildlife. Much of the property sits on the former Choctaw Island, known as Island No. 78. The levee runs along the 1830 Meander Line where a channel of the Mississippi River made this an island.

The property is managed and owned by the Arkansas Game and Fish Commission. It is used for recreation, wildlife watching, hunting and fishing, and is managed for trophy-sized white-tailed deer. Small game such as squirrel and rabbit are also plentiful. While the area is prone to flooding, there are four primitive campsites and almost ten miles of nature trails. There are also boat ramps on Rocky Hole Lake and the Mississippi River.

The Wildlife Management Area was named for Freddie Black of nearby Lake Village. Black, chairman of the Arkansas Region for Simmons Bank, is a hunter and a major supporter of the many wildlife management areas in the state. In 2002, he was appointed commissioner of the Arkansas Game and Fish Commission by then Governor Mike Huckabee.

84.0 SPRAGUE STREET – Sprague Street heads north and becomes Arkansas Highway 4. This is probably the busiest street in Arkansas City as it passes the post office, city hall, a restaurant, and a grocery store. Several old buildings still stand in the area, mostly unused. Arkansas City's historic Commercial District, which is listed on the National Register of Historic Places, is in this area. To the south, the road crosses the levee and provides access to Rocky Hole Lake and the Rocky Hole Trail, both in the Freddie Black Choctaw Island Wildlife Management Area and Deer Research Area East Unit.

This sign marks the entrance to the East unit of the Freddie Black Choctaw Island Wildlife Management Area, just across the levee from Arkansas City.

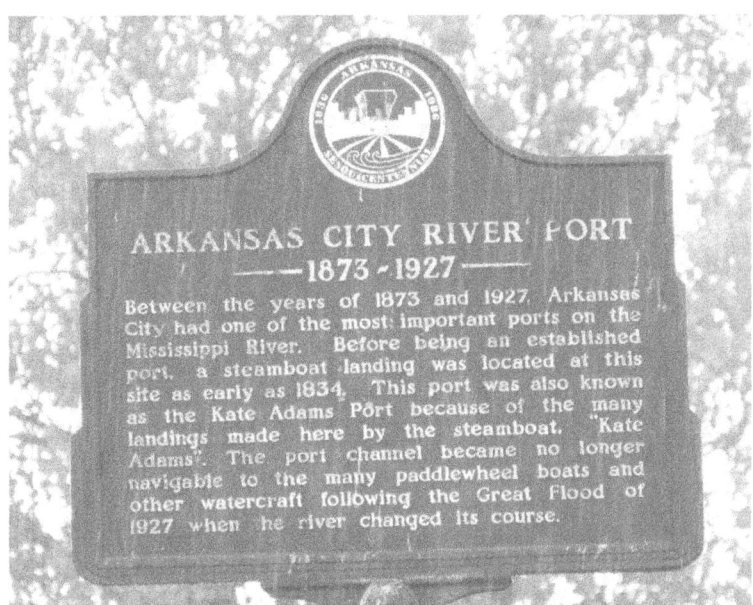

For many years during the late 1800s and early 1900s, Arkansas City was an important Mississippi River port. This historical marker alongside the levee at Arkansas City provides a bit of the detail.

84.2 ARKANSAS CITY TRAILHEAD – Located just north of here at the intersection of Weatherwood and Desota is the Arkansas City Trailhead, opened on October 18, 2018. This trailhead probably has the most facilities of any along the Delta Heritage Trail except for the visitor center at Barton. Besides the typical parking, information signs, picnic tables and benches, this facility also has restrooms, a bathhouse, a bicycle repair station, and a large group charcoal grill. There is also a ranger station in the building that resembles a railroad station.

This view of the Arkansas City Trailhead is from the paved trail on the levee.

Arkansas City

Arkansas City is located in the Arkansas Delta at a natural steamboat port, and for almost a century, steamboats docked right on the levee at Kate Adams Landing. Settlement in the area began when Mr. and Mrs. John R. Campbell and their sons, as well as Mr. and Mrs. Oscar Bowles and their son, moved to the area in 1835. A steamboat landing was already here, serving settlers to the west. Campbell bought land in the area for 25 cents an acre, and a small community began to grow, known as Arkansas City on December 12, 1838. Oscar Bowles arrived soon after, bringing Campbell's slaves and many of his possessions. Bowles became Campbell's overseer for the next seventeen years before he bought his own land, located north of Arkansas City. This land included the Mississippian culture mound on which he was later buried. Some of the first work in the area was the erection of levees to protect the new farms. Initially, these were simply additions to natural levees, but larger levees were built during the late 1850s. Further work was halted by the Civil War, but more work occurred through the late 1800s, and then again after the Flood of 1927.

The Arkansas City post office opened in 1872, and the town was incorporated on September 12, 1873. An issue with the incorporation came up soon after because it was done by the Chicot Circuit Court. About the same time, the county line changed and Arkansas City was in Desha County, where it was made the county seat in 1879. In the 1880 census, the population was recorded to be 503 residents. Because the questionable incorporation had been recognized for so long, the Supreme Court of Arkansas legalized it during November 1881.

During the mid-1800s, railroads added to the transportation benefits of the area. Arkansas City was one of the earliest port cities in southeast Arkansas to gain access to a railroad, making it an important water-to-rail terminal. Reports from about 1900 state that Arkansas City was a thriving river town with a dock full of steamboats, two railroads, three large sawmills, an opera house, two doctors, several churches, fourteen saloons, and 1091 residents. The Bank of Arkansas City was chartered on January 24, 1912, to handle the business. The Arkansas City Sporting Club sponsored several events that drew people from around the region, including a boxing exhibition on March 8, 1891, by John L. "Boston Strong Boy" Sullivan, the first heavyweight champion of gloved boxing (1882-1892), and Jack

Dempsey, the world heavyweight champion from 1914 to 1927, who held a boxing exhibition there in 1924.

As Arkansas City grew, a number of social and fraternal organizations were started up. This large two-story wooden building on Capitol (formerly 3rd Street) once housed a lodge of one of these organizations.

Arkansas City was a very large producer of lumber, and the Interstate Commerce Commission investigated the matter in 1916-1917, looking at the railroad freight rates and how they impacted the ability to serve markets across the country. The report, *Investigation and Suspension Docket No 827 – Lumber from Arkansas City, Ark.*, determined that Arkansas City was producing a great deal of lumber for a community of its size, and that the railroad rates had something to do with that.

> Memphis, a city of approximately 150,000 inhabitants, is a great hardwood center; Helena, with approximately 15,000 inhabitants, has 20 hardwood

mills; and Arkansas City, with a population of 1,500, has 3 hardwood mills. Nevertheless, Arkansas City manufactures about one-fourth as much hardwood as Helena and one-tenth as much as Memphis.

It is in evidence that by reason of its location on the river, and perhaps by reason of favoritism from a former management of the Iron Mountain, rates on hardwoods from Arkansas City have been much lower than the rates from intermediate points on respondent's line and from other points in the immediate neighborhood.

Arkansas City was at its peak in 1920 with a census population of 1482, although some sources state a population of 15,000. The U.S. Census recorded a population between 1400 and 1500 from 1910 until 1940. The 1921 *Arkansas Marketing and Industrial Guide* provided a list of businesses operating that year. These included the Arkansas City Cooperage Company, Breece Lumber Company, Brock & Foster Lumber Company, and Thane Lumber Company. Farming was represented by the Arkansas City Cotton Gin Company, while mining had The Ark Gravel Company. There was a City Bakery, Lambe & Denmark which supplied city water and light, and the *Democrat* newspaper, published for evening distribution daily except Sunday.

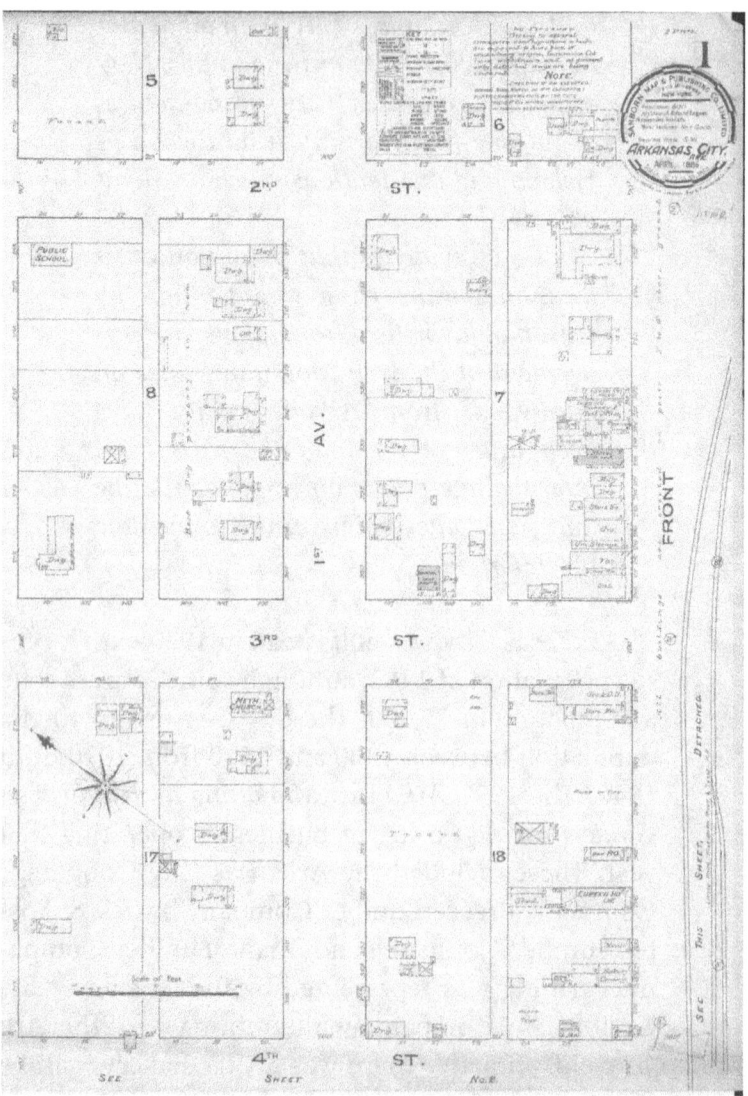

This early insurance map shows a warehouse and other buildings at the Arkansas City docks. Located between 3rd and 4th Streets. It also shows how close the Mississippi River used to be to Front Street and the railroad tracks that ran along the levee. *Sanborn Fire Insurance Map from Arkansas City, Desha County, Arkansas.* Sanborn Map Company, Apr, 1886. Map. Retrieved from the Library of Congress, https://www.loc.gov/item/sanborn00193_001/

Things were slowing down some when the Flood of 1927 hit Arkansas City, and most of its neighbors. For weeks, the levees around Arkansas City held as massive amounts of water flowed down the Mississippi River. However, rains across Arkansas and other states added to the flows, and levees began to break along the Arkansas River and Mississippi River. Water rushed south, causing the failure of more levees. As reported by an article in the September 1927 *National Geographic*, at noon on April 24th, the streets of Arkansas City were dry and dusty. By 2:00pm, "mules were drowning on Main Street faster than people could unhitch them from wagons." By the end of the day, every building in town was sitting in six to thirty feet of water, with most only showing their rooftops. Most people fled to the levee along Front Street where they lived for weeks in tents, boxcars, boats, and pretty much anything they could use. More than 2000 people had to be rescued.

At the time of the flood, there were two large hardwood sawmills that produced approximately 40 million feet of hardwood lumber a year, employing approximately 700 men. There was also a flooring plant and one large gravel plant that produced 1200 yards of gravel per day. The Standard Oil Company of Louisiana also had a facility at Arkansas City. Oil was brought in by barges, stored in tanks, and then distributed by the Missouri Pacific Railroad.

This marker at Arkansas City covers the basics of the Flood of 1927 and its impact on the community.

By the time the flood waters receded on August 12th, the fields were ruined for the year and the Mississippi River had moved east about a mile, leaving Arkansas City high and dry. Most of the timber businesses never reopened, and the river docks became useless. With no business, the railroad provided less and less service to the town. The Flood of 1927 and the end of the timber industry hurt Arkansas City, but it was the end of the need for farm laborers that really finished local prosperity. The population held steady between 1400 and 1500 through the 1940 census, but by 1950 was at 1018, down almost thirty percent. This decline continued with 783 residents in 1960 and 615 in 1970. Additionally, the larger stores and selections at surrounding towns led many to shop elsewhere, and eventually to move away.

Rohwer to Arkansas City

This foundation tells part of the story of Arkansas City, a boom and bust community. What was once a proud local business – Palace Confectionery – is now simply an impressive floor, located just east of the Arkansas City Trailhead.

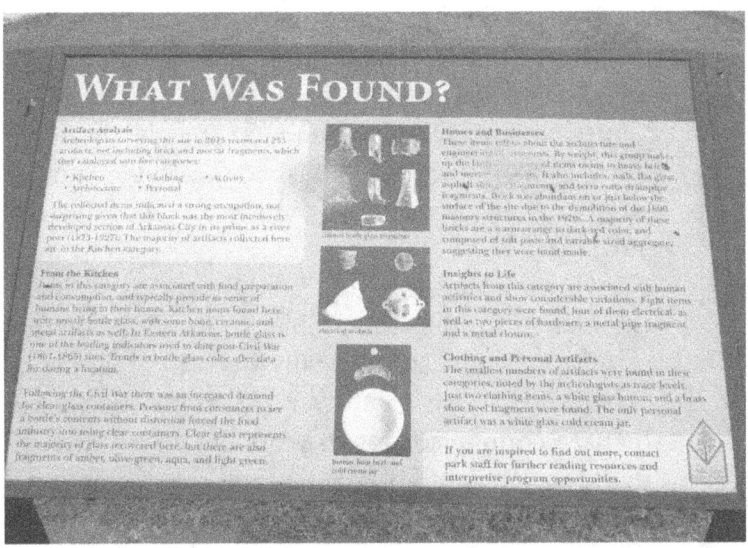

During the past decade, a cultural resources survey was conducted of the area, some of which is explained by various signs at the Trailhead.

There were efforts to bring commerce back to Arkansas City. On March 29, 1928, Congress passed an act that would allow Henry Thane "to construct, maintain, and operate a bridge across the Mississippi River at or near Arkansas City, Arkansas." With ferries no longer running between Arkansas City and several Mississippi towns, transportation across the river was needed, and if built at Arkansas City, it would pour traffic through the community.

Henry Thane was involved with almost everything at Arkansas City. He was born in Germany on February 10, 1850, and moved to the United States in 1852 with his family. He grew up in Illinois and then worked for the Bolenhuse Ice Company in Memphis. In 1872, he came to Arkansas and was engaged in merchandising before moving to Arkansas City in 1876. He studied law and was admitted to the bar in 1879. He then became justice of the peace, town mayor, postmaster, and eventually a member of the State Senate and then the circuit clerk and ex officio county clerk of Desha County. Thane also built the Thane Bank Building, established the Thane Lumber Company, and controlled the Desha County Bank and Trust.

Following the April 1927 flooding, Thane began a campaign to solve the problem. His effort focused on what would have basically been a straightened and ditched Mississippi River. He proposed that this ditch be completed in two years between Cairo, Illinois, and the Gulf of Mexico, and that a ship canal for ocean-going ships be built along the west bank of the river. Naturally, this canal would pass through Arkansas City. Thane's reports and plans generally ran for dozens of pages and were often included in committee reports from the U.S. Senate and House of Representatives. Thane's efforts to build a Mississippi River canal and bridge resulted in little, but there were efforts during the 1930s to modernize Arkansas City, and to honor some of its past.

Looking down onto Arkansas City from the Delta Heritage Trail on the levee, one can only imagine what was once there. When originally platted, the avenues were aligned parallel and streets perpendicular to the Mississippi River and its levee. Originally, Front ran parallel to the levee and then subsequent parallel streets numbered 1st through 6th Avenue. Today, Front is Desota Avenue, and 1st Avenue is Kate Adams Avenue. Where did the name Kate Adams come from? It came from a fast passenger and cargo ship that regularly stopped at Arkansas City.

During the 1930s, most of the streets and avenues received names honoring various boats and people. At the east end of town, President Street replaced what had been 1st Street. 2nd Street became Natchez Street (another riverboat) and 3rd Street became Capitol Street. 4th Street, the primary north-south street, was renamed Sprague Street after a large towboat, while 5th Street was given the name Weatherwood Street. While the plat of town went as far as 13th Street, the area west of 6th Street, which no longer extends all the way to the levee, was primarily industrial, once the site of the railroad's shops and later the home of Thane Lumber and Union Sand & Material. Those that wander throughout Arkansas City will find other streets and avenues carrying the names of riverboats. 5th Avenue is now Sadie Lee (a small riverboat that ran between Memphis and Vicksburg), 4th Avenue/Arkansas Highway 4 is now Delta Queen Avenue, and 3rd Avenue has been given the name Morning Star.

Following the flood, there were also efforts to move the county seat to one of the larger cities, such as McGehee or Dumas. However, it is still located here. A small boost in population occurred during the late 1970s and early 1980s, caused by the construction of the nearby Potlatch boardmill plant, but it has since dropped to about 300. Part of downtown Arkansas City is now the Arkansas City Commercial District, listed on the National Register of Historic Places in 1999. This Commercial District is actually three buildings near the intersection of Desota Avenue and Sprague Street. The buildings include the Cotham Drug Store and the Red Star Grocery, both built about 1900. The two-story buildings, both facing south towards the levee, stand attached just east of Sprague Street. Sanborn insurance maps from the 1930s show that these two buildings were once part of a larger complex, which included an undertaker and a moving pictures theater on the first floor, and a commercial hotel on the second floor. The third building in the historic district is the Ramus Brothers Market, a unique two-story building built out of poured, reinforced concrete in 1910. This building is on Sprague Street, just around the corner from the Cotham Drug Store.

The Arkansas City Commercial District, which includes the Cotham Drug Store and the Red Star Grocery, is easily visible from the Delta Heritage Trail.

Another historic tip about Arkansas City is that it is the birthplace of John Harold Johnson. Johnson was born on January 19, 1918, and his mother moved to Chicago, Illinois, so he could get a full education. John Harold Johnson was the founder of Johnson Publishing Company, the producer of magazines like *Ebony* and *Jet*. This made Johnson Publishing Company the largest African-American-owned publishing company in the country. Johnson was the first African-American to be named to the *Forbes Magazine* list of the 400 wealthiest Americans and he later received the Presidential Medal of Freedom.

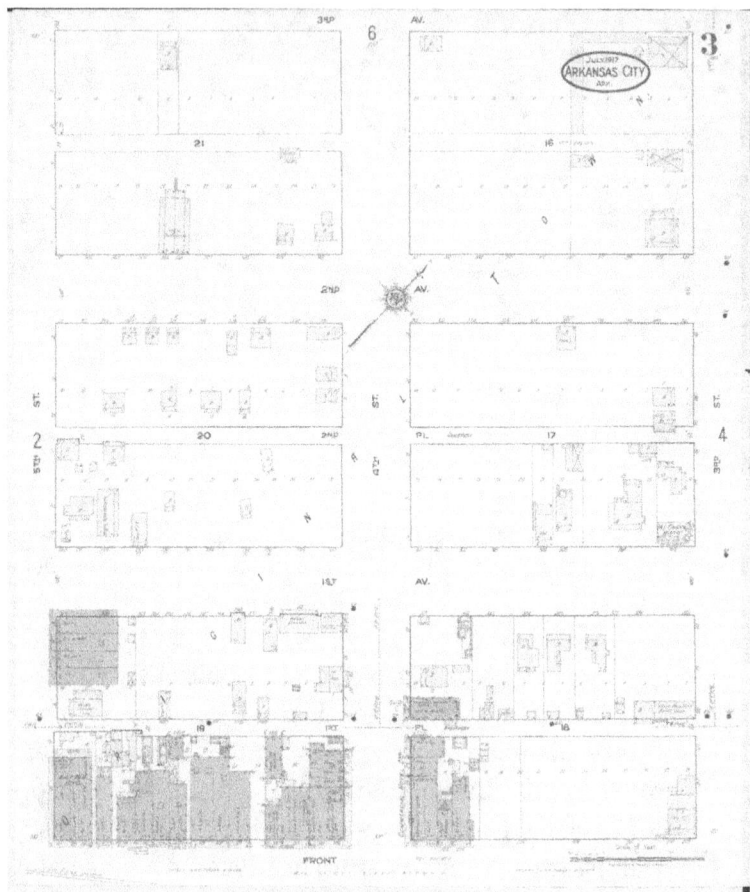

The Sanborn Map Company showed what the Front and 4th Street area looked like in 1917. Note that today's Arkansas City Commercial District was busier, with a post office and the Commercial Hotel. *Sanborn Fire Insurance Map from Arkansas City, Desha County, Arkansas.* Sanborn Map Company, Jul, 1917. Map. Retrieved from the Library of Congress, https://www.loc.gov/item/sanborn00193_004/

The Timber Companies of Arkansas City

Anyone who travels the Delta Heritage Trail should realize that all of the open farmland was once bottomland hardwood forest, full of gum, oak, elm, ash, cottonwood, and bald cypress trees. A few scenes of this type of land can still be seen along the Mississippi River levee and in the bottoms of the Arkansas and White Rivers. But even here, most has been cut-over and what is there is second generation growth.

To do this cutting, dozens of both large and small timber companies were here from the late 1800s until the 1920s. Many were based at Arkansas City and had operations in the woods to the north and south. The combination of rail and water service made Arkansas City the perfect location, or at least until the timber was cut and Helena and other production centers took over. Therefore, the timber industry brought the town to its peak of business in the early 1920s, and quickly led the exodus by the 1930s.

While sawmills operated here soon after the Civil War, the history of Arkansas City states that "some of the bigger operations were the Kimball-Lacy Lumber Company and later the Thane Lumber Co. & Sawmill and Grayling Lumber Co. & Sawmill. Most of these companies had their own logging railroads, or at least operated a plant railroad at their mills. The **Desha Lumber & Planting Company** opened at Arkansas City by 1888, and operated several different mills. The firm was backed by investors from Boston, Massachusetts, and advertised itself as a "Manufacturer of Hardwood Lumber for Bridge and Car Builders." The firm made and sold freight car timbers, car sills, cross ties, bridge timbers, and building timbers at Arkansas City until about 1916. The company operated a railroad that extended seven-and-a-half miles north from Arkansas City, known as the Mississippi River & Northwestern Railroad Company. The railroad was incorporated on November 18, 1886, and apparently used the right-of-way of the original Little Rock, Pine Bluff & New Orleans. It was abandoned in 1899 and the rails were sold to the Empire Lumber Company.

Goodspeed Publishing's *Biographical and Historical Memoirs of Southern Arkansas* (1890) provided a great amount of information about the timber firm and its railroad. "The Mississippi River & Northwestern Railroad, extends from Arkansas City five miles west, and is operated by the Desha Lumber & Planting Company, its owners, to haul logs and materials to saw mills at Arkansas City." The company's first locomotive was a small steam locomotive built by Porter (Shop Number 967) in November 1888, that was later sold to the Alliance Lumber & Manufacturing Company in 1906.

The next major mill was owned by the **Paddock-Hawley Iron Company**, a St. Louis rail manufacturer. The firm had their **St. Louis & Arkansas Lumber & Manufacturing Company** here by 1903, and operated a woodworking plant and saw mill on the east side of town. The firm was here until June 1907 when it was acquired by the **Kimball Lumber Manufacturing Company**, incorporated by A. Kimball. Kimball operated here for a year and then moved south to a new mill at Laark, Louisiana, and built a company-owned tap line called the Arkansas & Gulf Railway from the Missouri Pacific Railroad at Kimball, Arkansas.

The Kimball family was also involved with the **Kimball-Lacy Lumber Company**, which had their mill at Arkansas City by 1898 and operated several logging lines along the Memphis, Helena & Louisiana Railway. The firm operated a small 13-ton Shay locomotive (Shop Number 1629, built in 1906) which it bought secondhand. In 1903, the Sanborn Map Company showed the mill to be southwest of downtown, built on fill between the levee and the Mississippi River. In November 1914, Kimball-Lacy opened a sales office in the Railway Exchange Building in Chicago, Illinois. About the same time, the *American Lumberman* reported on a fire at the company's Arkansas City mill that burned $75,000 of lumber, but stated that it was fully insured. The firm also operated the Lacy-Kimball Store Company (incorporated June 8, 1912) at Arkansas City.

On July 1, 1907, the **Delta Cooperage Company** was incorporated to acquire an older Delta Cooperage hoop mill, and to add a mill to manufacture specialty cottonwood staves. The mill was located just east of the Kimball-Lacy Lumber Company sawmill where the old Little Rock, Mississippi River & Texas Railway shops once stood. A connection to the nearby Kimball-Lacy mill was that A. Kimball was listed as the secretary and treasurer of the cooperage company.

The next major timber firm was the **Grayling Lumber Company**, incorporated in 1908 and created by the merger of the Standard Tie Company and Desha Land & Timber, using Henry Thane as its agent. The new company had 95,000 acres of land in Desha County, as well as Union and Ouachita Parishes in Louisiana. In 1911, the Grayling Lumber Company arrived at Arkansas City, establishing one of the largest mill complexes in the town's history. The large sawmill complex was located north of 6th Street, also known as Campbell Avenue, and west of 4th Street. Today, this is north of Georgia Lane Avenue and west of Arkansas Highway 4, an area that is used for apartments. To serve the mill, the railroad operated up the center of 6th Street.

Grayling also created one of the most complex histories of any timber company in Desha County. According to *Moody's*, the company had a mill with a capacity of 75,000 feet per day on one shift. At Monroe, Louisiana, the company had a mill which operated two shifts a day, producing 150,000 feet of lumber a day. There were also planing mills and dry kilns at Monroe.

Grayling Lumber had a mill and logging railroad, operated using a new Shay steam locomotive built in early 1913 (36-ton Shop Number 2611). A roundhouse and carshop was located on the east side of the sawmill. The Shay later operated on Grayling's Monroe & Southwestern Railway at Monroe, Louisiana. The Monroe operation was leased to the O. S. Hawes Lumber Company in 1922 before being acquired by The George E. Breece Lumber Company. The Shay then went to Breece's operation in New Mexico at Breece, and then Grants, before being scrapped.

The *American Lumberman* (December 18, 1920) had an article on the company which explains its history up until that time.

> *A typical, modern manufacturer of southern hardwoods of the above character is the Breece Manufacturing Co., with a double band mill at Arkansas City, Ark., and a fine manufacturing*

plant in Portsmouth, Ohio. The mill at Arkansas City was built by the Grayling Lumber Co. about eight years ago and shortly after completion was taken over by the West Virginia Timber Co. In 1919 the Arko Lumber Co., composed of the Breece Manufacturing Co. and P. E. Selby, both of Portsmouth, Ohio, took over the mill with all the timber holdings formerly owned by the West Virginia Timber Co. in Arkansas, and in addition about 22,000 acres in northern Louisiana.

In August last the Breece Manufacturing Co. bought Mr. Selby's interest in the Arkansas property of the Arko Lumber Co. and the sawmill has since been operated under the name of the Breece Manufacturing Co., with headquarters at Portsmouth, Ohio.

The sawmill at Arkansas City, as mentioned before, is a double band mill and has a capacity of 100,000 feet a day. The manufacturing and shipping facilities are second to none and there is an unlimited supply of timber behind the mill and it can, therefore, be run indefinitely. In addition to the stumpage owned outright by the Breece Manufacturing Co. a good deal of gum and other hardwoods is obtained along the Arkansas and White rivers and some is obtained from the Mississippi River.

By 1932, the sawmill was smaller and was operated by **Vestal Manufacturing Company**.

In 1921, *Poor's and Moody's Manual Consolidated* reported that the West Virginia Timber Company still had a mill at Arkansas City that produced 65,000 feet per day. Grayling Lumber became associated with the **Arko Lumber Company**, which had its own mill and logging railroad, and then both were acquired by the **Breece Manufacturing Company** in 1920. In January 1923, the **Breece-White Manufacturing Company** was incorporated to succeed the Breece Manufacturing Company. On April 9, 1925, the Breece-White Manufacturing plant burned, but reports showed the firm was still operating a sawmill at Arkansas City in 1926. The company also had a company store at Arkansas City, issuing script tokens as pay to its employees.

One of the most interesting details about the Breece Manufacturing Company was its attempt to incorporate the **Coon Bayou & Arkansas City Railway Company**, and to receive a Certificate of Public Convenience and Necessity from the Interstate Commerce Commission. The application was submitted on December 24, 1920, and decided on January 19, 1921. The plan was to build about two miles of track from a connection with the Missouri Pacific Railroad near McArthur into the timber holdings of the Breece Company. It would then lease an existing 1.3 miles of Arko Lumber Company track, plus one locomotive and forty log cars, located about three miles north of McArthur. To connect the various logging lines, the company would acquire trackage rights over the Missouri Pacific Railroad to reach Arkansas City, since Missouri Pacific had told the timber company that they had no freight cars or trains to handle the business. The application also stated that the Coon Bayou & Arkansas City Railway would operate for about two years and be abandoned after the timber was cut. The Interstate Commerce Commission denied the application in its typical grandiose manner. "We are, therefore, unable to find upon the record presented, that the present or future public convenience and necessity require or will require the construction of the line in question, the lease of the existing line, or the operation by the applicant of its trains over the line of the Missouri Pacific. An order will accordingly be entered denying the application."

Also related to Grayling Lumber Company was the **Desha Land & Timber Company**. This firm was part of the creation of Grayling, but it was incorporated again at Arkansas City in early 1914. It was capitalized at $200,000 with W. M. Lewis as president, and it reportedly owned about 50,000 acres. Incorporated about the same time was the **Detroit-Arkansas Logging Company** (some sources use Detroit-Arkansas Lumbering Company), with B. J. Terry as president. Terry was also involved with the Arkansas City Cooperage Company, Arko Lumber Company, Grayling Lumber, and the Arkansas Lumber & Manufacturing Company. Another timber company with a connection to Grayling Lumber was the **O. S. Hawes Lumber Company**. Hawes was the company secretary and treasurer of Grayling, and his company was based at Arkansas City by 1915, but leased the Monroe operations in 1922.

The January 25, 1915, issue of *The Tradesman* reported that the **Thane Lumber Company** was incorporated at Arkansas City with H. Thane, A. Kimball, and F. O. Johnson as the incorporators. Henry

Thane was an important leader in the growth of Arkansas City, holding many different political positions, controlling the local bank, and obviously this lumber company. In 1917, Thane Lumber bought "all of the river timber" owned by the Grayling Lumber Company. An article in *The New York Lumber Trade Journal* (August 1, 1917) stated that the "Thane Lumber Company brings in practically all of its logs by water and likewise ships a large part of its output by the same method." In 1918, Thane Lumber opened "general sales offices in Memphis to handle the output of the three mills it operates." In 1920, E. O. Johnson (president of Thane Lumber) and J. Clayton Johnson (sales manager of Thane Lumber) left the company to form their own Johnson Brothers Hardwood Company to handle the sales of the Arko Lumber Company. At the same time, Thane Lumber moved its sales office back to Arkansas City. By 1926, the Chicago Lumber & Coal Company was the sales company for the Thane Lumber Company.

Thane Lumber had their complex west of Arkansas City, between what would have been 8th and 12th Streets. The mill was located south of the levee with the lumber stacks north of the levee and tracks. Just to the west was the Union Sand & Material Company, which had a dredge in the river and several gravel bunkers for loading railcars.

The June 1916 issue of *The National Coopers' Journal* reported that the "plant of the Arkansas City Cooperage Co., Arkansas City, Ark., is nearing completion and will shortly be in operation. The mill will have a daily capacity of 40,000 staves. A dry kiln is also being erected." B. J. Terry and J. C. Henry, a former saw filer for the Grayling Lumber Company, established the **Arkansas City Cooperage Com-**

pany to manufacture barrel staves. This company was located immediately west of the Grayling Lumber Company facility, at the north end of 7th Street (Linda Street).

The Railroads of Arkansas City

The **Mississippi, Ouachita & Red River Railroad** was planned to connect the Mississippi River with the Red River, crossing southern Arkansas. It was incorporated on August 12, 1852, and received a charter from the State of Arkansas on January 22, 1855. The construction began at Eunice, south of Arkansas City, with a ground-breaking ceremony on July 6, 1854. About seven miles of track was built and is considered to be the first railroad to begin construction in Arkansas. Completion of significant construction and actual operation of the railroad did not occur until well after the Civil War. To help the railroad, a number of land grants were made available to the company, but by 1871, there was only forty miles of right-of-way graded, bridged, and tied, and only twenty-nine miles of railroad were in operation. The line finally reached Warren, Arkansas, in July 1872. The Mississippi, Ouachita & Red River Railroad never made a profit and failed to make payments on its bonds.

The **Little Rock, Pine Bluff & New Orleans Railroad** also dated back to one of the earliest railroads chartered in Arkansas. On January 9, 1839, the Arkansas General Assembly granted a charter to build a railroad from Little Rock to Napoleon, located on the Mississippi River. The **Little Rock & Napoleon Railroad** built a few miles of track, although the *United States Railroad Directory of 1856* showed the railroad to be "From Little Rock to Napoleon, 100 miles" with its offices at Pine Bluff, Arkansas.

Construction on the Little Rock & Napoleon Railroad started during the late 1850s, but no track was built before the Civil War ended all construction. A lack of money after the war kept the line from being completed, and on July 2, 1869, the rights to the route were sold to the Little Rock, Pine Bluff & New Orleans Railroad. This railroad had plans to build a line from Little Rock to Pine Bluff and then south to the Louisiana state line, passing through Drew and Ashley counties, west of Desha County. It was also going to complete the Napoleon line, using a route from Pine Bluff to Red Fork Bayou, and then to "a good landing on the Mississippi river near the mouth of Cypress Creek" and then south to a junction with the original Mississippi, Ouachita & Red River Railroad. Soon, about 65 miles of track along the former Napoleon route was completed.

By the mid-1870s, both the Mississippi, Ouachita & Red River Railroad and the Little Rock, Pine Bluff & New Orleans Railroad were in financial trouble, and they merged on November 11, 1873, to create the **Texas, Mississippi & Northwestern Railroad Company**. Floods and the failure to pay off bills led to the company being sold at foreclosure on December 16, 1875, to the bondholders, who then sold it to a Jay Gould organization, **The Little Rock, Mississippi River & Texas Railway**, on December 18, 1875.

The Little Rock, Mississippi River & Texas Railway had a charter to build a railroad from Chicot, on the Mississippi River, to Little Rock, Arkansas. The railway had been completed to Pine Bluff in 1873, but more improvements were necessary. For example, yearly flooding around Chicot led the railroad to move its Mississippi River terminus to Arkansas City in 1878. In 1881 the railway completed a line from Pine Bluff to Little Rock. About the same time, the railroad received permission to build a straighter line from Varner to McGehee, leading to the abandonment of the mainline through Watson and Arkansas City. This left just track from Arkansas City westward to the mainline.

For a number of years, The Little Rock, Mississippi River & Texas Railroad had a large presence at Arkansas City. Railroad tracks ran parallel to, and just along the edge of, the levee. A roundhouse and railroad machine shops were located southwest of town near the levee until about 1900. Several different depots were built at Arkansas City over the years, with the earlier depot becoming the freight depot when a newer station was built. The railroad also had a large freight warehouse on the Mississippi River. The last remaining railroad depot that stood in town has been moved to the property of Robert Moore, Jr.

In 1886, Gould had his own Little Rock, Mississippi River & Texas foreclosed on so it could be reorganized free of any outstanding debts. Gould bought the railroad through foreclosure on January 28, 1887, and it was deeded to the **St. Louis, Iron Mountain & Southern Railway** on February 1, 1887. During the 1890s, the line to Arkansas City was shown as having several different names. In one railroad document, the Trippe to Arkansas City line was known as the Arkansas City Division. In another document, it was listed as the Little Rock, Mississippi River & Texas Division, and was 11.86 miles long. The January 21, 1894, train schedule showed that passenger trains #221 and #222 operated daily between Arkansas City and Little Rock. Train #222 would depart Arkansas City at 12:30pm, McGehee at 2:00pm, and then arrive at Little Rock at 6:55pm. Train #221 departed Little Rock at 8:40am, McGehee at 1:40pm, and then arrived at Arkansas City at 2:45pm.

With the construction of the Memphis, Helena & Louisiana Railway, Arkansas City was left at the end of 8.45 miles of track from Trippe Junction to Arkansas City, shown as being part of the Warren Branch in 1903. In 1908, the railroad headed along the Mississippi River levee to serve companies like Kimball-Lacy Lumber, Delta Cooperage, the Hamett Grocery Company warehouse and a cold storage warehouse labeled as the beer depot, both at 6th Street. By the early 1910s, the railroad had a wye at the south end of 6th Street, plus a track northward to reach the Grayling Lumber Company and the Arkansas City Cooperage Company.

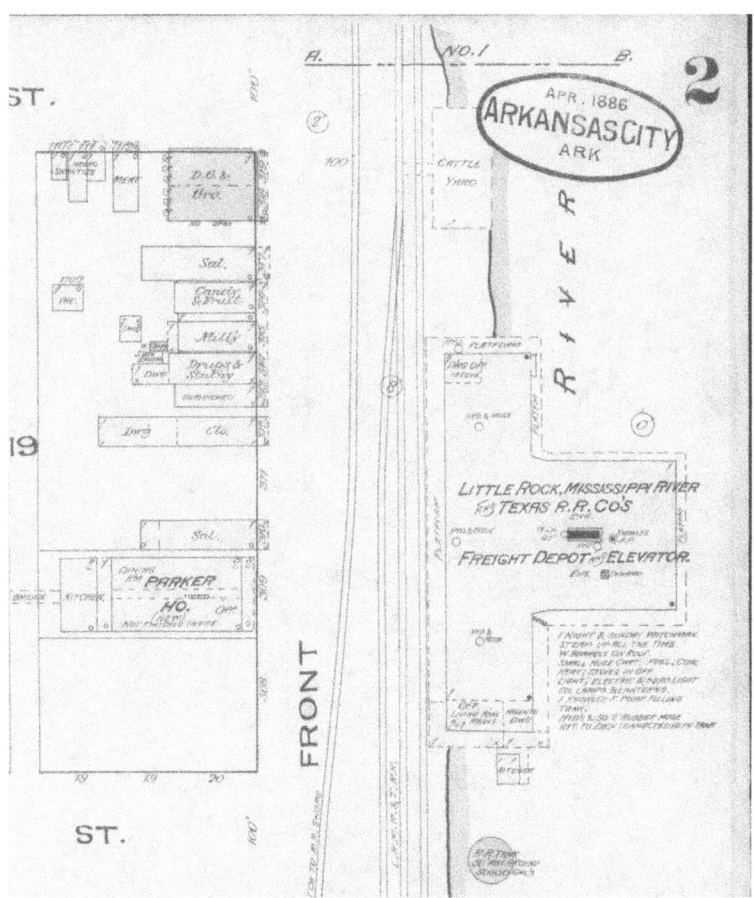

During the 1880s, the Little Rock, Mississippi River & Texas Railroad Company had a number of facilities at Arkansas City. Between Front Street and the Mississippi River, the railroad had a small passenger depot and freight office at 5th Street, plus a large dock and freight depot, elevator and dock on the river. *Sanborn Fire Insurance Map from Arkansas City, Desha County, Arkansas.* Sanborn Map Company, Apr, 1886. Map. Retrieved from the Library of Congress, https://www.loc.gov/item/sanborn00193_001/

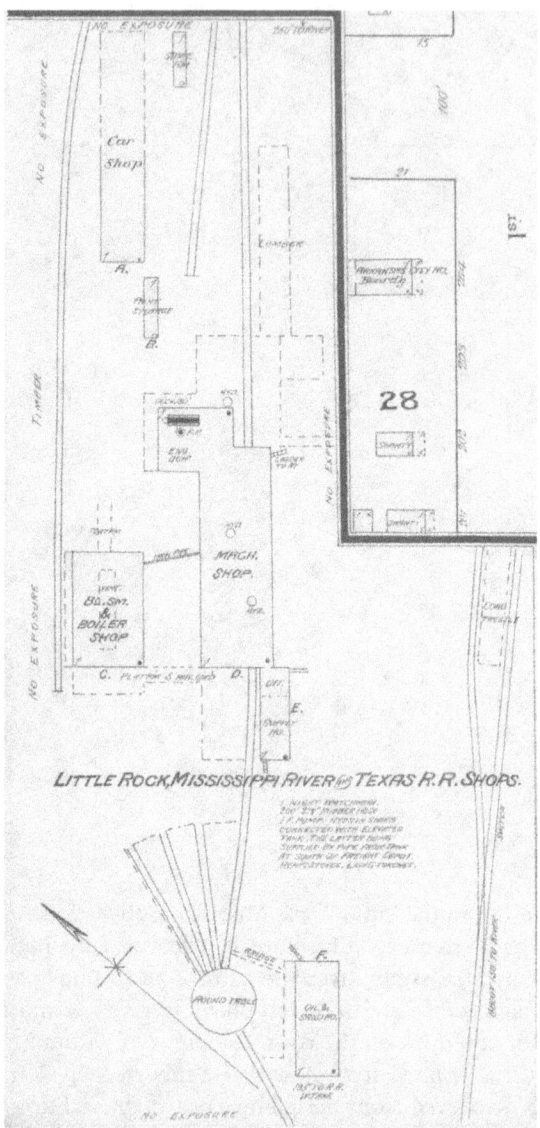

During the 1880s, the Little Rock, Mississippi River & Texas Railroad Company had a significant shop complex at Arkansas City, including a turntable, machine shop, boiler shop, and car shop, all located west of 6th Street on property that is now covered with trees. *Sanborn Fire Insurance Map from Arkansas City, Desha County, Arkansas.* Sanborn Map Company, Apr, 1886. Map. Retrieved from the Library of Congress, https://www.loc.gov/item/sanborn00193_001/

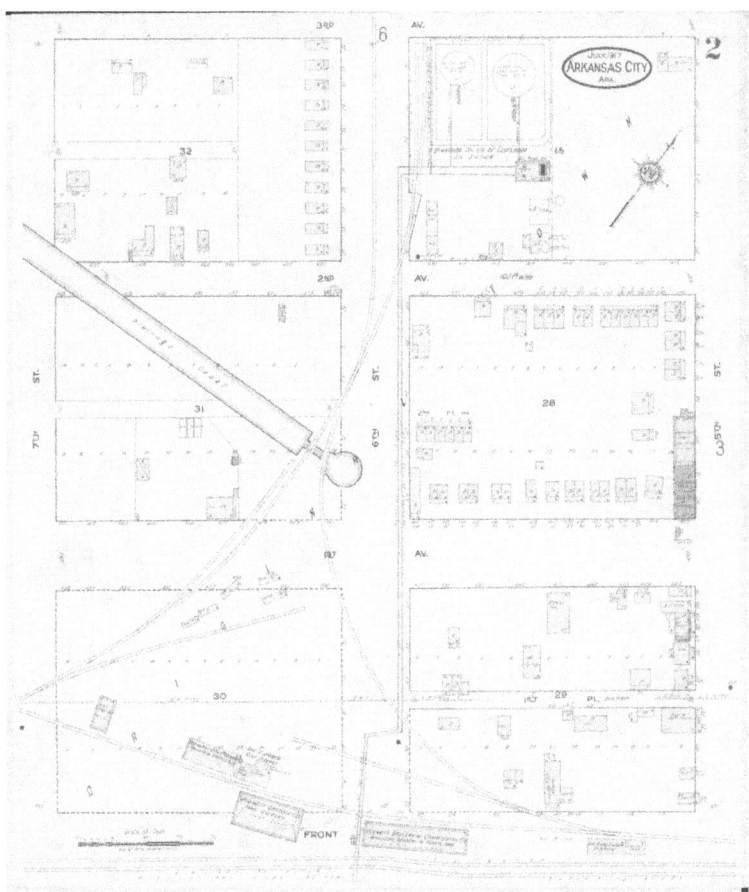

The Sanborn Map Company showed how busy the area around 6th Street and the Mississippi River levee was in 1917. *Sanborn Fire Insurance Map from Arkansas City, Desha County, Arkansas.* Sanborn Map Company, Jul, 1917. Map. Retrieved from the Library of Congress, https://www.loc.gov/item/sanborn00193_004/

Delta Heritage Trail: History Through the Miles

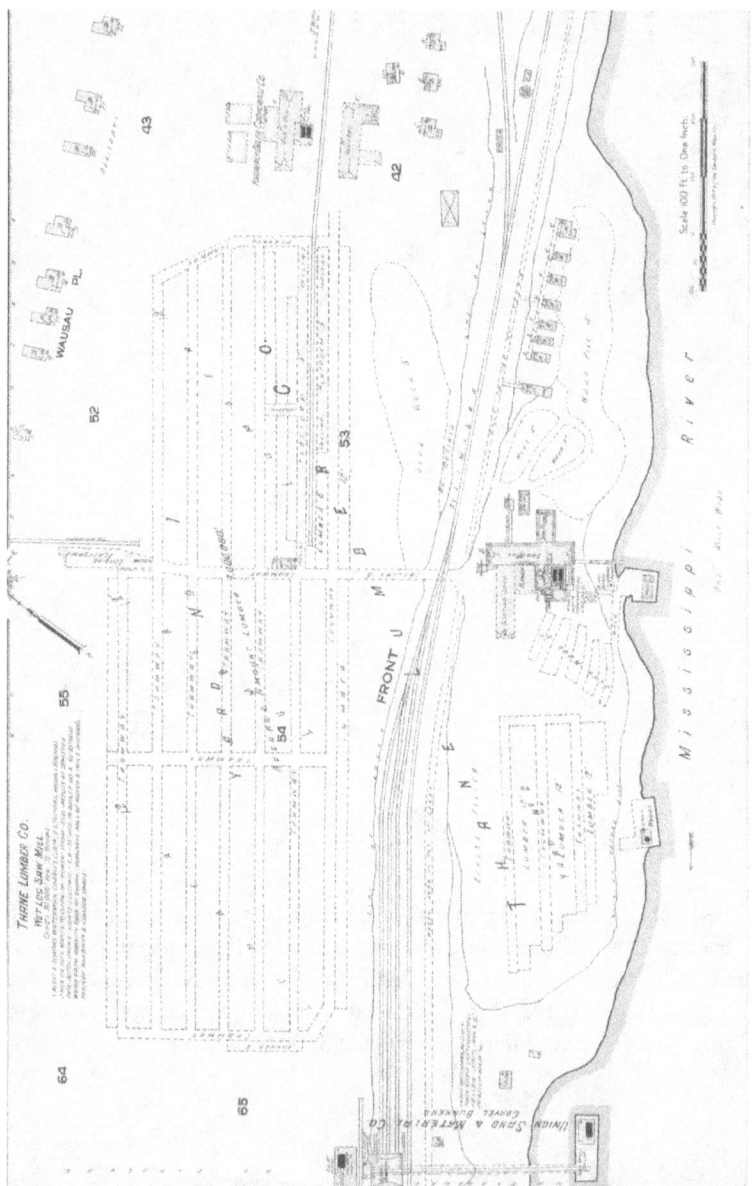

By 1917, the Thane Lumber Company and the Union Sand & Material Company had facilities where the railroad shops were once located. *Sanborn Fire Insurance Map from Arkansas City, Desha County, Arkansas.* Sanborn Map Company, Jul, 1917. Map. Retrieved from the Library of Congress, https://www.loc.gov/item/sanborn00193_004/

In 1912, the St. Louis, Iron Mountain & Southern brought another business to Arkansas City, the Union Sand & Material Company. The construction of the facility was reported on in *Cement and Engineering News* (January 1913). "The new mill of the Union Sand and Material Co. at Arkansas City, Ark., which represents an investment of about $100,000 is now in operation. The mill will be operated indefinitely, the company having a contract to furnish the Iron Mountain road 1,000,000 cars of ballast. About 60 hands are employed at the plant." At the time, Union Sand and Material had a contract to supply ballast for a number of projects across the Gould system, and they operated a half-dozen plants to provide the materials.

All of the major rail lines in the area were part of a large merger on May 12, 1917, that created the **Missouri Pacific Railroad Company**. With the merger, the line to Arkansas City became simply a smaller part of a larger railroad. In early 1926, the town was served by a pair of passenger trains from and to Memphis, Tennessee. Train #344 would depart Arkansas City daily at 9:35am and arrive at McGehee at 10:15am. It would then depart at 10:35 with a scheduled arrival time of 5:40pm at Memphis. The return train, #343, departed Memphis at 9:00am, McGehee at 6:35pm, and arrived at Arkansas City at 7:15pm.

During the 1920s, there were efforts to strengthen the levees at Arkansas City. As a part of this, on July 27, 1923, the Arkansas Railroad Commission ordered Missouri Pacific to remove its tracks off of the levees of the Southeast Levee District at Arkansas City. This impacted the riverfront freight dock that the railroad had in the city.

The Flood of 1927 greatly affected the railroad at Arkansas City as many of the businesses moved away or simply never reopened. The logging railroads also suffered as about twelve miles of railroad and siding, all owned by Thane Lumber and Breece-White Manufacturing, was destroyed by the flood. With many companies moving away from Arkansas City and other Delta towns, Missouri Pacific proposed to replace many of their branch line trains with motor coach service for passengers and small packages. By 1952, the Arkansas City line was seeing little freight business, with only 104 freight cars being moved over the route. On December 30, 1953, the Interstate Commerce Commission granted authority to Missouri Pacific to abandon the 8.3-mile line between Trippe Junction and Arkansas City, effective in 40 days. Parts of the abandoned grade are still used as farm roads, and the remains of a few of the timber trestles can still be found where they once crossed some of the larger streams.

Despite the railroad to Arkansas City being abandoned in early 1954, the wooden depot still stood here during the summer of 1988. It has since been moved to a nearby farm.

84.3 DESOTA AVENUE – This street, which replaced Front Street decades ago, turns away from the old grade and climbs the levee to connect with Levee Road. Heading south on the Delta Heritage Trail, the views to the north now include woods, but this was once the location of the railroad shops of the Little Rock, Mississippi River & Texas Railroad, and later the sawmill of the Thane Lumber Company.

One issue that should be addressed is that while the local street signs use the name Desota Avenue, many maps show it to be DeSoto Avenue.

As can be seen by this street sign, the spelling is Desota, not DeSoto, as some sources state.

The paved levee trail actually goes beyond the Arkansas City Trailhead of the Delta Heritage Trail. This is the Milepost 85 sign, located near the park at Kate Adams Lake Access.

85.3 KATE ADAMS ROAD – Kate Adams Road turns south off of Arkansas Highway 4 and crosses the levee at this location, providing access to the Moore Farms Access of Kate Adams Lake. For many years, the road on top of the levee in this area was known as Summit Street.

Rohwer to Arkansas City

This sign points the way toward the Moore Farms Access to Kate Adams Lake. The sign can be found alongside Arkansas Highway 4.

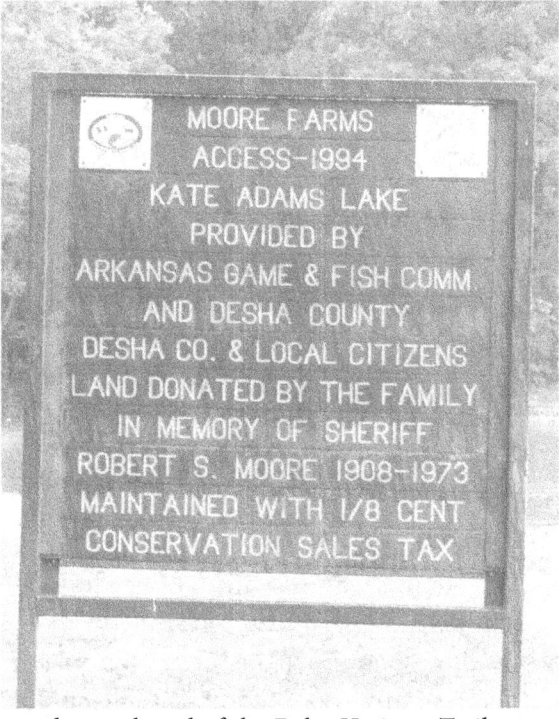

Welcome to the south end of the Delta Heritage Trail, or at least the south end in 2021. There are numerous plans to tie together a series of trails to follow the Mississippi River across Arkansas, and even the country, so future plans can certainly change.

Delta Heritage Trail: History Through the Miles

85.4 MOORE FARMS ACCESS TO KATE ADAMS LAKE – This location features parking, picnic grounds, a fishing pier, and a boat ramp. The access area was made available when the Arkansas Game & Fish Commission swapped nine acres of property for seven acres on the lake that was owned by the Moore family of Arkansas City. The 150-acre Kate Adams Lake was once part of the main channel of the Mississippi River, but is now an oxbow lake left behind after the Flood of 1927. Fishing for bream, bass, crappie and catfish is popular.

This dock on Kate Adams Lake provides terrific views of the lake and the local wildlife.

Kate Adams was the wife of Major John D. Adams, a prominent Memphis citizen and entrepreneur who operated a steamboat business. The primary route of the company was Memphis-Vicksburg, stopping at ports like Helena, Arkansas City, Greenville and Natchez, handling freight, passengers and mail. The company started in 1882, and over the years, there were three ships that carried the name *Kate Adams*.

About the same time that the Memphis, Helena & Louisiana was being built, the Memphis & New Orleans Railroad was being planned by the St. Louis & San Francisco Railroad (Frisco). The two railroads would essentially have paralleled each other through east Arkansas. During early 1903, A. L. Phillips, chief engineer of the Frisco, arrived at Arkansas City on the *Kate Adams* to check on the eight groups of engineers surveying the line. A month later, surveying stopped. Apparently the two railroads realized that it was crazy to build two railroads along the route as a few months later, Russell Harding, General Manager of Missouri Pacific, stated that their line would also be used by the Frisco, although that never happened.

There are several large brick structures on the banks of Kate Adams Lake. There have been many explanations for them, but they are located near where Union Sand and Material once had a dredge operation and conveyor system to a number of bins used to load railroad cars.

This park on Kate Adams Lake marks the south end of the Delta Heritage Trail in 2021. However, there are those who support extending trails southward along the levee system all the way to Louisiana, and even the Gulf of Mexico. Should this take place, later editions of this book will include this information. It is hoped that you enjoy your visit to Southeast Arkansas and the Delta Heritage Trail.

Delta Heritage Trail: History Through the Miles

Several large brick structures still stand alongside Kate Adams Lake, the remains of Mississippi River docks and businesses that once operated in the area.

About the Author

Writing about the Missouri Pacific's Wynne Subdivision, today's Delta Heritage Trail, was a trip back in time for the author, as he was once the Manager of Track Maintenance (Roadmaster) in charge of much of the line. While working for Union Pacific Railroad, he made numerous trips over the railroad during its final days. During some of these trips, he took the time to explore some of the history found along the line. Today, Bart Jennings, after years working in the railroad industry, is a professor emeritus of supply chain management and teaches transportation operations. He also still teaches workshops for the railroad industry, a way to stay in touch with the industry he loves.

For almost three decades, Barton Jennings has been organizing charter passenger trains and writing the route descriptions, both for planning purposes and for the enjoyment of the passengers. These trips have been from coast to coast, often covering operations that haven't seen a passenger train in decades. In addition, he has written a number of articles about various railroads for rail hobby magazines, plus almost a dozen books in the series *History Through the Miles*. His home has several rooms full of books, timetables and other documents about this and other railroads – important research items from a time long before today's internet. This book on the Delta Heritage Trail is part of this effort to preserve railroad history.

Bart was born in Northwest Arkansas and has worked across the country, but he and his family have lived along this east Arkansas line, and he still regularly visits the area. He is happy that his former office in the Missouri Pacific depot at McGehee is now part of a museum. He has been fortunate to get to know many of those who have known and researched the railroad, and has long shared ideas and information. This book is an outgrowth of all of these experiences and previous writings about the Missouri Pacific Railroad in southeastern Arkansas.

This route description was begun in the late 1980s as remains of the railroad's history were explored. With the creation of the Delta Heritage Trail, the notes were dusted off and additional research was conducted. Much of the information comes from internal railroad records, government and public records, and conversations with old and new friends. It is hoped that you enjoy your adventure with the Delta Heritage Trail.

The author, Barton Jennings, visited Barton Junction a number of times while writing this book.

www.ingramcontent.com/pod-product-compliance
Lightning Source LLC
Chambersburg PA
CBHW071216080526
44587CB00013BA/1391